About the Authors

Malcolm Joseph "Joe" Thurman was born on 26 August 1928 at Mulvane, Kansas. During World War II, while in high school, he was a member of the 3rd Missouri Infantry, Missouri State Guard. In late 1945, Joe became a merchant seaman and made voyages to the Middle East, Belgium and Japan. He enlisted in the US Army on 13 November 1946. Joe was sent to Japan in early 1947 and was assigned duties as a page at the International Military Tribunal– Far East (IMTFE). He remained in that duty assignment until the trial of the major Japanese war criminals was concluded. Joe remained in the Army for 29 years and retired as a chief warrant officer (W4) in 1975.

During his military service he was station in numerous European countries, Korea and Japan. While stationed in Berlin, Germany, he met and later married Christine Langner. They had two children: a daughter, Christine and a son, Joseph. After leaving military service, Joe was employed for 15 years by Litton Industries and Teledyne. Upon this final retirement he moved to Scottsdale, Arizona. Joe died at his home on 15 July 1997, survived by his widow Christine, and their two children.

Joe's daughter and co-author, Christine Sherman was born on 11 February 1955 at Berlin, Germany. She has lived in various European countries, Korea and the U.S. She obtained her juris doctorate in 1980 in Los Angeles, California. Subsequently, she was career prosecutor with the Los Angeles County District Attorney's Office. She is currently residing in Nairn, Scotland with her husband and two children, Nicholas and Matthew, where she has begun researching her next book.

Throughout the history of mankind there have always been wars and their resulting after effects. Normally, these wars have ended through negotiated settlements amongst the parties concerned or with the total destruction and subjugation of one side by the other. In the negotiated settlement what each side was to receive from the other was spelled out usually in the settlement documents. However, in the case of one side being vanquished by the other, the victors would normally enforce their will on their opponents, including what they wished to be done with the populace and their leaders.

It soon became apparent that with the size of the armies rising to the millions and the populace of the nations involved on both sides of the conflict growing to the hundreds of millions there was also an increased need for greater rules and controls of warfare.

Included in the rules and controls were the responsibilities of senior military commanders and national leaders with respect to the treatment and protection that was required to be accorded to POWs, internees, and the populace of conquered lands.

"*WAR CRIMES: Japan's World War II Atrocities* demands a prominent place in military history. Mr. Thurman and his daughter, Christine Sherman, bring to life the atrocities which the tribunal was formed to prosecute. War crimes remain a part of world history, and the world should know about them."

– Turner Publishing Company

This book is dedicated to the memory of the men, women, and children who were and are the victims of war crimes

War Crimes: Japan's World War II Atrocities

M.J. Thurman
Christine A. Sherman

TURNER PUBLISHING COMPANY

Turner Publishing Company Staff:
Editor: Dayna Spear Williams
Designer: Susan L. Harwood

Library of Congress Control No: 20-01092657

ISBN: 978-1-68162-132-6

Additional copies may be purchased
directly from the publisher.
Limited Edition.

Table of Contents

Authors' Biographies

Malcolm Joseph "Joe" Thurman was born on 26 August 1928 at Mulvane, Kansas. During World War II, while in high school,

Malcolm J. Thurman

he was a member of the 3rd Missouri Infantry, Missouri State Guard. In late 1945, Joe became a merchant seaman and made voyages to the Middle East, Belgium and Japan. He enlisted in the US Army on 13 November 1946. Joe was sent to Japan in early 1947 and was assigned duties as a page at the International Military Tribunal– Far East (IMTFE). He remained in that duty assignment until the trial of the major Japanese war criminals was concluded. Joe remained in the Army for 29 years and retired as a chief warrant officer (W4) in 1975.

During his military service he was stationed in numerous European countries, Korea and Japan. While stationed in Berlin, Germany, he met and later married Christine Langner. They had two children: a daughter, Christine and a son, Joseph. After leaving military service, Joe was employed for 15 years by Litton Industries and Teledyne. Upon this final retirement he moved to Scottsdale, Arizona. Joe died at his home on 15 July 1997, survived by his widow Christine, and their two children.

Joe's daughter and co-author, Christine Sherman was born on 11 February 1955 at Berlin, Germany. She has lived in various European countries, Korea and the U.S. She obtained her juris doctorate in 1980 in Los Angeles, California. Subsequently, she was a career prosecutor with the Los Angeles County District Attorney's Office. She is currently residing in Nairn, Scotland with her husband and two children, Nicholas and Matthew, where she has begun researching her next book.

Christine A. Sherman

General of the Army Douglas MacArthur, Supreme Commander Allied Powers, International Military Tribunal - Far East Convening Authority.

Preface

Throughout the history of mankind there have always been wars and their resulting after effects. Normally, these wars have ended through negotiated settlements amongst the parties concerned or with the total destruction and subjugation of one side by the other. In the negotiated settlement what each side was to receive from the other was spelled out usually in the settlement documents. However, in the case of one side being vanquished by the other, the victors would normally enforce their will on their opponents, including what they wished to be done with the populace and their leaders.

It soon became apparent that with the size of the armies rising to the millions and the populace of the nations involved on both sides of the conflict growing to the hundreds of millions there was also an increased need for greater rules and controls of warfare.

Included in the rules and controls were the responsibilities of senior military commanders and national leaders with respect to the treatment and protection that was required to be accorded to POWs, internees, and the populace of conquered lands.

War Crimes

The Potsdam Conference had declared that stern justice should be meted out to all war criminals, including those who had visited such cruelties upon our prisoners. The justice or even the legality of war crimes trials as such will not be discussed in this book.

Such was the fate of General Tomoyuki Yamashita, who had fought so cruelly and effectively against General Mac-Arthur during the Philippine campaign and was among the first to be executed. Yamashita was cut off from most of the units under his command during this campaign. It is hardly surprising that the discipline of many Japanese troops suffered and many horrible atrocities were committed.

Yamashita surrendered on 3 September 1945 and was charged with being a war criminal on the 25th of September. General MacArthur established a military tribunal in November which convicted Yamashita of having failed to provide the required effective control over his troops and sentenced him to death for a crime which had been, prior to that time, unknown in the annals of jurisprudence. An appeal to the U.S. Supreme Court was rejected as the Court said that they were not empowered to dispute the findings of a military court. When President Truman refused to take any action on a petition for clemency, Yamashita's death was certain. Shortly after 6 a.m., 23 February 1946 General Yamashita "The Tiger of Malaya" was executed by hanging until he was dead.

General Homma's case was far clearer cut than was that of General Yamashita. As the instigator of the infamous Bataan death march, the Emperor stripped Homma of his officer's commission when the facts were made known to him. Homma was rapidly sentenced to death by the war crimes tribunal. In an effort to save him, Homma's wife appealed to General MacArthur, but MacArthur, who probably wanted Homma's scalp more than anyone else's, declared that if Homma did not deserve his fate, then no one in 'jurisdictional history ever did'. Homma's sentence was carried out under MacArthur's orders.

Emperor Hirohito

Another issue that had to be dealt with was whether Emperor Hirohito should be tried as a war criminal or not. Many Allies, primarily the Russians and to some extent the British, thought Hirohito should be indicted as a war criminal. General MacArthur strongly resisted every such proposal, even one put forth by President Truman. The suggestion of the President was quickly withdrawn when he saw how adamant General MacArthur was on the subject. From the outset, General MacArthur believed that there should be some continuity maintained with the old order for the benefit of the Japanese people. The reduction of their Emperor from a godhead to a constitutional monarch was shocking enough without having him tried and maybe even executed. This would have been counter-productive to the American efforts to conciliate their former enemy.

Additionally, by attempting to execute the Emperor, a 'last stand' form of mentality among the Japanese might be created and the Allies, primarily the United States, would have to field a substantial army to put down the uprisings that would inevitably follow to restore order. It would have taken several generations to rebuild a viable relationship between America and a conquered Japan if this took place. General MacArthur was aware of this and had already decided not to try the Emperor.

The war was officially ended when the Japanese Delegation signed the surrender documents aboard the American Battleship USS *Missouri* in Tokyo Bay and General MacArthur symbolically accepted the surrender by formally signing the documents for the Allies.

Japanese delegation headed by Defendants Mamoru Shigemitsu and General Yoshijkiro Umezu aboard the American battleship USS Missouri *for the signing of the Japanese surrender.*

Defendant Shigemitsu, as the representative for the Japanese Imperial Government, signs the surrender document aboard the American Battleship USS Missouri. Defendant Umezu later signed the document as the representative of the Japanese Armed Forces. General MacArthur then signed the documents accepting the Japanese surrender for the Allied Forces.

The International Military Tribunal for the Far East (IMTFE) could finally render its decisions there after in due course. The Tribunal sat for nearly three years, and although there were many persons tried and sentenced both inside and outside of Japan by the individual countries concerned, this was the primary show trial involving major war criminals, who numbered four former prime ministers amongst themselves.

Despite the presence of such figures, the Tokyo and other Far Eastern War Crimes Trials received only a fraction of the publicity given to the European Trials at Nuremberg. It is possible that the names at Nuremberg were better known, but given the hatred that most Americans felt for the Japanese, it was surprising that the Tokyo trials were so relatively unpublicized. It would seem that the leaders in Germany having committed suicide, there would be more interest in the Far East trials. (Hitler and Goebbles shot themselves in the Hitler Bunker in Berlin during the last days of the war, and Goering stood trial. He died by biting into a poison capsule that had been embedded in his jowl.) Tojo attempted to commit suicide by shooting himself in the chest below his heart because he did not want to mess up his head. Correspondents and photographers who had accompanied the American agents who came to Tojo's residence to arrest him moved Tojo's body from the chair where he had shot himself to a cot nearby, which inadvertently saved his life, as stated by an American doctor who arrived two hours afterwards. This doctor said that if the blood had not drained out, it would have filled his lungs and drowned him. Tojo was transported to a Yokahoma American military hospital where half a dozen transfusions with American blood helped to save his life and he was transferred to Tokyo's Sugamo Prison in late 1945.

Perhaps the fact that some of the most important happenings took place well after Nuremberg, as long as three years after the end of hostilities, made them somewhat anti-climactic. By that time most Americans had their attentions turned towards different affairs at home and abroad. They did their best to forget or at least push the recent past from their minds and concentrate on future events and the restoration of products such as new vehicles to the marketplaces. The troops had been or were being mustered out of the military services and were returning to family, friends, jobs, and schooling and did not want to recall the events of the war years.

IMTFE Organization
CHAPTER 1

The International Military Tribunal for the Far East was established by General MacArthur in his capacity as the Chief of the Allied Powers for the Far East to make use of facilities available at the Japanese War ministry in Tokyo. The trial was to be the show case trial for the more noted individuals who were accused of the commission of criminal actions, namely: conspiracy to wage aggressive wars against their neighboring countries; the furtherance of actions to accomplish the intents of these aggressive wars and responsibility for the inhumane treatment of POWs, internees, and the populace of the captured nations through their own actions or the actions of individuals under their command without providing proper guidance and control.

This would be the first chance for most Japanese personnel to observe the workings of a trial under the new Japanese Constitution. The trial was to be as open as possible so as to allow the maximum number of people to attend the proceedings while the security and control of the trial was being maintained. This was accomplished by the establishment of an Attendance Control Office which had responsibility for securing permanent passes for all individuals accredited to the court and getting temporary passes which were valid for one of the two sessions each day for spectators, both Allied and Japanese.

Tribunal personnel were derived from citizens of the 11 Allied Nations that made up the tribunal. This included the Justices, their assistants and advisers, and clerical help as well as the members of the International Prosecution Section and their clerical help and any assistants. Translation teams were also provided to insure that all of the documents required for the trial were properly translated and each was certified as being accurate.

The Defense consisted of the accused, their legal counsel, and a small number of clerical personnel.

The Marshall of the Court and his personnel, the Provost Marshall and the military police for security purposes, and administrative personnel to perform required support services were provided by the United States Army.

Tribunal Personnel
CHAPTER 2

Justices

The Panel of Justices consisted of an individual from each of the following Allied nations:

The Commonwealth of Australia

The Dominion of Canada

The Republic of China

The Republic of France

The United Kingdom of Great Britain and

Northern Ireland

The Government of India

New Zealand

The Kingdom of the Netherlands

The Commonwealth of the Philippines

The Union of Soviet Socialist Republics

The United States of America

The Justice from Australia (Sir William Webb) was named the President of the Tribunal and the remainder were Tribunal Members.

Only one Justice failed to complete the trial but there was no lost continuity due to his replacement since it came early in the trial. Major General Myron C. Cramer of the US Army replaced Justice John P. Higgins as the American Justice.

Panel of Justices

President of the Tribunal:
Commonwealth of Australia, Sir William Webb

Tribunal Members:
Dominion of Canada, E. Stuart McDougall
Republic of China, Ju-Ao Mei
Republic of France, Henri Bernard
The United Kingdom of Great Britain and Northern
    Ireland, Lord Patrick
Government of India, R.B. Pal
New Zealand, Erima Harvey Nordcroft
Kingdom of the Netherlands, Bernard Victor A. Roling
Commonwealth of the Philippines, D. Jaranilla
Union of Soviet Socialist Republics, I.M. Zaryanov
United States of America, John P. Higgins
Replaced by Major General Myron C. Cramer

International Prosecution Section

The 11 Allied nations of the court each named a counsel
to act on their behalf during the trial. The counsel for the
United States of America was named the Chief Counsel of
the International Prosecution Section (IPS) and the remainder were Associate Counsels.

IPS Chief Counsel

Mr. Joseph B. Keenan on behalf of the United States of
America.
    IPS Associate Counsels:
Justice A.J. Mansfield on behalf of the Commonwealth
of Australia.

IMTFE International Justices July 1946. This picture was the first group picture taken after Major General Myron C. Cramer replaced Justice J.P. Higgins as the Justice from the United States of America. Distinguished members, seated, first row, left-to-right: Justice Patrick, Great Britain; Justice Cramer, USA; Chief Justice Webb, Australia; Justice Mei, China; Justice Zaryanov, USSR; Distinguished members, standing, second row, left-to-right: Justice Pal, India; Justice Roling, Netherlands; Justice McDougall, Canada; Justice Bernard, France; Justice Nordcroft, New Zealand; Justice Jarnilla, Philippine Islands.

IMTFE Tribunal President Sir William Webb of Australia and newly appointed Justice Major General Myron C. Cramer of the United States of America at the entrance to the War Ministry Building, Tokyo, Japan.

US Congressional Party visits war crimes trials. Representative Michael A. Feighan, House Judiciary Committee, and Representative John E. Sheridan, Military Affairs Committee discuss court procedures with Sir William Webb at a tea given by the IMTFE President.

Brigadier J.G. Nolan on behalf of the Dominion of Canada.

Judge Hsiang Che-Chun on behalf of the Republic of China.

Mr. Robert Oneto on behalf of the Republic of France.

Mr. A.S. Comyns Carr on behalf of the United Kingdom of Great Britain and Northern Ireland.

Mr. G. Menon on behalf of the Government of India.

Justice W.G.F. Borgerhoff Mulder on behalf of the Kingdom of the Netherlands.

Brigadier R.J. Quilliam on behalf of New Zealand.

Mr. Pedro Lopez on behalf of the Commonwealth of the Philippines.

Mr. S.A. Golunsky on behalf of the USSR.

Also included in the IPS were the assistant counsels appointed to help the associated counsels in the preparation and presentation of their portion of the prosecution's case; the clerical help involved with the preparation and presentation of the prosecution case and the translation teams required to translate the vast amounts of documents needed for the prosecution's case.

The prosecution had a much easier time in the preparation of their case since they could draw on the facilities of the 11 Allied Nations by way of the Associate Counsel assigned to function on that country's behalf, a luxury not afforded to the Defense.

Marshall of the Court Personnel

Many of the vital functions that are required at a trial of this nature are performed by the person filling the position of the Marshall of the Court. Captain D.S. Van Meter of the

US Army was assigned to perform these functions during the IMTFE trial.

A qualified person had to be present in this position at all times the court was in session. The US Army assigned another officer to assist Captain Van Meter and to insure this requirement was fulfilled. Senior noncommissioned Officers in the Section were qualified to handle these functions for short periods when neither the Marshall of the Court nor his assistant were available.

The Marshall of the Court was responsible to announce the start of each court session by stating that the International Military Tribunal for the Far East was now in session or had now resumed.

Personnel assigned Court Page duties were responsible to the Marshall of the Court and had to insure that the courtroom was properly arranged prior to the start of each court session. While the court was in session, these Court Pages were strategically placed around the Courtroom to aid the Justices and Counsels or to perform errands for them when they could not leave.

Although the duties of personnel assigned to the attendance Control Office were related to security, they were responsible to the Marshall of the Court and had no MP duties.

Miscellaneous Personnel

The Clerk of the Court was responsible for the assignment of a court document number using either the prosecution or defense document number for identification purposes to insure continuity of the documents used during the trial.

Personnel assigned as translators/interpreters were responsible for the interpretation and /or translation of all items spoken or presented during the court session thereby providing multi-language court records.

Security Personnel

Security for the accused and for the Tribunal was provided by US Military Police under the command of the Tribunal Provost Marshall, Lieutenant Colonel Aubry S. Kenworthy.

The accused were transported from Sugamo Prison to the War Ministry and back to the prison each day on a United States military bus with the windows covered so that the defendants could not be seen from the outside of the bus nor could the accused see out of the bus. The bus was driven by Military Police and there were also other fully armed Military Police guards who rode on the bus. The bus was escorted by two jeeps loaded with fully armed Military Police. When the bus arrived at the War Ministry, one jeep would park in front of the bus and the other to the rear, the military Police would dismount from their vehicles and the defendants would be escorted to a holding area in the War Ministry until it was time for that session of the court.

Military Police were stationed at each entrance to the court and no one was allowed to enter the court without proper authorization. All personnel assigned to the Tribunal, who required access to the court, had badges which authorized their entrance. Additionally, spectator passes for both Allied and Japanese spectators were issued for each of the two daily sessions of the court, one in the morning and one in the afternoon.

Defense Personnel
CHAPTER 3

The Defense personnel consisted primarily of the defendants and the Legal Counsel for each Defendant.

There was also a small number of clerical personnel but not nearly as many as those that were assigned to the Prosecution Section.

Defendants

Originally there were 28 defendants at the start of the trial but as the trial progressed three of the accused were relieved from any further participation in the trial due to their physical and/or mental condition. The Tribunal passed judgment on the remaining 25 accused at the conclusion of the trial.

Araki, Sadao
Dohihara, Kenji
Hashimoto, Kingoro
Hata, Shunroku
Hiranuma, Kiichiro
Hirota, Koki
Hoshino, Naoki
Itagaki, Seishiro
Kaya, Okinori
Kido, Koichi
Kimura, Heitro
Koiso, Kuniaki

Matsui, Iwane
Matsuoka, Yosuke *
Minami, Jiro
Muto, Akira
Nagano, Osami *
Oka, Takasumi
Okawa, Shumei *
Oshima, Hiroshi
Sato, Kenyo
Shigemitsu, Mamoru
Shimada, Shietaro
Shiratori, Toshio
Suzuki, Teichi
Togo, Shigenori
Tojo, Hideki
Umezu, Youshijiro

* Relieved from trial due to physical or mental disability.

Defense Legal Counsel

The Defense Legal Counsel was made up of a Chief of Counsel and the American and Japanese counsel assigned to prepare and present the defense for a specific defendant. The defense had only a limited number of clerical personnel who were organized in a pool fashion.

Chief Defense Counsel: Captain Beverly M. Coleman, USNR
Counsel for Accused Araki, Sadao: Mr. Lawrence McManus, Yutaka Sugawara
Counsel for Accused Dohihara, Kenji: Mr. Franklin E.E. Warren, Naoyoshi Tsukazaki

Counsel for Accused Hashimoto, Kingoro: Itsuro Hayashi

Counsel for Accused Hata, Shurroku: Lieutenant Aristides G. Lazarus, USMCR, Masayoshi Kanzaki

Counsel for Accused Hiranuma, Kiichiro: Captain Samuel J. Kleiman, AC, Rukuyo Usami

Counsel for Accused Hirota, Koki: Mr. David S. Smith, Tadashi Hanai

Counsel for Accused Hoshino, Naoki: Mr. George C. Williams, Goichiro Fujii

Counsel for Accused Itagaki, Seishiro: Hanzo Yamada

Counsel for Accused Kaya, Okinori: Tsuruo Takano

Counsel for Accused Kido, Koichi: Mr. William Logan, Shigetaki Hozumi

Counsel for Accused Kimura, Heitaro: Mr. Joseph C. Howard, Toksaburo, Shiohara

Counsel for Accused Koiso, Kuniaki: Captain Alfred Brooks, Shohei, Sammonji

Counsel for Accused Matsui, Iwane: Mr. Floyd J. Mattice, Kiyose, Ito

Counsel for Accused Matsuoka, Yosuke: Mr. Franklin E.N. Warren, Shunzo, Kobayashi

Counsel for Accused Minami, Jiro: Kintaro Takeuchi

Counsel for Accused Muto, Akira: Shoichi Okamoto

Counsel for Accused Nagano, Osami: Hachiro Okuyama

Counsel for Accused Okawa, Shumei: Captain A.W. Brooks, AUS, Shinichi Ohara

Counsel for Accused Oshima, Hiroshi: Mr. Owen Cunningham, Naoyoshi Tsukazaki

Counsel for Accused Sato, Kenryo: Mr. James N. Freeman, Ichiro Kiyose

Counsel for Accused Shigemitsu, Mamoru: Mr. George A. Furness, Kenzo Takayanagi

Counsel for Accused Shimada, Shigetaro: Mr. Edward P. McDermott, Yoshitsuigu Takahashi

Counsel for Accused Shiratori, Toshio: Charles B. Caudle, Dr. Somei Uzawas

Counsel for Accused Suzuki, Teiichi: Motokichi Hasegawa

Counsel for Accused Togo, Shigenori: Mr. George Yamaoka, Shigetaka Hozumi

Counsel for Accused Tojo, Hideki: Ichiro Kiyose.

Counsel for Accused Umezu, Yoshijiro: Major Ben Bruce Blakenney, AC, Shotaro Miyake.

Japanese lawyers were conspicuously absent who were willing to defend Tojo in court with only one relatively inexperienced barrister offering his services. Eventually he was joined by a second veteran lawyer.

As for American defense counsel for Tojo, two lawyers came and went before the Occupation Headquarters was satisfied with the third.

Defense Attorney D.F. Smith proposes the dismissal of the case against Defendant Koki Hirota at the war crimes trials at Tokyo, Japan.

Defense Witness Kisaburo Ando signs a statement presented to him by the Marshall of the Court. Mr. Ando was a lieutenant general in command of the 9th Depot Division in 1937 and served as Home Minister from April 1943 to July 1944 when he retired.

Attorney and defendant confer through precautionary screen. During the noon recess at the war crimes trials in the War Ministry Building, Defendant ex-Gen. Muto confers with his attorney through the double screen installed in the interview room as a military policeman stands guard nearby.

Tribunal Physical Layout
CHAPTER 4

The IMTFE used the entire War Ministry Building plus some of the other buildings located on the compound for administrative functions or for the trials themselves. Billets were provided in the War Ministry Building itself for the enlisted members of the court's personnel and the military police. Messing and lounge facilities for these personnel were provided in other buildings on the compound.

Offices were provided in the War Ministry Building for the Justices, legal counsel, other court officials and their assistants and staffs.

There was also a holding area where the defendants were placed upon their arrival at the War Ministry until it was time to escort them into the courtroom. The defendants were also placed in this holding area during court recesses.

The IMTFE courtroom where the war crimes trials of former Japanese Premier Hideki Tojo and other upper level defendants were conducted in the War Ministry Building at Tokyo, Japan is shown below. On the right: The IMTFE Panel of Justices were seated at the upper level bench and on the lower level were aids/assistants and the Clerk of the Court. The Marshall of the Court is standing at the near end of the lower level together with one of his Court Pages. On the left: Docket for the Defendants with MP Guards behind them. In the center: Between the Justices and Defendants were work spaces and desks provided for use by members of the prosecution and defense legal teams as required when the court was in session. Located on the right front was the witness stand. The rear portion was for spectators, with Japanese spectators on the left and Allied spectators on the right. Reserved seating for the press were provided in the front of the center sections for both Japanese and Allied members of the press.

In the balcony: Divided for spectators the same as the lower level with Japanese on the left and Allied, on the right. Not Shown: Elevated, soundproof, glass-fronted booths were provided for the court interpreters. All court proceedings were translated into English, Russian and Japanese, with all three versions being available by switches associated with the headsets that were provided at every seat in the court. In front of the interpreters booths but at various lower levels were seats which provided an unobstructed view of the courtroom for seating of any distinguished visitors and spectators.

Prosecution Presentation
CHAPTER 5

General Warfare

The United States, Great Britain, France, and Japan, by a treaty which was concluded on 13 December 1921, undertook to respect each others rights in respect to their Pacific Ocean possessions and dominions. They agreed to settle all differences among themselves on this subject by peaceful means only.

Although the Netherlands was not among the signatories to this treaty, a solemn declaration was issued by each of the contracting governments on 4 February 1922 stating that the rights of the Netherlands in relation to its Pacific Ocean possessions would be respected. At no time did the Japanese government give any indication that they no longer considered themselves to be bound by this Pact. However, in the final years prior to their military expansion southward, the Japanese government repeatedly declared that Japan's intentions were totally peaceful but all the while they were planning and preparing for this onslaught.

Numerous Japanese government officials made statements that Japan was satisfied with this situation from the time of this declaration up to as late as 1940 and early 1941.

However, the Netherlands Indies with its vast natural resource deposits, great amount of agricultural products, and huge petroleum reserves was one of the most desired assets in the Asiatic area that was coveted by Japan.

Japan's desire to acquire the Netherlands Indies was indicated by a comprehensive plan dated in September 1940 that was found in the files of the Japanese government after the end of the war. This plan listed in some detail how a military conquest in the Netherlands Indies could be achieved without causing too severe damage to its natural resources nor its industrial equipment. Also shown in this plan was the method on how to make the Netherlands Indies a puppet state within Japan's sphere of influence by stirring up an independence movement.

A similar policy was to be followed in all other regions from Burma to the Philippines.

When the Netherlands East Indies did not yield to Japanese pressure and threats, aggression and military conquest of the area was decided upon. One of the main motives for the December 1941 Japanese aggression in the Pacific was the Japanese advancement into the Netherlands Indies and the surrounding territories. The Japanese intent in the capture/occupation of these areas was to facilitate construction of a new Japanese empire.

The Geneva Prisoner of War Convention of 1929 provided that in respect to the punishment of POWs while they were incarcerated any punishment of a corporal nature, imprisonment in quarters without daylight, and the use of any form of cruelty whatever was forbidden. It also stipulated that collective punishment for individual acts were also forbidden. These, together with other important POW punishment limitations, were included to insure humane treatment of POWs. Arrest was listed as being the most severe form of punishment that could be imposed on a POW and the duration of a single punishment could not exceed 30 days.

That the Japanese government understood the contents of this convention was shown by their objection to its ratification in 1934. They stated that POWs under the Convention would be treated less severely than would Japanese forces under the Japanese Military and Naval Disciplinary Codes unless these codes were revised to place them on an equal footing. The Japanese government further stated that such code revisions would not be desirable in the interests of discipline.

During the entire period of the hostilities with the Chinese, the Japanese government did not create any special agency for dealing with the administration of POWs and civilian internees, nor was a Prisoner of War Information Bureau maintained as required by The Hague and Geneva Conventions. Defendant Muto stated that the question of whether or not the Chinese captives were to be treated as POWs presented quite a problem. It was not until 1938 that it was decided that since the Chinese conflict was officially known by the Japanese government as an "Incident" or "The Chinese Incident", and not a war, that the Chinese captives would not be regarded as POWs.

Throughout the late 1930s and early 1940s the Japanese always cited the "China Incident" as one of the major problems in Asia and that of the providing of arms and supplies to the Chinese by the Americans and British.

Even with these reservations, the Japanese government gave their word early in the Pacific War that they would apply these provisions towards the treatment of any Allied POWs and civilian internees that came under Japanese control during the course of the conflict.

The Japanese government circumvented the aims of these Conventions by the enactment of ordinances and regulations that were contrary to these provisions. In 1943, a regulation was published which specified that if a POW was guilty of an act of insubordination, he could be subjected to imprisonment, arrest, or any other measure of punishment that was deemed necessary for discipline. Citing this regulation as the authorization, corporal punishment as well as torture and mass punishment was ordered and administered with thousands of deaths being attributable to this punishment.

An ordinance was issued on 9 March 1943 which provided for the death penalty, life imprisonment, or confinement for 10 years or more for a variety of offenses.

This ordinance also provided for death or other severe penalty for the 'so called' leader of a group whose actions resulted in the commission of an offense and the same punishment or slightly less severe penalty for all others involved. Mass punishment was therefore imposed on groups for no more than an act by an individual.

Punishment of this type was used in many cases where a POW attempted to escape or succeeded in escaping. The death penalty was often imposed not only on the escapee if he was recaptured but also on any other persons who helped or were suspected of helping in the escape.

In some cases all of the prisoners were divided into groups and if a member of a group escaped, all members of the group were killed. The formality of a trial was dispensed with in most instances. Imposing of the death penalty for escape or attempted escape was widespread within the entire Asiatic Pacific area.

This same ordinance provided for the death penalty for any POW who defied or disobeyed the orders of any person supervising, guarding, or escorting them and also provided for five years imprisonment for any POW who, publicly or privately, insulted persons functioning in any of these capacities.

These are but a few examples of how the Japanese government departed from the requirements in respect to treatment of

POWs and internees as contained in the Geneva Convention which Japan had agreed to comply with by altering their regulations and ordinances.

The indictment had specific counts dealing with Japanese aggressive wars against its neighboring countries or areas. There was very little lateral communications between these areas. The Japanese Armed Forces commander in the area was held responsible for the establishment of the occupational government for the area as well as maintaining facilities for the control of POWs and internees until they were transported to the camps established under the Japanese government for this purpose.

The primary data for these occupied area governments and all prisoner facilities was provided in the directives from the Japanese government in Tokyo regardless of the area or the armed force having responsibility for the area, the Japanese Army or the Navy. The directives published by the Japanese government provided for such strong centralized control that even with such little exchange of information between areas there was very little difference between them and usually then they only dealt with problems clearly of a local nature.

War Against China
CHAPTER 6

As a part of their plan to subjugate China, the Japanese leaders used opium and narcotics as weapons to prepare for and to further Japanese aggression in China. This was in violation of their obligations under several Conventions relating to the suppression of opium and narcotic drugs of which Japan was a signatory.

Japanese agents, both military and civilian, engaged in widespread illegal traffic in opium and narcotics in advance of Japanese armed aggression in any area. These agents introduced the production of heroin, morphine, and other opium derivatives into areas where the use of these drugs had not been prevalent before. Due to the existence of Japanese extra-territoriality rights in China, they operated almost with immunity. The intent of this illegal activity was to neutralize or completely negate Chinese listless and incompetent to resist aggression. Japanese consular authorities failed to prevent Japanese nationals from engaging in narcotics trafficking or punishing those adequately who were apprehended for narcotic violations. This was in sharp contrast to the drastic action taken by Japanese authorities where Japanese nationals sold narcotics to other Japanese.

The Japanese conspirators launched their aggressive war against China in 1931 and conquered Manchuria and Jehol. The Japanese had started to infiltrate into North China by 1934, garrisoning the land and setting up puppet regimes designed to serve their purposes.

As the Japanese achieved domination in each area of China, that area served as a base of operations for the narcotics offensive against the next area marked for that form of armed aggression. Japanese controlled puppet governments followed a uniform pattern in the creation of opium monopolies that were designed to appear as opium suppression agencies but actually became in fact the sole traffickers in opium and narcotics in their territory. These Japanese controlled puppet regimes received vast amounts of revenue from opium and narcotics trafficking under the guise of the control of opium for its suppression. A Japanese loan made to Manchukuo for the purpose of financing operations of the puppet government was secured by pledging the profits of the opium trade.

Thus the prosecution presented evidence to show that Japan sponsored the opium and narcotics traffic for the following two purposes: To weaken the stamina and undermine the will to resist on the part of the Chinese people; and to provide substantial revenues to finance Japanese military and economic aggression.

The commission of atrocities against civilians and crimes against humanity by Japanese troops took place in every province of occupied China and covered the entire period that Japanese troops were there.

These offenses included: murder and massacre, torture, rape, robbery, looting, and wanton destruction of property.

A heinous example of the commission of these barbarous acts occurred following the capture of the city of Nanking. The Japanese Army under the command of the defendant Matsui captured the city on 13 December 1937 and an orgy of killing, raping, looting, and burning began immediately and continued unabated for more than forty days until February 1938. The total of these crimes collectively came to be know historically as the "The Rape of Nanking."

Some of the acts committed by Japanese troops during this period of time are included in Chapter 10 as provided by eye witness testimony and the extract of data from documents and affidavits during the trials.

These actions commenced with individual acts by simple or small numbers of individuals and culminated with widespread actions by large groups of Japanese troops against vast numbers of the Chinese populace.

Acts such as those alleged to have taken place in Nanking occurred in other areas of China but not in such vast and concentrated numbers.

Some of the puppet regimes that the Japanese established in occupied Chinese territory were:

1) Provisional Government of the Republic of China, Peking, 14 December 1937, headed by Wang Keh-Min, a one time Minister of Finance in one of the former Chinese Nationalist Governments.

2) Autonomous Federation of Mengchang, Kueihua, November 1938 with Prince The or The-Weng as he was known in China, as its leader. This regime was made up from the following three local puppet governments: Northern Shansi Province; Inner Mongolia, Kueihua; Kalgan.

3) Reform Government at Nanking.

4) National Government of China at Nanking, 30 March 1940, established by combining the Reform Government at Nanking and the Provisional Government of the Republic of China at Peiping, with Mr. Wang, Ching Weh as the leader. He spoke in vague terms of cooperation with Japan and stated that the policy of his government was peace, anti-communism, and reconstruction.

One of the Chinese puppet regimes was headed by Mr. Henry Pu-Yi, who was the last Chinese Emperor. Mr. Pu-Yi was born in Peking in 1906 and was enthroned as Emperor in 1909. A revolution started in China in 1911 under Sun Yat-Sen. The royal family continued to reside at the Peking Palace until being forced out during the revolution in 1924. Mr. Pu-Yi was a resident of Tientsin when the Japanese occupied that area. General Kashii commander at Tientsin compelled Mr. Pu-Yi to move to Port Arthur. General Honjo, Commander-in-Chief of the Japanese Kwantung Army insisted that Mr. Pu-Yi become the head of the Manchurian state or there would be danger against his life, so he accepted.

Japanese in the various offices of these puppet regimes, particularly on the economic and financial side, had the figures and the authority to speak out on matters while the Chinese in these regimes had very little authority. Japanese absorption of China's industries was for the benefit of Japan and in particular the Japanese Army. Methods concerning China's industries were handled differently in various areas of China.

In Shansi Province these industrial plants resumed work controlled by the Japanese Army Special Service Mission.

In other areas the Japanese Army turned seized industrial plants and the like over to be operated by Japanese civilian companies such as in North China to subsidiaries of the North China Development Company and in Central China to those of the Central China Development Company.

The Japanese financial policy for North China created a new currency and a new government bank known as the Federal Reserve Bank. Afterwards regulations followed that required all exporters and importers, Chinese and non-Chinese alike, except Japanese, who traded with Japan had to clear their foreign exchange through this bank. This single Japanese imposed policy in itself resulted in the gradual strangulation of all foreign trade with the occupied areas other than that with Japan and the effect on domestic China was to actually cut occupied China in two, economically.

In 1940 Mr. Okinori Kaya, one of the defendants, then president of the North China Development Company, stated in his words, as interpreted by a Japanese Army spokesman, stated that the plan for the material mobilization in the North China area occupied by the Japanese Army encompassed three main points. These were: (1) to supply Japan with the war material being consumed during the conduct of the Sino-Japanese hostilities; (2) to expand the armament of Japan; (3) to meet the needs of peace time industry.

Mr. Kaya added that the plan was not necessarily limited to the needs of only one nation but rather for the requirements for the regular daily needs of China, Japan, and Manchukuo as well.

Mr. Kaya, in elaboration as to what the North China Development Company was doing in China, referred to one of its subsidiary, the North China Communications Company, which was operating 3,750 miles of railway in North China, 6,250 miles of bus lines, and 625 miles of inland waterway communications.

Mr. Kaya also referred to the following other subsidiaries of the North China Development Company: The North China Telephone and Telegraph Company, The North China Aviation Company, The North China Salt Company. The Tatung Coal Mining Company, and The Lung Yen Iron Mining Company.

Thereafter, while the Japanese continued to pursue their policy of attempting to acquire control over the Netherlands, East Indies and other resource rich areas of Asia through peaceful means as well as the threat of the use of arms, they were gradually changing their policy towards China. When they abandoned the peaceful method to achieve their aims and swung towards the use of force for this purpose, they concentrated their efforts in China for the capture and occupation of the larger urban areas and by-passed the vast rural agricultural areas in between. This was particularly true along the coast where there was a series of Japanese occupied enclaves around the cities with open or unoccupied areas around them. Under this policy, the Japanese could maintain control over larger numbers of captured Chinese with a much smaller force of their own. Much of central and western China remained unconquered throughout the war.

Southern Regions
CHAPTER 7

Extract from Japanese Foreign Office Announcement, 1 August 1940:

The world stands at a great historic turning point, and it is about to witness the creation of new forms of government, economy, and culture, based upon the growth and development of sundry groups of states. Japan, too, is confronted by a great trial such as she has never experienced in history. In order to carry out fully at this juncture our national policy in accordance with the lofty spirit in which the country was founded, it is an important task of urgent necessity to us that we grasp the inevitable trends in the developments of world history, effect speedy fundamental renovations along all lines of government, and strive for the perfection of a state structure for national defense. Accordingly, the general lines of the country's fundamental national policies have been formulated as follows:

The basic aim of Japan's national policy lies in the firm establishment of world peace in accordance with the lofty spirit and principle of Hakko Ichiu, in which the country was founded, and in the desired idles for the construction of a New Order in Greater East Asia, having as a first step for its foundation the solidarity of Japan, Manchukuo, and China.

Japan will, therefore, devote the total strength of the nation to the fulfillment of the above policy by setting up swiftly an unshakable national structure of her own adapted to meet the requirements of new developments both at home and abroad.

Japanese Tentative Plan for Policy towards the Southern Regions, dated 4 October 1940:

Although the objective of Japan's penetration into the Southern Regions cover, in the first stage, the whole area to the west of Hawaii excluding for the time being the Philippines and Guam; French Indo-China, the Dutch East Indies, British Burma, and the Straits Settlements are the areas where we should first gain control. Then, we should gradually advance into the other areas. However, depending on the attitude of the US Government, the Philippines and Guam will be included.

To avoid the danger that the natural resources in the Dutch East Indies may be destroyed, within the possible limits of war strategy, we should use force in the areas of British Malaya and the Strait Settlements prior to using it in the Dutch East Indies. (There is a necessity that we investigate the strength of Singapore, and also in case we lay our hands on one of the British territories, whether or not we are strategically forced to extend to the other British territories immediately thereafter.)

We should conclude a military alliance between Japan and Thailand, with Japan using Thailand as a rear area base. However, in order to delay her in making preparations, it is well to pretend that the current diplomatic relations between Japan and Thailand are not deemed to be secure until we start military action. (In case we consider that the military alliance cannot be kept in strict secrecy because of internal affairs in Thailand, there is room for consideration that we should set up a secret committee based on the non-aggression treaty between Japan and Thailand to enable us to enter into a military alliance as soon as we start military action.)

Military operations shall be started simultaneously with Germany's military operations to land on the British mainland or after the lapse of a proper period. However, we must maintain close contact with Germany, asking her to act in concert with us.

In case Germany gives up her intention to land on the British Mainland, we, maintaining liaison with Germany, should start our military operations at the time when Germany carries out her most severe battle, or when an appropriate period has passed after that. In case Britain should yield to Germany prior to the common cement of our military action, even though the internal situation is not favorable to Japan, we must at least by diplomatic means, on the occasion of peace between Britain and Germany, make Britain remove the defense installations on Singapore and make her conclude an economic treaty with Japan which will be advantageous to Japan.

In case we are forced to act without relation with our plans in regard to Chiang Kai-shek, by using the pretext that Britain is aiding Chiang Kai-shek by the Burma route, and in case the plans have proved to be a success, by using the pretext that we cannot stand the Oriental peace being threatened by the British military forces based in Singapore, we should request Britain to return Hong Kong, British Malaya, and the Strait Settlements (Including British Borneo depending on the overall circumstances) to the races in East Asia and upon her refusal, start war. (The above pretexts hamper in some ways our relations with the United States, but it is likely that something which we can use as a direct reason, will rise by that time.)

Following the case of French Indo-China, the former territory of Thailand shall be returned to Thailand and other regions shall be made protectorates. But the Strait Settlements must be placed under the direct rule of Japan.

In the newly established independent countries the enterprise rights of the nationals of third countries with which we are at peace shall follow the case in French Indo-China.

While the attack on Singapore is going on, or immediately after it, by presenting the following requests pertaining to the Dutch East Indies, and if they are not admitted, we should use military force:

As the Dutch Government in England, which the people of the Dutch East Indies considers law, the Dutch East Indies shall at once declare its independence for the peace of Greater East Asia, and announce an appropriate name for itself.

The sovereign and the constitution will be decided by a committee consisting of several Japanese, Dutch people born there, natives, and Chinese. (It must be arranged that the total number of Japanese and natives number more than half the committee.) Until the sovereign and the constitution are decided, this committee shall carry out the administration.

The Governor-General and all other Dutch officials of the highest rank shall be forced to resign. But the official titles, honors, and pay should be left as they are. The position of the Dutch people other than the aforementioned will be recognized as they are.

If any of the important natural resources should be destroyed, all the persons connected with the raw material, the government officials concerned shall be punished as being the responsible persons. (This matter should be announced widely beforehand by radio and other means.)

We should, if possible, at a proper time before pre-senting the aforementioned requests, cause an independence movement to be aroused among the natives.

If it is considered a better plan from the viewpoint of strategy that we act first with the Dutch East Indies, the time to start the activity against this area would be at the same time as the opening of Germany's military operation to land on the British mainland, or after the lapse of a proper period.

In case that Germany gives up her intention to land on the British mainland, we should start action choosing an appropriate time before Britain and Germany cease hostilities.

After the Dutch East Indies become independent, we must conclude a protective treaty under the guise of a military alliance, and appoint Japanese military and economic advisers to fill powerful positions under such an agreement. Places deemed to be important from a military point of view must be leased.

The enterprise rights of the nationals of the third countries with which we are at peace shall follow the case of French Indo-China.

After we have grasped real power in the Dutch East Indies and in Singapore, we must take proper measures to get real power in British Borneo and other British territories.

Hong Kong is to be returned to China. (However, if it is important strategically, it shall be reconsidered.)

Following what has been stated about French Indo-China, the Dutch East Indies, Malaya, etc., we shall consider locally the administrative system in each place.

Australian territories are to be considered separately.

Extract from a memorandum for the German Foreign Minister concerning German-Japanese economic relations during and after the war, Berlin, 21 March 1941: Notes on German-Japanese economic questions for the conversation with the Japanese Foreign Minister.

Raw Material Orders Through Japan

We shall have to buy raw materials from third countries through Japan and get them into Germany, e.g. rubber and tin from the Netherlands Indies and Thailand; Wolfram from South China; tin from Bolivia. For this purpose we are ready to place foreign bills of exchange at the disposal of Japan. Thus far, in deference to England and America, and because of her own supply situation and lack of tonnage, and so forth, Japan has done little in this direction. But even where such reasons did not exist, bureaucratic restraints and involved procedural regulations have produced difficulties and delays On the basis of a promise by Matsuoka, the Wohlthat delegation should probably be able to obtain improvements.

We are likewise counting on Japanese help with blockade runners and auxiliary cruisers for the transportation of such raw materials to Germany.

New Form of Economic Relations After the War

According to the German conception, the great possibilities which exist for the new order of economic relations between the European-African economic sphere under the leadership of Japan can only be fully realized if matters are carried out in a grand manner. For this reason the freest possible trade exchange should take place. As a matter of principle one should reserve to oneself preferences over third countries. Over-centralization with its unavoidable hindrances should be shunned. Rather, Japan should be able to carry on business and make its own trade agreements directly with the independent countries in the German-Italian Sphere, and conversely, Germany and Italy with the independent countries according to previous statement of government representatives in Tokyo is that Germany should have trade dealings with countries like China, Indo-China, and also the Netherlands Indies not directly, but only through Japan. No fundamental aggravation of this question had yet occurred, as we have been dependent anyway on Japanese support in imports in our trade during the war with the countries mentioned.

There was a report of a conversation between the German and Japanese Foreign Ministers on 29 March 1941, in which an attack towards the South was again discussed as well as the construction of German and Japanese spheres of domination. During this discussion, the Japanese Foreign Minister expressed his fears that should Japan attack the Netherlands Indies, the oil fields there would be set on fire.

Extract from a decision by Imperial Headquarters in April 1941:

Gist of Imperial Headquarters, Army/Navy Department Policy concerning Measures to be taken in the South.

The aims of the measures to be taken by the Empire in the South are to promote the settlement of the China Incident as well as to expand our overall national defensive power in the interests of self-existence and self-defense. For these purposes: To establish close and inseparable joint relations in military affairs, politics, and economy with French Indo-China and Thailand; to establish close economic relations with the Netherlands Indies; to maintain normal commercial relations with the other various countries in the South.

The foregoing purposes shall, on principle, be accomplished through diplomatic measures.

In executing the foregoing measures resorting to arms in the interest of self-existence and self-defense will be taken only when the following instances should occur and when no means for solution of same can be found: In case the Empire's self-existence should be threatened by the embargoes of the United States, Great Britain, and The Netherlands; in case the situation of the Anti-Japanese encirclement by the United States, Great Britain, the Netherlands, and China become so tense that it cannot be tolerated in the interests of national defense.

When a Japanese attempt to obtain a foothold in the Netherlands Indies failed in June 1941, the Japanese began making preparations to occupy bases in the southern part of French Indo-China, which were needed for a military advance into the Netherlands Indies.

Decision of the Imperial Headquarters Government Liaison conference, 25 June 1941, Re Acceleration of Measures in the South.

In view of the various existing conditions, the Empire shall, in accordance with its fixed policy accelerate its measures towards French Indo-China and Thailand. Especially, in connection with the return of the Japanese Delegate from the Dutch Indies, a military union shall be established with French Indo-China as soon as possible for the purpose of stability and defense of East Asia. Concerning this establishment of joint military relations with French Indo-China, the essential factors which the Empire should stress upon are as follows: The establishment or use of air bases and harbor facilities in specified areas in French Indo-China stationing of the necessary troops in the southern part of French Indo-China; furnishing of facilities in connection with the stationing of Imperial troops.

To open diplomatic negotiations for the purpose of the preceding paragraph.

In case the French Government or the French Indo-China authorities do not comply with our demands, we shall attain our objective by force of arms.

In order to deal with such circumstance as mentioned in the above paragraph, preparations shall be commenced beforehand for the dispatching of troops.

In the Imperial Conference of 2 July 1941 the principle of Japan's policy was laid down in three points: Japan would adhere to the principles of establishing a Greater East Asia Co-prosperity Sphere regardless of any change in the international situation; Japan would follow up the southward advance to establish for herself a basis for self-existence and self-defense; Japan would remove all obstacles for the achievement of the foregoing purpose.

There can be little doubt that the Japanese government was studying the consequences of various war situations as evidenced by the answers that were contained in an extract from a document prepared by the Foreign Ministry to questions that they were tasked to provide answers to at the Liaison conference between the Government and Imperial Headquarters in October 1941:

Q: In case of the outbreak of war against Britain, America, and the Netherlands, how much cooperation can we make Germany and Italy promise?

A: It is impossible to expect a great deal.

a) In case war breaks out this autumn: Germany has hitherto given us the impression that she would attack America in case of war breaking out between Japan and America. In view of the Tripartite Treaty obligations, we can expect both Germany and Italy to begin war against America depending on our attitude. But in this case, either country's declaration of war against America would only mean they would take further steps in their present relations against America. Their attacks on American vessels and warships in the Atlantic would be intensified, and they would play an effective role by diverting America in their landing operations on the British mainland, which would help us indirectly.

But it is difficult to expect all these from Germany (or Italy) which might require a preparation period for other operations after she comes to a pause in attacking Russia. Furthermore, now that contact with Germany through the Siberian Railway has been cut off, it is impossible to expect materials and economic assistance from Germany.

As for the case of our advance into the Dutch East Indies, Germany has contemplated pressing Dutch people in Holland to bring pressure upon the Dutch East Indies, but we doubt its effect at present since a considerable number of German prisoners still remain in the Dutch East Indies.

b) In case war breaks out next spring: The German forces are hinting at the carrying out of landing operations on the British mainland next spring and operational preparations for this purpose on the French coast seems to be considerably advanced, but we cannot affirm that the operations will be carried out. The attack on the British mainland will indirectly help Japan to fight against Britain and America, but no more direct assistance can be expected except the operations of the Japanese and German forces which will indirectly benefit each other, since the hope of our contact with Germany through Siberia will be difficult even next spring. As we are not sure if the landing operation on the British mainland will take place next spring, it is dangerous to rely on it.

In both cases of (a) and (b) the greatest help that we can expect from Germany and Italy will be the advance of German and Italian forces to the Near East, Central Asia and India. In as much as our advance must be carried out in accordance with them, a full arrangement would be required beforehand.

c) In case war breaks out later than next spring: When Germany has consolidated her occupied areas and completed the establishment of a new order in Europe, her attack on Britain will be much more intensified. Consequently it may be of considerable advantage for us to fight America, but we must consider the possibility of peace between Germany and Britain.

Q: Can our opponents in war be restricted to the Netherlands or both to Britain and the Netherlands?

A: There is no possibility of restricting them only to the Netherlands or to Britain and the Netherlands. As for the attitude to be taken by Britain and America provided that Japan advances by force to the South, namely Thailand, Burma, Singapore, and the Dutch East Indies, we have certainly not heard of any military alliance among them.

Nor has there been any settlement providing for cooperation among Britain, America, and the Netherlands (or the Chungking regime), but it is almost certain that they have mutual understanding for joint defense in case Japan car-

*ries out an armed advance against any one of these coun-
tries. The attitude of Britain and America will also be affected to a great degree by the time and manner of our advance to the South, the international situation at the time,
and the internal situation of both Britain and America. It is
necessary to take into consideration all probable cases which
may take place in this connection, but at any rate it is impossible for us to restrict our opponents to the Netherlands
only or to Britain and the Netherlands in case of our southward advance, and we must also be ready for Russia to enter the war.*

*Now we have made the following general assessment per-
taining to each country, judging from the present situation:*

Britain (including Australia, Canada, etc.): *When we
advance to the Dutch East Indies we might expect Britain to
carry out, first of all, a diplomatic campaign regarding us
and the Dutch Indies, but we can expect that she will probably make up her mind to take up arms for her own self-
defense. (Whether she will take up arms immediately or not
will depend on the situation at the time.) Judging from
Britain's reports and behavior until the present, we are considerably sure of this view.*

America: *In a case as pointed out above, Britain may
immediately ask America for assistance. Therefore, even if
America does not participate in the war immediately, she
most assuredly will, of course, accelerate strengthening her
military preparation. Then we can suppose that in such a
situation she will take the following steps: Diversionary measures against us by way of diplomacy; close her consulates;
recall ambassadors; and severance of her diplomatic relations.*

*Demonstrations by her navy and air forces. But it is dan-
gerous to form such a view that America would take gradual*

steps toward us, judging by her attitude towards Germany. For we cannot but expect America to take much more prompt steps in case we advance to the south, compared with the case where Germany swept over the European countries. America would not be able presumably to overlook the Japanese southward advance as "another's business" because of the following reasons:

In a sense she considers the southwestern Pacific area as being in the zone over which she has the power of utterance (as seen in the Japanese-American negotiations).

Some materials of the above mentioned area are necessary in America (gum, tin, etc.).

She fears that in Chinese problems, she could entirely lose her right of utterance.

She is afraid of our occupation of the Philippines.

The American public opinion would be more excited than in case of the European war.

Advantages and disadvantages for our foreign relations in case war breaks out about March of next year.

Advantages: As a result of the Russo-German War, Soviet forces in European Russia may suffer a crushing blow and be very busy with its reconstruction from this winter until next spring. Consequently, a considerable transfer of the strength of the Soviet Far Eastern Army and an increasing unrest within the country are anticipated. Therefore, we think that for us the threat and burden in the north will be less than at present.

Depending on the situation there may also be some slight chance of taking diplomatic measures regarding Russia so as to mediate Russo-German peace.

German winter operations are expected to be directed toward Africa, the Near East and Central Asia, and thus Britain must exert herself to defend these areas. With the preparations to meet German landing operations on the British homeland, etc. the European Theater will become busy; consequently her position in East Asia will be weakened and German's diversionary role will be more effective than at present.

Even if America does not participate in the war next March, her preparation for entering the war will be further advanced; consequently internally she will be increasingly troubled by difficult problems in her domestic administration and finance; militarily there is a possibility that she will have to divide her strength in the Pacific; while diplomatically she may have to soften her attitude toward us.

We should gain time to improve and strengthen our diplomatic position within the Thailand and the French Indo-China areas.

Disadvantages: *We think that our economic difficulties will rather increase by March of next year.*

Militarily there may be danger in also giving the opponents time for preparation.

War Against the United States of America and the Philippine Commonwealth
CHAPTER 8

Pearl Harbor

During the early 20th century, there was a competitive struggle for naval supremacy in the western Pacific between Japan and the United States. This naval armaments race began in earnest in 1916 and Japan continued to expand the size and power of her Imperial Navy until by the Autumn of 1941 it was more powerful than the combined British and US fleets in the Pacific area. In their fleet were not only the two largest battleships the world had ever seen but they also possessed ten aircraft carriers while the British had only one and the United States had three. While most of the world's navies, including, the United States, at the time still regarded the aircraft carrier as useful only to provide a defensive air umbrella for the battle ships, the Imperial Navy adopted the strategy of using them as an offensive weapon. Most of the Japanese Army leaders, based on their successes in China, were for expanding the war and the promotion of the Greater East Asia Co-prosperity Sphere but most of the admirals were not. This situation changed when President Roosevelt ordered the US Pacific Fleet to leave the West Coast ports and concentrate at Pearl Harbor.

Admiral Isoruku Yamamoto, who was appointed commander-in-chief of the Japanese Combined Fleet, the senior executive command in the Imperial Navy, on 30 August 1939, was the person who conceived of and pushed the plan to strike at the American Pacific Fleet in Pearl Harbor utilizing aircraft armed with bombs and torpedoes. Yamamoto, who had always been opposed to actions which could precipitate a conflict between Japan and the United States and Britain, was often accused by Japanese political extremists of being pro-American and a traitor because of his outspoken philosophy against policies which risked such a war. He had already been threatened with assassination in his previous position as Vice-Minister of the Imperial Navy because of his anti-war beliefs.

After assuming his new position as commander in chief of the Combined Fleet, he began reflecting on how to destroy the American Pacific Fleet if Japan's politicians should involve her in a war with the United States.

Based upon the success of the British in the sinking of three Italian battleships at Taranto while losing only two out of 24 of their attacking aircraft, Yamamoto concluded that the chances of success of an air strike against the fleet while at anchor in Pearl Harbor would be excellent.

The Pearl Harbor task force under the command of Rear Admiral Chuichi Nagumo would set sail from Tankan Bay in the Kurile Islands destined for an aircraft launch point some 230 miles north of Oahu. The task force would consist of six aircraft carriers, two battleships, two heavy and one light cruiser, seven destroyers, and assorted support ships such as tankers since the fleet would have to be refueled on the way. Aboard the aircraft carriers were an estimated force of 360 aircraft that would be armed with bombs and torpedoes. Three submarines were to go ahead of the task force to reconnoiter the route in advance and two destroyers had the job of destroying the US air base at Midway Island simultaneously with the attack on Oahu.

The task force set sail for the aircraft launch point on 26 November 1941.

An advance expeditionary force consisting of five midget and twenty I-class submarines together with their supporting screen departed separately on a different route that would have them approaching Oahu from the southwest. The midget submarines could not make the trip on their own, so they were transported to the vicinity of Pearl Harbor clamped to the deck of an 'I' class mother ship.

Japanese representatives in Washington, D.C. continued the negotiations during the time that the task forces were sailing toward Hawaii for their surprise attack.

At 0615 on the morning of 7 December 1941 (Washington DC time) the first wave of 181 aircraft lifted off their aircraft carriers led by Commander Mitsuo Fuchida and headed for Pearl Harbor arriving at 0755 where they attacked American warships and airfields on Oahu. Surprise of the attack was so great that even though the signal on its extent was misinterpreted that attacks by the bombers and torpedo planes occurred simultaneously and not one after the other as the plan called for, there was not very much opposition to either. At 0824 a second wave of 172 Japanese aircraft arrived to continue the attack.

The attacks resulted in 18 ships being sunk or seriously damaged, 188 aircraft destroyed and 159 damaged, with total American casualties of 2,403 killed and 1,178 wounded. Nearly half of the personnel killed were lost when the magazine on the battleship *Arizona* blew up. Also during the attacks, bombs and American anti-aircraft fire caused damage to the city of Honolulu that was estimated at 500,000 dollars.

Admiral Yamamoto criticized Admiral Nagumo for failing to: Locate and cause great damage to or the destruction of the aircraft carriers assigned to the US Pacific Fleet; and destroy the fuel for the Pacific Fleet stored in the tanks at the Fleet Fuel Storage area.

Nagumo rejected Yamamoto's criticism by saying that he had obeyed his orders to the letter.

However, it can be readily seen that had the Japanese attack achieved either of the above the outcome of the war could have been greatly prolonged or changed. The outcome would have drastically changed if the Japanese attack had destroyed or heavily damaged the machine shops on Oahu, proven to be invaluable in repairing the stricken ships. If the tanker *Neosho,* which was berthed near the fuel storage tanks on Ford Island, had been hit it would not only have created an inferno on the four battleships moored nearby, *Maryland, Tennessee, Oklahoma,* and *West Virginia*, but would probably have destroyed the storage tanks also.

Japanese losses during the attack included 29 aircraft, one I-class, all five midget submarines, and 185 personnel.

The Japanese Pearl Harbor task force arrived back in Japan on 24-26 December 1941.

Vast amounts of material has been published in both the written and pictorial forms pertaining to the events leading up to and the happenings during the attack, both fact and fiction. It would serve very little to add much of anything more than a chronology on the planning and execution of the attack but to state the obvious. An extremely devastating blow had been rendered against the US Navy and hostilities were initiated in the Pacific Asiatic conflict that was to have deadly and dire effect on the lives of millions of persons.

The following is an abbreviated chronology of the Pearl Harbor attack from the time of Admiral Yamamoto's appointment as Commander-in-Chief of the Japanese Imperial Navy until the attack force returned to Japan.

August 1939: Admiral Yomamoto was appointed Commander-in-Chief of the Japanese Imperial Navy.

April-May 1940: Japanese Combined Fleet held maneuvers, paying special attention to mock air attacks.

11 November 1940: Royal Navy aircraft sank three Italian battleships during a daring night attack at the Taranto base in the Mediterranean.

December 1940: Suggestion that anti-torpedo nets be erected in Pearl Harbor was rejected. Admiral Yamamoto confided his idea for an attack on Pearl Harbor to his Chief-of-Staff.

27 January 1941: US Ambassador Grew reported from Tokyo a rumor that Japan was planning a surprise attack on Pearl Harbor.

1 February 1941: Admiral Kimmel was appointed Commander-in-Chief of the US Pacific Fleet succeeding Admiral Richardson who had always opposed the fleet being based at Pearl Harbor and urged that it be returned to the US West Coast.

February-March 1941: In Tokyo, plans for the attack on Pearl Harbor were prepared in draft form.

7 February 1941: General Short assumed duties as Commanding General, Hawaiian Command.

14 February 1941: President Roosevelt received the new Japanese Ambassador, Admiral Nomura.

8 March 1941: US passed Lend-Lease Bill, authorizing aid to any country opposing members of the Tripartite Pact of September 1940 (Japan, Germany, and Italy).

9 April 1941: Admiral Nomura presented the first of a Japanese series of proposals for resolving US/Japanese difficulties. Each of these proposals was rejected by the US.

15 April 1941: US began Lend-Lease shipments to China.

20 June 1941: US stops oil shipments from Atlantic and Gulf ports to all countries except Britain and Latin America.

2 July 1941: Japan calls up 1,000,000 men for their armed forces.

24 July 1941: Japanese troops occupy Southern Indo-China with consent of French Vichy Government.

26 July 1941: President Roosevelt freezes Japanese assets in the United States, closed all US ports to Japanese vessels, and announced an embargo on sale of US petroleum products to Japan.

6 August 1941: Admiral Nomura presented a Japanese proposal in which Japan agreed not to advance beyond Indo-China and to evacuate Indo-China when an agreement was reached with China, if the US would restore free trade with Japan, stop aid to China, persuade China to negotiate a treaty favorable to Japan, and recognize Japan's interests in Indo-China.

9-12 August 1941: Churchill for Britain and Roosevelt for the US agreed in principle on the Atlantic Charter.

17 August 1941: President Roosevelt insisted that fundamental issues be reached at the Ambassadorial level first on Japanese Prime Minister Konoye's proposal for a summit meeting between the two of them.

6 September: Japanese Imperial Conference decided on war if an agreement was not reached by early October with the United States.

24 September 1941: US intercepted a message from Tokyo to the Japanese Consulate-General in Honolulu, ordering spies to report on US naval vessels on Pearl Harbor.

9 October 1941: US succeeded deciphering the Japanese message of 24 September 1941. This was one of the decoded messages given the code name Magic and provided with limited distribution among high-ranking US officials.

16 October 1941: Japanese Prime Minister Konoye was forced to resign. After the fall of the Konoye Cabinet, Tojo became Prime Minister and formed a new Cabinet with Togo as Foreign Minister.

16 October 1941: Admiral Stark, US Chief of Naval Operations, warned Admiral Kimmel that Japanese aggression was possible.

3 November 1941: US Ambassador in Tokyo, Grew, cabled Washington that dangerous Japanese action might come with dramatic suddenness which could render armed conflict between the two nations unavoidable.

5 November 1941: Admiral Yamamoto issued Combined Fleet Top Secret Order #1 which contained detailed plans for the attack on Pearl Harbor.

5 November 1941: The Japanese Privy Council authorized submission of further proposals to the US. The US rejected both plans by 20 November.

5 November 1941: The US intercepted a message from Tokyo to Ambassador Nomura stating the deadline for agreement with the US was 25 November.

15 November 1941: Special Envoy Kurusu arrived in Washington to assist Admiral Nomura in his negotiations with the United States.

15 November 1941: The US intercepted a message to the Japanese Consul General in Honolulu from Tokyo directing their spies to provide their ships in harbor reports twice a week.

17 November 1941: Ambassador Grew in Tokyo cabled Washington warning that Japan may strike suddenly and unexpectedly.

20 November 1941: Japanese negotiators in Washington presented the final Japanese proposal.

22 November 1941: The US intercepted a message from Tokyo to Japanese negotiators stating that the 25 November deadline was extended to 29 November but no further extension was possible.

24 November 1941: Admiral Kimmel was warned by the US Chief of Naval Operations that Japanese surprise aggressive action was possible.

26 November 1941: Admiral Natumo's Pearl Harbor task force sailed from Tankan Bay in the Kuriles destined for the initial aircraft lift off point some 200 miles north of Oahu.

26 November 1941: US Secretary of State, Cordell Hull, handed the US reply to the 20 November Japanese note to Japanese negotiators.

27 November 1941: US Chief of Naval Operations and the US Army Chief of Staff separately notify Admiral Kimmel and General Short that diplomatic negotiations with the Japanese had collapsed and Japanese aggression might occur at any time.

27 November 1941: US Chief of Naval Operations suggested that Admiral Kimmel arrange to deliver 25 aircraft each to Wake Island and Midway ASAP.

27 November 1941: Tokyo tells Nomura and Kurusu that even with the rupture in negotiations, they were not to give the impression they had broken off.

28 November 1941: Admiral Kimmel ordered that submerged submarines in the vicinity of Pearl Harbor were to be regarded as hostile.

29 November 1941: The US intercepted a message from Tokyo to the Japanese Consulate-General in Hawaii directing his agents to report absence of ship movements at Pearl Harbor.

30 November 1941: The Japanese Cabinet approved the text of a note to be sent in answer to Cordell Hull's proposal dated 26 November. Emperor Hirohito insisted that the note should be delivered before hostilities began.

1 December 1941: The Japanese Privy Council, meeting in the presence of the Emperor, authorized the attack on Pearl Harbor.

2 December 1941: The US intercepted a message to the Japanese Embassy in Washington from Tokyo directing the Ambassador to destroy his codes.

6 December 1941: The US intercepted two messages from Japanese agents in Honolulu to Tokyo stating that there was still a lot of advantage in the surprise attack and there did not appear to be any air reconnaissance being done by the fleet air arm. This message was not deciphered until 8 December.

6 December 1941: By about 0930 a.m. President Roosevelt had read the deciphered Japanese note of 30 November, which the Japanese Ambassador had been directed not to deliver until a time specifically designated by Tokyo.

7 December 1941: (9:20 a.m. Washington time; 3:50 a.m. Honolulu time). The mine sweeper USS *Condor* sighted a submarine periscope outside the entrance to Pearl Harbor.

7 December 1941: (11:00 a.m. Washington time; 5:30 a.m. Honolulu time). The US Chief of Staff and Chief of

Naval Operations received deciphered copies of the final part of the Japanese note and a message from Tokyo that the note was to be delivered at 1:00 p.m. Washington time. The Chief of Staff cabled General Short at 12:18 p.m. (Washington time; 6:48 a.m. Honolulu time) with a copy for Admiral Kimmel telling the time specified for the delivery of the note but neither received the message until after the attack.

7 December 1941: (12:15 p.m. Washington time; 6:45 p.m. Honolulu time). The destroyer USS *Ward* sank a submarine outside the Pearl Harbor boom.

7 December 1941: (1:25-1:55 p.m. Washington time; 7:55-8:25 a.m. Honolulu time). Japanese aircraft attacked US ships in Pearl Harbor and airfields on Oahu where the US aircraft were lined up wing-tip to wing-tip for anti sabotage defense.

7 December 1941: (1:55 p.m. Washington time; 8:25 a.m. Honolulu time). A second wave of Japanese aircraft attack Oahu.

7 December 1941: (3:15 p.m. Washington time; 9:45 a.m. Honolulu time). Japanese aircraft depart Hawaii to return to their carriers.

7 December 1941: At the same time as the attack on Pearl Harbor, the Japanese launched attacks on the Philippines, Malaya, Hong Kong, Thailand, Guam, and Wake Island.

7 December 1941: (4:00 p.m. Washington time; 10:30 a.m. Honolulu time). An Imperial Rescript, signed by Emperor Hirohito, declaring war on the United States and Britain was issued.

8 December 1941: The US Congress passed a resolution declaring war on Japan.

8 December 1941: Britain declared war on Japan.

9 December 1941: Secretary of the Navy Knox left the United States for Hawaii to assess damage at Pearl Harbor.

11 December 1941: In accordance with the Tripartite Treaty, Germany and Italy declared war on the US and the US declared war on Germany and Italy.

24-26 December 1941: The Japanese Pearl Harbor task force arrived back in Japan.

One of the documents entered by the prosecution as evidence described the bombing of Manila by Japanese planes in December 1941 after the city was declared to have been an open and undefended city. Many buildings were damaged or destroyed as a result of the bombs dropped during these raids, including churches, schools and colleges, as well as those private residences destroyed by the ensuing fires.

The Japanese placed troops ashore in the Philippines during five landings there and began the drive towards the capture of Manila and the complete subjugation of all island areas.

General MacArthur moved his Headquarters to Corregidor Island at the entrance of Manila Bay. MacArthur and selected members of his staff were evacuated from there to Australia and it was during this move that he made his famous statement, "I shall return."

Another of the prosecution documents was the affidavit of Major General Edward P. King, the Commanding General of the American/Filipino forces that surrendered on Bataan in April 1942. When asked when his forces surrendered to the Japanese, General King replied that he sent three officers from his staff forward under a flag of truce at 2:00 a.m. on 9 April 1942 to make an appointment for him to meet with the Japanese Commander on Bataan. On the way forward to the arranged rendezvous point General King's party were delayed often by stopping and taking cover from attacking, low-flying, Japanese aircraft. It was nearly 10 o'clock when they arrived. They were met by a Japanese Major General who said that he was the commander of one division of the Japanese forces, and that he had reported the coming of General King to Japanese headquarters in the Philippines. He further stated that he had no authority to meet with him, that another officer was to be sent from the Japanese headquarters to meet with him and that his own forces would not advance for 30 minutes while General King decided what he was going to do. When no such officer arrived and the Japanese forces resumed the advance, General King sent word back for his units to display a white flag and to surrender to the first Japanese who approached them.

Soon a Japanese Colonel, who was identified as General Homma's Chief-of-Staff, arrived, said he would act as General Homma's representative, and demanded an unconditional surrender. General King's main concern was for his forces to be treated as POWs and he asked for some assurance on this but the Japanese Colonel accused him of attempting to set a condition for the surrender instead of being unconditional.

After some lengthy debate, the Japanese Colonel finally said that the soldiers of the Imperial Japanese Army were not barbarians and with that assurance General King surrendered. After the surrender General King asked that the motor transport and gasoline that had been left operational be used to move the POWs out of Bataan. He even offered to provide assistance but the Japanese said that they would take care of the POW movement as they desired, that General King was to have nothing to do with it, and that his wishes could not be considered.

With the surrenders at Bataan and Corregidor, organized resistance in the Philippines ceased to exist and only irregular forces continued to resist the Japanese occupation aided by those members of the US forces and Filipino militia who had managed to escape and remain hidden.

Subsequently, the United States established and maintained two separate commands for the pursuit of the Pacific War, one in Australia commanded by General MacArthur and the other commanded by Admiral Nimitz in Hawaii. This command structure remained in force until Japan surrendered due to the destruction of the cities of Hiroshima and Nagasaki by the atomic weapons that were unleashed in 1945.

Less than six months after Pearl Harbor, four of Yamamoto's precious carriers were at the bottom of the ocean, casualties of the Battle of Midway. After the overwhelming defeat at Midway and the costly evacuation of Guadalcanal, the Japanese feeling of invincibility, which had followed the Pearl Harbor attack was undermined and Yamamoto's encouragement was badly needed.

Admiral Yamamoto would in all probability have been included as one of the defendants in this major war crimes trial if he had survived the war. He was killed when the aircraft he was in was shot down over Bougainville on 18 April 1943. Admiral Yamamoto and his party were making a morale building tour of forward bases in the south Pacific. They were being flown from one point of their tour to the next in two bombers that were being escorted by six Japanese fighters when they were intercepted by American fighter aircraft. After two short bursts of cannon fire, the plane that Admiral Yamamoto was flying in, trailing black smoke, crashed into the trees and was quickly engulfed in flames with no survivors. The American fighter aircraft had been provided the precise itinerary for Admiral Yamamoto's party since the Americans had broken the Japanese code. At no time did the Japanese give any indication that they knew that their code had been compromised.

United States forces started to complete the reversal in the recapture of the Philippines by the invasion of Leyte Island. General MacArthur was depicted wading ashore onto the beach of this island, whereby he was symbolically fulfilling his famous vow to return to the Philippines that he had made upon his evacuation to Australia.

Admiral Nagumo died by committing hara-kiri when he shot himself in a hut on Saipan and an aide set fire to the hut. His body was never found.

After the surrender at Bataan, some of the war's worst atrocities were committed during the Bataan Death March and later during the final months of Manila's occupation by Japanese forces. Both the Japanese Commander during the final period of Philippine occupation, General Yamashita, and General Homma, the Commander responsible for the Bataan Death March, were tried shortly after the end of hostilities, convicted of being responsible for allowing the commission of the atrocities, and executed by hanging.

Admiral James D. Richardson, former commander in chief, US Fleet, testifies at the War Crimes Trials in the War Ministry Building, Tokyo.

G.C. Hardin, associate council in the Prosecution Section, introduces the affidavit of Ex-Ambassador Grew as an exhibit during the War Crimes Trials at the War Ministry Building, Tokyo.

Three former POWs look over a map during a session of the War Crimes Trials at IMTFE. The map showed the extent of the Japanese Empire in 1942.

War Against The Netherlands and the Netherlands East Indies
CHAPTER 9

Mr. Justice Borgerhoff Mulder, associate prosecutor from the Kingdom of the Netherlands, presented the prosecution's case as it relates to the Japanese aggression against the Netherlands. However, before Mr. Mulder could get started, the defense counsel for defendant Oshima raised objections to introduction of the Netherlands phase of the case by the counsel for the Government of the Kingdom of the Netherlands and to their participation in the trial for the following reasons:

- Nothing in the record of this case officially or otherwise granted the Court jurisdiction for the presentation of the Netherlands phase of the case by any counsel other than American counsel, if any authority exists for that.

- That the Appointing Authority had no power over Dutch forces and therefore, no jurisdiction to enforce trial for offenses to their national honor and dignity nor for the violation of land warfare against their armed forces.

- That the Appointing Authority had no power over the Netherlands prosecutors and that the Chief of Counsel had no authority to delegate responsibility to them.

- That no oath of office, notice of appointment, or letters of authority have been filed by the Netherlands prosecution staff in these proceedings, as is required to all courts appointed by the Supreme Commander under his congressional or presidential authority.

- That the Netherlands Government was not a party to the Potsdam Agreement and, as such, is not a proper party to these proceedings, and that the terms at Potsdam cannot be enlarged upon or extended to any nation not a party to that agreement.

- That the views expressed in the Indictment and those in the opening statement of this phase of the case represent those of the Imperial Government of the Netherlands and not those of the leaders of the Dutch East Indies, that the Imperial Government of the Netherlands was in exile at the time the acts complained of occurred and, therefore, not a legally constituted government under international law but a government functioning in exile.

- That the defendants were entitled to know by whose and/or what authority the Netherlands Government's complaint was being pressed against them and the nature of the appointment of the prosecutors and the government to whom they were responsible.

- That international law requires strict proof of the right of the prosecution and evidence of the nature of the appointment and the extent of the representation since the prosecution was attempting to prove the crime "Charge Against Humanity."

The defense counsel stated that to permit them to prosecute this cause before a tribunal created by the American Supreme Allied Commander would constitute a fatal error and require vacation of the proceedings if the record stands as it now stands. He further said that he expects these objections to grow to even greater proportions as this phase of the case progresses and that was why the question was raised before the prosecutor made his opening statement.

The Tribunal President ruled that the objections had no foundation in fact, law, or reason and that they were overruled.

Mr. Mulder said that since the subject of this phase of the case was Japanese aggression against the Netherlands, the evidence to be presented would relate more especially to Counts 1 and 32 of the Indictment but would also substantiate charges set forth in other counts.

Japan, when a speedy conclusion of its war with China seemed improbable at the end of the 1930s gradually turned her attention to a southward expansion and the acquiring of southern territories which were rich in mineral resources and possessed vast quantities of agricultural products. Japanese plans for the peaceful domination of the area were put into execution through: Negotiations with Germany; a Japanese advance into Indo-China; threats on the so-called 'orphaned' Netherlands Indies.

At the same time, in case of failure of the peaceful method, plans for a military expansion southward were prepared. When the Netherlands East Indies did not yield to Japanese pressure and threats, aggression and the military conquest of the area was decided upon. One of the main motives for the December 1941 Japanese aggression in the Pacific was the Japanese advancement into the Netherlands Indies and the surrounding territories. The Japanese intent in the capture and occupation of these areas was to facilitate the construction of a new Japanese empire.

The prosecution introduced as evidence copies of several telegrams from the German Ambassador in Tokyo to the German Foreign Minister in May 1940 in which the German Ambassador reported his statement to the Japanese government that Germany was not interested in the Netherlands East Indies and that the Japanese press considered this German declaration to be a 'carte blanche' for Japan.

The prosecution also introduced a copy of a telegram from the German Ambassador in Tokyo to the German Foreign Minister, dated 24 June 1940, in which the German Ambassador reported that the accused, Koiso, then the Japanese Minister for Overseas Affairs, had inquired as to what Germany's attitude would be to military activity by Japan in Indo-China and parts of the Netherlands Indies.

The United States, Great Britain, France, and Japan, agreed by treaty on 13 December 1921, to respect each others rights to their Pacific Ocean possessions and dominions, and settle all differences on this subject by peaceful means only. Although the Netherlands was not among the treaty signatories, each of the contracting governments to the treaty issued a solemn declaration on 4 February 1922 stating that the Netherlands' right would be respected in relation to its pacific Ocean possessions. At no time did the Japanese government indicate that they no longer considered themselves bound by this Pact. In the final years prior to the military expansion southward, the Japanese government repeatedly declared that Japan's intentions were totally peaceful even while they were planning and preparing for this onslaught. Numerous Government officials stated that Japan was satisfied with this situation as late as 1940 and early 1941.

A comprehensive plan dated in September 1940 was found in the Japanese government files which listed in some detail how to achieve a military conquest in the Netherlands Indies without causing too much damage to its natural resources and industrial equipment. It also went into the method on how to make the Netherlands Indies a puppet state in Japan's Sphere by stirring up an independence movement.

In all other regions from Burma to the Philippines, a similar policy was to be followed.

The prosecution entered as evidence alternative drafts of demands to be made on the Netherlands Indies, dated mid August 1940, which stated that in the present world situation there were vast undeveloped areas with huge abundant resources, and on the other hand, there were nations suffering from a lack of resources and overpopulation while having great abilities for exploration and development. The Netherlands may control the Dutch Indies but geographically it is situated within the Co-Prosperity Sphere for the Far East and her rich resources should first be opened for the benefit of those races of East Asia and only thereafter for the benefit and prosperity of all mankind.

In line with the above views, the Imperial Japanese government, as the stabilizing power in East Asia, made the following demands on the Dutch East Indies Government:

Political Questions: (1) The Dutch Indies should cut off relations with Europe and should quickly take a position as a member of the East Asia Co-Prosperity Sphere; (2) complete self-government by the Indonesians should be allowed; (3) the Dutch East Indies should conclude the concrete agreement with the Japanese Empire necessary for self defense in order to maintain firmly the peace of the East Asia Co-Prosperity Sphere, which includes the above Dutch Indies.

Economic Questions: (1) The Subjects of the Japanese Empire should be afforded the same treatment as the subjects of the Netherlands in entering the Dutch Indies, in living in the Dutch Indies, in protection of persons and properties, in travel, in the acquisition of personal and real estate, in the management of business and enterprises (including aviation), and in all other matters in connection with navigation and trade. (2) The Government of the Dutch Indies should not only restrict or prohibit the exportation of goods, especially those by the Japanese Empire, among the products in the Dutch East Indies, but should also give facilities and use of its good offices with regard to the exportation of the goods to the Japanese Empire.

On 25 June 1941, at a Liaison conference between the Government and the Imperial Headquarters, it was decided that Japan must occupy the southern part of French Indo-China to establish air and naval bases for the further advance to the south since the Netherlands Indies refused to yield to Japanese demands.

During 1940, Japan kept pressuring the Netherlands Indies to ensure a continuous flow of raw materials for Japan's war production and for her partners under the Tripartite Pact. Japan was desirous of having the following concessions from the Netherlands Indies:

-To liquidate the Netherlands Indies economic relations with the European and American continents and remove existing restrictions on Japan's economic activities.

-To arrange for the joint development by Japan and the Netherlands of the Netherlands Indies.

-To place the production and export of essential war materials under Japanese control.

-To place the exchange/control of the Netherlands Indies under the guidance of Japan.

-To liquidate foreign financial holdings in the Netherlands Indies.

-To place the formation and execution of all economic policies under the control of a joint Japanese-Netherlands Economic Commission.

The Japanese occupation of the southern part of French Indo-China took place in July 1941 which resulted in the freezing of all Japan's assets in the Netherlands Indies. No further trade was possible and commercial relations between Japan and the Netherlands Indies practically came to an end from this time forward.

A telegram sent from Canton to Tokyo, dated 14 July 1941, stated that the purpose of the occupation of the southern part of French Indo-China was to allow the Japanese to launch a rapid attack from there when the international situation is suitable. The first step to be taken in this connection was the sending of an ultimatum to the Netherlands Indies.

An extensive espionage system had been established by the Japanese in the Netherlands Indies years before the outbreak of war between the two. A great many of the thousands of Japanese residing in the Netherlands Indies were kept closely under the control and supervision of Japanese authorities through many local Japanese associations to actively gather important military information. Japanese consuls and consular agents thought that one of their main tasks was the collection and dispatch of this military information through diplomatic channels. The Japanese Army and Navy each had their own agents in the more important places. Special emphasis was on Japanese propaganda among the Chinese and Indonesians of the Netherlands Indies on whom large sums of money were expended. Many Chinese agents were brought over from Japanese occupied parts of China.

From July 1941 onward it became apparent that the continued advance to the south could only be accomplished through the use of military force. This was not a deterrent to Japanese plans, although some individuals were hesitant since they realized that to advance into the

Netherlands Indies and to the South in general would involve war with both the United States and Great Britain. It was decided at the Imperial Conference held on 6 September 1941, that the policy of advancing to the South would require a determination for war against the United States, Great Britain, and the Netherlands by mid-October, should Japan's demands for a British-American guarantee that they would not strengthen their positions in the South be rejected. Japan was willing to guarantee the Philippines neutrality but no mention was made of the Netherlands Indies. All of the Japanese plans provided that simultaneously with the start of hostilities against the United States and Great Britain, the Netherlands would be attacked. As far back as January 1941, occupation currency for the Netherlands Indies had been ordered with the first deliveries being made in March of that year. It was decided to begin hostilities sometime after 25 November at the Imperial Conference held on 5 November 1941. New negotiations were to be opened with the Netherlands Indies to conceal and disguise the plan for a Japanese attack on that country.

The final decision to declare war on the United States, Great Britain, and the Netherlands was made at the Imperial Conference of 1 December 1941. Japan attacked on 8 December 1941 and subsequently declared war on the United States and Great Britain but not on the Netherlands. This step would have been undesirable for strategic reasons according to Prime Minister Tojo. The Netherlands' government realized that the attacks on Pearl Harbor and Singapore were but a prelude to the eventual military conquest of the Netherlands Indies and formally declared war on Japan. The first Japanese troops landed in the Netherlands Indies on 12

January 1942. The Japanese government issued a statement which said that it regretted being compelled to fight a war caused by the aggression of the Netherlands.

Foreign Minister Tojo, on 22 January 1942 at the opening of the 79th Diet Session, again expressed his regrets at having been forced into war by the Netherlands.

One of the main concerns of the Japanese was how to gain control of the oil resources of the Netherlands Indies in an undamaged condition. When the first important installations on the Island of Tarakan were occupied and the oil wells were found to have been destroyed, the Commander of the town of Balikpapen in Borneo, one of the prime oil producing regions of the Netherlands Indies, was sent an ultimatum stating that if the oil installations were not surrendered intact the whole white population of the town would have to pay with their lives. When the Japanese attacked the town and the oil wells were destroyed, the entire white population was rounded up and murdered.

When the occupation of the Netherlands Indies was completed, the first measures taken were to eradicate the existing forms of government and to sever all contacts with Western influence and the outside world. All government officials of western origin were dismissed and interned, to be followed by the rest of the population, including women and children. The territory of the Netherlands Indies was split up and some parts were placed under the Japanese Army for military administration and some under the Navy. Centralized Japanese Army and Navy executive bodies staffed by Japanese personnel replaced existing Government Departments which were abolished. A completely new style of local government was formulated based on autocratic Japanese lines. Japanese judiciary took the place of the abolished law courts, administering radically different conception of the principles of law, which were unacceptable according to democratic standards.

All political parties were dissolved and all political activity was forbidden. All existing banks were closed down, liquidated, and replaced by Japanese banks, including the Central Bank.

All Western owned agricultural enterprises and public utilities were taken over by Japanese authorities.

Japan, through the measures they enacted, thoroughly exploited the country to strengthen the Japanese war machine and to enrich herself, thereby causing hardship, poverty, and hunger to the entire population. Hundreds of thousands of personnel were deported as slave laborers for the Japanese Army. The greater part of these people became victims who perished through the lack of food, shelter, and medical attention.

Japan's policy with regard the two Southern Regions were broadly laid down in Tokyo so that only insignificant local modifications were made, and then only in the application and not in the principal itself. In general, whatever applied in one region applied in the others also. The prosecution presented data pertaining to Java and only referred to occurrences in other regions where there were important deviations from the events on Java.

Throughout the east Indies, the entire occidental group of influential persons in the administration, commerce, and industry were immediately and systematically interned in prisons and camps hastily prepared for that purpose. From July 1942 these measures of internment were gradually applied to occidental women, so that by the end of 1943 virtually all occidentals, both male and female, had been interned.

Additionally, a large group of prominent Chinese were interned mainly on the ground that they had supported the Chiang Kai-shek regime in the past and on the suspicion of their anti-Japanese attitude.

As of 1 September 1945, according to official Japanese records, 62,532 persons were interned on Java of which nearly 50% were females and over 20% were children. Additionally, all occidental military personnel were made prisoners of war, approximately 45,000 men.

Those members of the former occidental community who were not interned were subjected to heavy pressure of being spied upon by the Japanese, of being intimidated by continuous wholesale arrests and trials, and by the fact that interrogation by the Kempei as well as treatment by Japanese Courts Martial were such that they were deprived of all rights and were subjugated to arbitrary maltreatment and starvation methods.

This class of persons were dismissed from their positions, both official and private, thus depriving them of their means of livelihood. In as much as their bank accounts were frozen in most cases, there was practically no alternative for these individuals other than to gradually sell off all of their possessions. The Japanese further handicapped them by the simple act of requisitioning whatever took their fancy, generally without any compensation.

During the occupation:

1. The use of Western languages was forbidden in public and business communications.

2. The Japanese began to close down all schools.

3. In April 1942 the listening to radio broadcasts from outside of the East Indies was banned and an announcement

in July 1942 provided that persons listening to foreign broadcasts despite the ban would be sentenced to death.

4. The possession of certain specified books in enemy languages was a punishable offense. These books had to be handed over to be burned.

5. Old monuments which were reminders of former occidental influence were destroyed, removed, or carried away to storage.

6. The names of streets and towns were changed to Japanese (sometimes Malay).

7. The names of shops, commercial concerns, trademarks, etc., had to be transcribed into Japanese or Malay as Western languages could not be used.

8. All existing Councils were abolished.

9. All existing law courts were abolished by ordinance dated 29 April 1942 and replaced "Japanese Law Courts of the Military Government." There was no provision for appeals. All lower court decisions were declared to have been affirmed by the Appellate Court.

All meetings, associations, etc., were forbidden by ordinances in March 1942, with the exception of those concerned with sports/recreation, scientific, cultural, charitable, and distributing organizations.

Even the exempted associations were restricted in their activities as they were subjected to police supervision and their activities could be resumed only after obtaining permission form the police and their being registered. The police had to authorize their meetings. In practice, activities were permitted only for those organizations which accepted Japanese leadership and could be used for propaganda purposes.

The Japanese authorities built up a very extensive propaganda machine from the outset. The vanguard of this propaganda machine came along with the first troops to land on Java. They attempted to establish immediate contact with Indonesian and Chinese politicians who were known to be disaffected. They seized control of all means of public expression at once with all public and private radio broadcasts and cinematographic activities as well as the entire Press were placed under their immediate control. The Dutch language continued to be used for two months but when the propaganda machine became sufficiently organized all newspapers were forbidden and new papers using the Malay language were introduced. There was also a Japanese language paper, the Java Shimbun, which was published in Batavia.

Japan's propaganda referred to herself as the 'liberator,' who came to establish a 'New Order,' and stated that 'New Java' was to be educated to become a worthy member of the Greater East Asia Co-Prosperity Sphere under the leadership of Japan.

Rigid censorship was instituted by the Japanese which not only affected all postal, telegraphic, and telephonic communications but also extended to photographs given to photographers for development. Additionally all public utterances were subject to censorship including not only radio broadcasts and the press, but also the theater, sermons, etc. Eventually the propaganda service took over all theatrical companies. The Japanese by using these methods of censorship had control of all expressions of public opinion.

The Japanese began at once to establish schools taught in Japanese only but when schools for Indonesians were reopened the important subjects of Japanese language, songs, and dances were added to the curriculum. The programs in the East Indies in the fields of finance and economics were similar even though some areas were administered by the

Japanese Army and some by the Navy. Java and Sumatra were occupied and administered by different Japanese Armies and the Celebes, Borneo, Moluccas, Timor, etc., were occupied by the Japanese Navy. There was virtually no contact between areas but the basic principles of their administration were very similar in reality.

The Japanese government began issuing its own military paper currency in March 1942 and reduced the East Indies guilder value to the same as that of the Japanese yen. At first the paper currency in circulation was retained. Later, however, when it commanded a greater value on the open market than the Japanese occupation money, it was withdrawn and the mere possession of this currency was considered a punishable offense.

Issuing of unlimited quantities of paper money without backing led to inflation in early 1943 which increased at an ever faster rate until by the middle of 1945 this paper money had only a fortieth of its original buying power.

All banks were closed down immediately at the start of the occupation. The banks that dealt mostly with Occidental clients were liquidated. Those that largely had Indonesian clients were reopened under Japanese names and direction, but balances due at the time of the closing remained frozen. Later, Indonesian cash deposits were partially unfrozen while occidental, internees, and prisoner's deposits remained frozen. These frozen assets were transferred to the Japanese established Enemy Property Administration Bureau which was charged with custody of enemy property.

This Bureau liquidated nearly all confiscated items and credited the owners, when known, in their books with the proceeds in Japanese paper money. After May 1945, this liquidation was hastened and Japanese were frequently the purchasers at so called public auctions but the proceeds in Japanese occupation money bore no reasonable relation to the price of the same property on the open market.

Before the war, Occidentals were the primary investors or owners of the agricultural enterprises and industries in the Netherlands Indies. After the occupation, the Japanese took over control of all these agricultural concerns, including those operated with Indonesian or Chinese capital. The Japanese followed a policy directed towards carrying out a rigorous war effort and maintaining the required production. Enterprises that were of no immediate importance to the war effort were switched to other production whenever possible. Tea and rubber plantations were seriously restricted during the later stages of the occupation since the Japanese gave precedence to food crops. Tea plants and rubber trees were cut down and used as firewood, and the estates were split up and parceled out to the local farmers to increase food crops production.

Public utilities were seized by the Military Administration, including those that were privately owned, and were operated without compensation. Private Japanese companies were allocated these facilities in some cases. Private railway, tramway, and bus companies were consolidated with the State Railways. Private company railway equipment was shipped mostly to the Burma-Siam Railway.

At first, the Military Government was part and parcel of the Army with its basic functions being laid down in a March 1942 directive by the Japanese Commander-in-Chief in which he assumed all powers that had been previously exercised by the Governor-General. Military administration was divided into nine departments under the supervision of the Chief of the Military Government who was the Chief of Staff to the Japanese Army Commander-in-Chief. The Chief of the Military Government was assisted by three Army officers, each administering his respective area. At the local level, administration was carried out by Commanding Officers of occupational detachments. All leading positions in the departments were occupied by Japanese. On 1 September 1945, 23,242 Japanese nationals were employed by the Military Government of Java, which amounted to half the number of service personnel stationed there according to official Japanese information.

Legislative powers were exercised by the Imperial Government at Tokyo, the Supreme Commander in the Southern Area, the Commander-in-Chief of Java, and the Chief of the Military Administration. The ordinances and laws of the first bodies were not published locally even though thousands were arrested, tortured, and sentenced under them.

Beginning in August 1942, the provisional set-up was replaced by the permanent Administration. An ordinance issued by the commander-in-chief, Java, created an entirely new system of local administration. Java was divided into 17 areas, equal to the former 'Residencies' geographically and one Special City Area for Batavia. The former "Provinces" of West, Central, and East Java were eliminated but similar organizations were re-established in early 1945. These local organizations replaced the former decentralized and autonomous local administration and placed them directly under the control of the Chief of the Military Administration in a rigidly centralized mode. The Fuehrer principle was initiated with area officials being held responsible only to their superiors, as they possessed a large measure of liberty in the performance of their duties, had real powers for dismissals and appointment in their areas, and had almost unrestricted disciplinary power over their staffs.

Early in the occupation certain activities were strictly prohibited by ordinances issued by the occupation government. By virtue of these prohibitions, some Indonesian nationalist leaders were arrested in April 1942 and many were not released until much later. A large scale round up was conducted in December 1942 to January 1943 of Indonesians who had engaged in any kind of activity that was or might be construed as being anti-Japanese. These individuals, except for those sentenced to death or who had died in prison, were not released until September 1945. The Kempei continued to guard against and spy upon all underground activity even after January 1943, which caused a very large number of victims.

The Japanese sought further contact with the Indonesian world, mainly those individuals who had been dissatisfied with the former government and the rate that the country was being prepared for independence. Chief among these individuals was Sukarno, brought to Java by Kempei in July 1942, who formed the so-called 'Ampat Serangkai' (four-leaf clover) with three other nationalists. These four became the leaders, under Japanese supervision, of those nationalists prepared to cooperate with Japan as they saw in the Japanese promises a means of attaining early independence for which they were striving.

The first request to the Japanese was for the leaders to be allowed to form a party. No action was taken by the Japanese on this request until 8 December 1942, where the Commander-in-Chief, at a propaganda meeting commemorating Pearl Harbor, promised that an Indonesians only party was to be permitted but that a decision from Tokyo must be awaited for the fulfillment of this promise.

On 9 March 1943 a peoples movement with leaders and advisory councils was created but it was not a party. The Commander-in-Chief appointed the movement's leaders who were assisted by an advisory council consisting of nearly equal numbers of Japanese and Indonesian members. The object of the movement was the arousal of the strength and effort of the people to support all measures for winning final victory in the Greater East Asia War. To accomplish the object of the movement, the commander in chief advised that all leaders must possess profound knowledge of, and have a deep abiding faith in the aims and objectives of the Dai Nippon Army. The functions of the movement were officially set forth in ten points which included the need to impress on the Indonesian people their duties and responsibilities in the establishment of a "New Java", and to participate in the defense of Greater East Asia by fostering the needed self-discipline in order to bear and overcome any mental or physical privations which might provide a detrimental effect in the ability to the accomplishment of this ultimate victory.

The elimination of occidental influences was another of the movement's aims as well as the deepening of mutual understanding between the Japanese and Indonesians. Since the movement was only for Indonesians, the Japanese introduced a new social hierarchy which was comprised of the following groups: Japanese, Indonesians, other Asiatics, mixtures of Indonesians with other groups and Europeans.

Indonesians were treated as a special category by virtue of being the original inhabitants and groups 3-5 were treated as foreigners with the worst treatment being allocated for the Europeans and the Eurasians. Around the same time, restrictions on foreigners were strengthened with the establishment of forbidden zones covering the entire South coast and the two Eastern and Western extremities of Java. No foreigners were allowed to enter these areas and even Indonesians required a pass to be there. It was also ordered that immediately everyone must inform the police when providing lodging for someone from outside his place of residence.

During this period important events were taking place outside the East Indies. Japan had been forced into a defensive position rather than an offensive posture and her lines of communication were being threatened seriously. Prime Minister Tojo stated during a speech he gave in the Diet on 16 June 1943 that since the people of Java had shown that they were willing to cooperate with the Japanese, it was time for them to be provided with the opportunity to participate in the government. He also promised during this speech so called independence for Burma and the Philippines. Subsequent to this speech, the prime Minister visited the Southern Regions in person and repeated the promise for independence for Burma and the Philippines during visits to Singapore and Manila. In Java no independence promise was made but only the right to participate in the government. Indonesians were nominated to advisers to seven government departments but the Japanese retained all real power and the Indonesians were there strictly for rubber stamp approval.

Beginning in August 1943, a Volunteer Corps started being created for the defense of Java based on the principle of joint defense of Greater East Asia. It was emphatically stated that this Corps: would not be formed as part of the Japanese Army; would consist solely of volunteers; would have its own officers; would be trained by Japanese instructors; would not be used outside of Java.

After the first recruiting levy, it became apparent that the enthusiasm for this Corps was insufficient, so that with every new levy from then on, each of the Regencies were told just how many "volunteers" were required to bring the formations up to strength.

Training of the Corps' Officers started in October 1943 and lasted for three months. Tasks assigned to the Corps consisted mainly of guarding road junctions, bridges, and other strategically important points. Most training took place using wooden guns and where weapons were supplied it was only for the duration of the drills.

Prior to the formation of this unit, the Japanese had made use of "Heihos" (auxiliary soldiers) which were used by both the Japanese Army and Navy. These were Indonesian soldiers who were recruited but also compelled to serve in units formed as part of the Japanese forces, wore Japanese uniforms and insignia, and were generally used to guard camps occupied by women and civilian internees. These units could be used off the island, were taught to speak Japanese, and had their regulations written and orders given in Japanese.

One important area where the Japanese expected Java to increase was in the production of farm products and the delivery to the Japanese Military Administration. Java had previously been barely capable of meeting its own essential food requirements. Increases in foodstuff production was negated by lack of proper supervision by insufficiently trained Japanese personnel and the haphazard method of forcing the production of desired commodities that were unsuitable for climatic and geographic conditions.

The Japanese, from the outset, had adopted the policy of stabilizing the price of rice at a proper level. As the Japanese military guilder decreased in its purchasing value, the official price fell far below its former value relative to other commodities and it became less and less advantageous for the simple farmer to hand over his produce to the Japanese authorities who ordered that 60% of food products harvested had to be delivered to them. Far reaching measures to combat the black market in rice and other food products were taken.

Throughout the Southern Regions, Japan used labor everywhere for the building of military fortifications, airfields, strategic railways, etc. with Java being a source for such labor. At first, the Japanese were successful in encouraging the voluntary enlistment of these coolies. However, when the populace learned how the Japanese were treating these coolies, the desire to work for them practically disappeared. This became even worse when the coolies did not return to Java and no news was provided on their whereabouts. Conscription was adopted by the Japanese then to secure the number of coolies required for labor on Java as well as off the island and each Regency was informed of their share which they had to draft and provide.

These laborers received far less care than the POWs and internees, and their ignorance of hygienic precautions and medial care aggravated their condition. Japanese official figures received after the surrender, show that 27,000 men were transported off Java as coolies but that since the war's end only 7,000 had returned. Most of those who did return had suffered inhuman maltreatment. Not only were accommodations, food, and medical care thoroughly inadequate but they were absent altogether in many cases. Coolies who had died from starvation and contagious diseases were daily carried away from certain camps by the cart-load.

The propaganda service made an effort to obtain cooperation from the populace in religious matters. The Mohammedans, who formed the largest majority of the population, and the Chinese, while few in number, were the mainstay of the middle class, were the ethnic groups at which these activities were initially directed. The Eurasians, who occupied mainly the middle strata of the technical and administrative occupations, were at first ostracized. Eurasians were replaced by Japanese in the higher ranks but there were not nearly enough Japanese or sufficiently trained Indonesians to replace them in the more numerous ranks.

In September 1943, an effort was made to secure the cooperation of the Eurasian group. Where previously the Eurasian group had been regarded as 'aliens,' they finally came to be regarded as belonging to the indigenous population group next to the Indonesian group. Eurasians were told by the Japanese that they must renounce their Western ancestry and had to realize that they were to feel like and act as members of the Greater East Asian community under Japanese leadership from then on.

Many of the Japanese promises to these groups were never satisfied and in some cases it appears that they were never meant to be.

Systematic prosecution by the Kempei-tai was brought about by their activities by the Eurasions for mutual support. Dozens of their leaders died in prison as a result of ill treatment, starvation, contagious diseases, and sentences by courts martial. Once someone had attracted suspicion, he was tortured in such a way that false confessions were a daily routine; and these in turn often brought more victims within the clutches of the Kempei-tai. On the west coast of Borneo, a typical example of this happened in 1944, where in excess of 1200 prominent Indonesian and Chinese, including the local nobility, were executed on an entirely unfounded suspicion of conspiracy. There were hundreds of cases where people of all races were cruelly tortured, on the strength of reports of a usually entirely innocent conversation. Tortures used included the 'water cure,' electrification, hanging by the limbs, the use of boa constrictors, etc.

The breakthrough at Saipan shook the very foundations of the Japanese defense. The Koiso Cabinet which succeeded the Tojo Cabinet, recognized that it must face the necessity for the Japanese troops in the Southern Regions to stand by themselves and that it was of greater importance to gain popular cooperation. Prominent Indonesians warned the Japanese that if they wanted to retain full cooperation they must accelerate satisfying nationalist aspirations in the Southern Regions. Prime Minister Koiso, in the Diet on 7 September 1944, made a promise of independence for the East Indies after having promised Korea and Formosa an equality of rights as those enjoyed by the Japanese.

In April and May of 1945 at conferences held at Singapore attended by representatives of all areas under Itagaki's 7th Area Army and included in correspondence with Field Marshal Terauchi's Headquarters at Saigon during this period, Java representatives emphasized the fact that there was no way to regain the population's confidence with the exception of following through on the promise of independence.

Since all concerned recognized that the war was turning against Japan, it was decided that Java be allowed to convene a committee for the study of preparations for independence.

On 28 May 1945 a committee for such a study was installed. The members of the committee took a solemn oath of loyalty to live and die with Japan. Originally the independence date had been set for sometime during the middle of 1946 but this date was continually being changed for earlier dates until Field Marshal Terauchi, early in August 1945 received orders from Tokyo to hasten preparations for the establishment of the Indonesian puppet-state and that this state was to be created in September 1945.

On 9 August 1945 Sukarno and two other prominent Indonesians were flown to Terauchi's Headquarters at Saigon where the Field Marshal received them on 11 August and stated that he had been instructed to transmit to the delegation the contents of Japanese Imperial Government Decree on the creation of the New State which would include the entire Netherlands East Indies territory. Sukarno was appointed Chairman of the Committee.

Newspapers in Java on 14 August reported on Sukarno's return and he was welcomed as the new leader of Indonesia. On 15 August the committee members were secretly informed of Japan's capitulation. During the night of 16-17 August it was decided that independence would be proclaimed the next morning. The draft constitution was hastily altered and the following morning Sukarno broadcast the independence announcement.

Between 17-21 August 1945, the newspapers controlled by the Japanese propaganda service, and local broadcasts mentioned nothing but the announcement of independence and the constitution. On 21 August 1945, the papers published the text of the Emperor's 14 August broadcast concerning the surrender of Japan. Thus, Japanese authorities had kept Japan's defeat a secret from 14 August until 21 August 1945. This time came to be called the 'stolen week.'

Lawyers assigned to present the defense for some defendants associated with this phase of the trial seemed to be more interested in arguing with the witness and attempting to elicit from the witness his agreement that the actions taken by the Japanese upon their occupation of the East Indies were correct and what was considered appropriate when one country conquers and occupies another. Some of these actions were:

- Personnel with European or occidental blood, including Eurasian, as a percentage of the overall population rather than a figure.
- Internment of influential persons in the administration of the Netherlands Indies affairs.
- The freezing of all bank balances.
- Prohibiting the Javanese from using their radios.
- Closing of schools and burning of certain books that they felt were anti-Japanese in nature.

The Tribunal President ruled the defense lawyers were indeed being argumentative with the witness and that they were not making proper use of cross-examination. He also sustained objections by the prosecution that some defense questions asked for opinions and/or decisions from the witness on subjects that were in the purvey of the Tribunal with the right to make rulings as to whether actions were in accordance with international law.

Above to right: Empty witness box on main floor of the War Ministry Building in Tokyo, Japan. Prosecution witnesses and the 25 defendants charged with war crimes would testify from this box over a three year period during the International War Crimes Trial.

Atrocities
CHAPTER 10

The prosecution presented evidence provided by living witnesses or that was derived from Japanese documents which indicated that the basic policy pursued by the accused and other Japanese leaders was one which had been designed to produce a warlike master race which was dead set upon world conquest.

In order for this policy to be implemented, it was necessary for the combined resources of the state-controlled press, radio, schools, stage, movies, literature and religion to be marshaled to indoctrinate the people of Japan with a fanatical martial spirit, blind worship of totalitarianism and ultra-nationalism, love for aggression and burning hatred and contempt for all enemies, either actual or potential.

The implementation of that basic policy resulted in a vast multitude of innocent persons being butchered, maimed, starved, and degraded; a host of cities, towns, and villages being sacked; and immense numbers of homes and farms being pillaged. This insidious internal propaganda of hatred succeeded in poisoning many Japanese minds and hearts to such a degree, that, during the military campaigns, their character and nature swung like a pendulum from one extreme of kindness and courtesy to the other extreme of cruelty and indecency which culminated with the commission of a vast number of atrocities.

These Japanese atrocities were not isolated incidents of individual misconduct but:

- Were general throughout the whole Pacific and Asiatic war areas.

- The technique and method used in wholesale murder, torture, and rape, and wanton destruction of property followed a consistent and similar pattern throughout.
- The stronger the resistance that was offered, the more abominable the invaders became.
- The strategy of terror was after a time identified as part of the Japanese form of warfare calculated to crush the resistance and the will to fight of the people of the overrun countries.
- Started on a large scale for the first time in 1937 at Nanking, and climaxed in 1945 with the Rape of Manila, a period of eight long years.
- Their areas of commission covered onefourth of the territorial space of the globe, including Burma, China, IndoChina, Malaya, Hong Kong, the Netherlands Indies, the Philippines, New Guinea, and various islands of the Pacific Ocean.
- The perpetrators came from both enlisted men's and officers' ranks of all branches of the Japanese armed services.
- The legion of victims included both civilians and POWs, the well and the infirm, the young and the old, men and women, and even children and babies.

The chronicle of murder and mistreatment was indicative of a pattern of warfare used by the Japanese government and military forces and included the massacre of 5,000 Chinese; brutal treatment of Europeans in Singapore; indiscriminate killing in all occupied areas of native inhabitants; the loss of lives of 16,000 Allied POWs; deaths of over 100,000 coolies and the gross mistreatment of almost every man during the Burma-Siam Railway construction; the Bataan and Borneo Death Marches; the massacres at Banka

Island, Palawan, The Tol Plantation in New Guinea, Bandermassin, Laha, Long Nawa, Pontianak, the Tarakan; murders on Wake Island, and the killing of survivors from ships which had been sunk.

Inadequate food, clothing, medicine, medical attention, and safe water contributed much to the unnecessary suffering and many deaths.

Torture, mass punishments, and beatings were widespread with severe punishments being meted out for trifling offenses. The punishment for attempting to escape was execution.

The prosecution devised a method to present evidence classified by area in a manner which could be followed easily and showed that in each area the mistreatment of POWs, civilian internees, and native inhabitants was similar throughout the territories occupied by the Japanese forces and that such mistreatment was not the result of independent acts by some of the Japanese commanders and soldiers but was the general policy of the Japanese forces and the Japanese government.

It also showed that the Laws of War were entirely disregarded by the Japanese forces in so far as they related to POWs, civilian internees, and native inhabitants of occupied territories in every area.

These areas were: Singapore and Malaya, Burma and Thailand, Hong Kong, Formosa, Hainan, Andamans and Nicobars, Java, Borneo, Sumatra and Banka Island, Celebes, Ambon, Timor, New Guinea, New Britain, Solomons, Gilberts, Nauru, Ocean Islands, other Pacific Islands, Indo-China, China (other than Hong Kong), sea transportation, Japan, and atrocities at sea

This division into areas was very efficient for the presentation of evidence but is not effective for the purpose of presentation here of such historical happenings. Atrocities committed prior to the start of the overall Pacific War with the attack on Pearl Harbor being listed first and those that took place after the attack coming next.

The commission of atrocities against civilians and crimes against humanity by Japanese troops took place in every province of occupied China and covered the entire period from the time Japanese troops first entered Chinese territory. These offenses included: murder and massacre, torture, rape, robbery, looting, and wanton destruction of property.

A heinous example of the commission of these barbarous acts occurred following the capture of the City of Nanking. The Japanese Army under the command of the defendant Matsui captured the city on 13 December 1937 and an orgy of killing, raping, looting, and burning began immediately and continued unabated for more than 40 days until February 1938. The sum total of these crimes collectively came to be known historically as "The Rape of Nanking." Numerous witnesses testified as to the activities of the Japanese troops during this period of time.

Providing the most telling testimony dealing with his own observations and accounts told him by other eye witnesses during this period was a Mr. John A. Magee, a minister of the Episcopal Church at Nanking from 1912-1940. He said that the killing began immediately and that it was unbelievable terrible. It started with individual men being killed but it soon grew to organized killing of great numbers of men and there were bodies of men living everywhere. Columns of men were being taken out to be killed. Generally these people were killed by rifle or machine gun fire but they had heard of groups ranging upward to several hundred being bayoneted to death.

One woman told him that her husband's hands were tied in front of him and he was thrown into a pond while she had to stand there and watch him drown since the Japanese would not let her rescue him.

Mr. Magee stated that the first proof as to what was happening to the groups of men being taken off was when their school cook's boy, 15 years of age, was taken off in a group of 100 men. Their hands were bound in front of them and the killing began with the people at the front of the group but the boy, who was in the rear of the group, managed to escape. He returned to the school approximately 38 hours later and told about what had occurred.

He also said that he saw long columns of Chinese with their hands tied in front of them and estimated the number to be a thousand men or more. The wounded began returning who after being shot or bayoneted, feigned death and would later escape to filter back to the mission hospital to give them authentic information as to what was happening to these vast numbers of people.

Mr. Magee also testified that on another occasion, he and three other foreigners, two Russians and one American, were standing on a balcony and saw two Japanese soldiers kill a Chinese. Both soldiers walked in front of him and stood not more than five yards from him when both shot the Chinese man in the face. Neither soldier stopped talking nor smoking their cigarettes, and after the shooting, they walked on with no more feeling than if they had taken a shot at a wild duck.

He spoke of another time when he saw three piles of Chinese bodies along the river side which he estimated to number between 300 and 500. The clothing was burned off these bodies and many of them were charred as it was evident that the bodies had been set on fire.

He told of taking moving pictures at another time of a group of 60 to 70 Chinese men being gathered on a road and women were kneeling in the street before the Japanese begging for their men folk but to no avail as the Japanese marched the men off.

In reply to a question as to the action of the Japanese soldiers toward the city's women and children, he replied that it was the same story, unbelievably terrible with rapings continuing day by day with many women and even children being killed. If a woman resisted or refused, she was either killed or stabbed and if the husband of the woman tried to help, he was killed. Mr. Magee testified on numerous different incidents of rapes that he knew about or had been told about including rapes of girls as young as 10 or 11 years of age.

Mr. Magee stated that if there had been any real effort to stop this conduct, it could have been stopped, but it was looked upon entirely too lightly. As an example he told of a colleague who had taken in several hundred Chinese women who were living in little huts in his garden. One day this colleague returned to his home accompanied by a Japanese officer. When they arrived at his house, they saw a Japanese soldier in the act of raping a woman in one of the huts and the extent of the Japanese officer's reaction was to slap the soldier's face. Mr. Magee's colleague was utterly disgusted by what he had seen and returned to the mission to tell him of the incident.

Early in 1938 a crisis arose because the Japanese wanted them to send the women that they had been protecting back home. As a compromise they advised the older women to go home but kept the younger girls under their protection. They started to hear stories immediately of rapings that began again of those women who went back home.

Mr. Magee went to investigate one of these cases with a Miss Vautrin, an American vice president of Gingling College, where at the worst time they had between 12,000-13,000 women and girls. When they entered the front of the house a woman was weeping and when asked why, she said that Japanese soldiers had killed her husband. The owners of the house lived in the rear, a widow in her 40s, her 12-year-old daughter, and her 77-year-old mother. When the Japanese first entered the house, the widow had been repeatedly raped so the three of them decided to escape to Gingling College. They became separated on the way and the 77-year-old mother was taken into a house and raped twice. The widow, after returning from the safety of Gingling College, to her home, was again raped. Altogether she had been raped between 17 or 18 times.

A Christian woman evangelist told Mr. Magee she was living with an 80-year-old Chinese woman. A Japanese soldier came to the house called the old woman to the door, and made motions for her to open her clothing. When the woman said, "I am too old," the soldier shot and killed her.

Mr. Magee described another incident in which only two children escaped out of 13 people in one house. The others, including two young girls of 14 and 16 were killed. Both girls had been raped and the maternal grandmother had taken a bamboo stick from the vagina of one of the girls. In another room where the mother was with her one-year-old child, the mother was raped, and both she and her child were killed. When the body was found there had been a bottle pushed into the vagina of the woman.

He repeated the story that a young girl of 15 told him after he had taken her to the hospital when he found her wandering the streets of the city in February 1938. She was from the city of Wufu, which was located about 60 miles from Nanking. Her brother had been killed by Japanese soldiers. They came to her house and accused him of being a soldier. These same soldiers had killed her older sister and her brother's wife when they resisted being raped and both her father and mother were also killed while kneeling before these soldiers. All of these members of her family had been killed with a bayonet and when the girl saw what the Japanese were doing to her family, she fainted.

Upon regaining consciousness, she found that the Japanese had taken her to some sort of barracks where she was kept for two months. She was raped repeatedly every day for the first month. She could not escape as her clothing had been taken from her and she was locked in a room. She became so diseased after the first month that the Japanese were afraid to have anything to do with her. She remained sick in the barracks for the entire second month, until one day when she was weeping, a Japanese officer came in and asked what was wrong. She told him her story and he took pity on her, drove her in his car to Nanking and wrote on a card "Gingling College," evidently knowing that they were taking girls there.

Mr. Magee's response to the question of what the Japanese soldiers' attitude was toward property in the city of Nanking was that they took from the people anything that struck their fancy: wristwatches, fountain pens, money, clothing, food, etc. The Japanese soldiers paid absolutely no attention to their own consular notices about foreign property or to those of the American Embassy. Practically all of the foreigners in the city signed a petition to the Japanese authorities on 21 December and took it in person to the Japanese Embassy, beseeching them in the name of humanity to stop the senseless burning of the homes of the people. This burning continued day by day in different parts of the city.

Mr. Magee was asked by the Defense during cross examination how many murders and rapes that he had actually seen and he replied only one murder and a couple of rapes but that he was told of many of both by other foreigners and Chinese. He was also asked by the defense if the big problem was not that of identifying those individuals guilty of these acts so that they could be punished and he replied that yes it was since the insignia on the soldiers uniforms were in Japanese which he could not read. As far as he was concerned, his chief means of identification was their faces he stated, and that he didn't get much of chance for that as the individuals fled when confronted by a foreigner.

Even though there continued to be atrocities committed in all areas as they were occupied by the Japanese forces, there was never such a large concentration after Nanking until those in Manila in 1945.

Later during the period prior to the attack on Pearl Harbor, while the Japanese continued to pursue their policy of attempting to acquire control over the Netherlands East Indies and other resource rich areas of Asia by peaceful means as well as the threat of the use of arms, they began to gradually change their policy towards China. When they abandoned peaceful methods to achieve their aims and swung towards the use of force for this purpose, they concentrated their efforts in China for the capture and occupation of the larger urban areas and by-passed the vast rural areas, which were mostly agricultural, in between. This was particularly true along the coast where there was a series of Japanese occupied enclaves surrounding the cities with open or unoccupied areas around them. Under this policy, the Japanese could maintain control over larger numbers of captured Chinese with a much smaller force of their own. Much of central and western China remained unconquered throughout the war.

One fact which aided the Tribunal in the determination of the guilt or innocence of the accused was the comparison between the number of persons who died in captivity in Germany and Italy and the numbers who died or were killed in captivity in Japan. In Germany and Italy, 142,319 British POWs were reported captured with 7,310 or 5.1% having been killed or died in captivity and out of 50,016 British POWs in the power of Japan 12,433 or 24.8% were killed or died in captivity.

Among the important reports of atrocities were those pertaining to the treatment of Allied Air Force personnel in Japan as they contain direct admissions that Allied aviators who had bombed the territory of Japan and were later captured were executed without any form of a trial.

Numerous sworn affidavits were submitted as evidence of atrocities that were committed in and around Singapore and Malaya which ranged from the execution of single individuals to groups of upwards of 50 individuals by decapitation, bayoneting, and rifle and machine gun fire on diverse ethnic groups from Australian and British POWs to Chinese, Malaysian, and Indian internees.

One such affidavit concerned the storming of the Alexandra Hospital in Singapore on 14 February 1942 by Japanese troops, who raced through the building, bayoneting and shooting all individuals they encountered, and left a path of death and destruction behind them even though appropriate markings were displayed at the hospital.

Both the inside and outside of the building had conventional markings, the beds had Red Cross counterpanes, and medical personnel were wearing the Red Cross brassard. Out of a total of 323 persons who were killed at the hospital, 230 were patients.

Stressful situations, beatings, and use of torture, including, burns by lighted cigarettes, by use of electrical shock and of the infamous water torture, usually accompanied interrogations and resulted in severe injury and sometimes death of the individual being questioned.

One of two girls, who escaped by tearing up some floor boards even though she was wounded, related in her affidavit how women and children, inhabitants of the village of Ebiang, were pushed into some houses and the Japanese fired on the buildings with machine guns until all moaning and crying ceased. The buildings were then set on fire.

The report of the President of the No. 4 War Crimes Court, Rangoon, describe the proceedings before the court and to summarize the evidence given concerning the massacre of Kalagon villagers. These villagers were interrogated by the Kempeitai, beaten, tortured, and taken in groups of 25 to nearby wells, where they were bayoneted and thrown down the wells. Of the 195 women, 175 men, and 260 children rounded-up by the Japanese only a very few escaped death.

One witness gave evidence that he gained by acting as an interpreter for a Japanese officer in May 1945, at Ongun, when seven Burmans were being questioned. He stated in his affidavit that these seven were taken to the Ongun cemetery to be beheaded. Although he placed his hands over his ears, he still heard the blows of the sword and cries of "Oh God!" coming from the trench.

The next day, two white men who had apparently witnessed the Burmans' execution, were murdered themselves in the same way.

Several affidavits provided statements as to conditions and lack of the necessary facilities for living and sleeping experienced by the prisoners during transportation by ship to the area where the Burma-Siam Railway was being constructed and in the construction camps after their arrival. The shortages of life's necessities and the lack of providing for the basic sanitation requirements resulted in wide spread infectious diseases and the high death rates among the prisoners. At least one camp had to be abandoned on account of its extremely bad condition and the lack of water.

In one particularly filthy camp, where 200 Allied POWs were kept, no one was fit and with an average daily death rate of two to six, sick men had to carry their comrades to the grave. Medical supplies could only be obtained by barter. The food supplied to the POWs consisted of an extremely small amount of rice. It was the policy of the area Japanese commander that the men received food only as long as they worked but if they became sick they were written off and sent to this particular camp to live until they died. It was in effect a living morgue.

Numerous deaths occurred among the POWs during Allied bombing raids at some of the camps that had been placed too close to bridges or other military targets and installations. The Japanese by refusing to provide any markings to indicate that there were POWs present in these camps were therefore responsible for these deaths.

In some coolie camps along the Burma-Siam Railway construction areas, extremely harsh measures were taken with those individuals who were too sick to work. In one camp, when the Japanese medical NCO thought that those sick with cholera were too ill to recover, they were forced into a small lean-to shelter and left to die, not being provided with any food or water.

In other camps, coolies who were seriously suffering from cholera were often forced into common pit graves and buried alive. When the coolies protested, they were beaten down by the Japanese orderlies.

While giving anti-cholera inoculation to the coolies in July 1943, the witness saw them beaten and humiliated. Disinfectant was deliberately sprayed into the eyes of some coolies, women were insulted, and even the Japanese doctor himself beat some of the coolies as they were being examined. The doctor explained to the witness that they were sub-human and not worthy of consideration.

In one affidavit, the witness described how he accompanied a Japanese trooper to interview the coolies in the hospital at one of the coolie camps. The trooper asked if any of them could not walk as they were to be transferred to the base hospital and that they would be carried if they could not walk. Several of the coolies staggered forward and each was given an injection of a red unknown fluid from a hypodermic syringe he produced. All coolies who received the injection died within a few minutes and the rest of the coolies, after seeing what had happened said that they could walk.

The Japanese trooper then proceeded to a dysentery hut where he looked around and then left. Sometime later he returned with a large tin of brown sugar mixed with a deadly poison. He gave this to the coolies and told them that it was good for them, but all who ate some of this poison died the same day.

Conditions at POW camps other that those associated with the building of the Burma-Siam Railway were the same as those at the railway with inadequate facilities, insufficient food and in many instances unsanitary water, and little or no medicine and medical facilities. The penalty for escaping and later being recaptured was automatic execution without the benefit of any trial whatsoever.

The affidavit of one witness states that she was interned at Jampong Tob with 21 other Europeans. Eight Indian soldiers were pushed into a room where the internees were living on 13 December 1941. Shortly thereafter, a Japanese soldier threw a hand grenade into the room but the witness was unable to move as her hip was injured. Two Japanese soldiers then entered the room, one firing an automatic weapon while the other was bayoneting people lying on the floor. The witness was saved from further injury as she was lying underneath other people. A number of people were killed with many others being injured and there was no explanation of the reason for the attack as the Japanese soldiers took off in a truck.

One witness testified that he was serving as a chaplain with one of the two Canadian Army regiments stationed in Hong Kong when that city was captured by the Japanese in December 1941. There were 160 to 175 patients and seven nurses in St. Stephens College Hospital (a boys school which was commandeered for use as a hospital at the start of the war). At 6 o'clock in the morning of Christmas Day, Japanese troops entered the hospital and bayoneted from 15 to 20 wounded men while they were still in their beds. They then began rounding up all those who could walk, both patients and staff. The nurses had originally been with the witness but shortly after being moved the nurses were separated from him. Before they were separated, the witness saw one of the nurses beaten over the head with a steel helmet, kicked and had been slapped in the face by a Japanese soldier. The Japanese took anything of value (jewelry, money. watches, etc.) from the prisoners. Two prisoners were taken from the group and as soon as the door was closed, screams were heard.

The prisoners were informed by sign language of the surrender of Hong Kong at 4 o'clock in the afternoon.

The next morning the witness made a tour of the hospital which was in a dreadful state. Both of the bodies of the men who had been taken from the group the previous day were found, badly mutilated, with their ears, noses, tongues, and eyes cut away from their faces. He saw about 70 men and his adjutant were found dead on the ground floor with their bodies badly mutilated.

At first only four of the nurses could be found and they told of the terrible time they had throughout the night when Japanese soldiers had repeatedly raped them. One of them told the witness how she had been forced to lie on two dead bodies as the Japanese used her as they chose.

Later in the morning a Japanese soldier took the witness, several other prisoners, and one of the nurses to a clump of bushes on the hospital grounds, where covered by blankets, under the bushes, the bodies of the other three nurses were found. The head of one nurse had been practically severed from her body in one of them.

The Japanese stopped the burial of bodies but ordered that a fire be built and that all the bodies around the hospital should be cremated. The witness cremated between 170 and 180 bodies that included not only those from the hospital but some from battle areas around the hospital.

The Japanese were observed looting the food in the hospital as well as large quantities of medical supplies and equipment that were taken away from the hospital by trucks.

On 30 December all troops at Stanley Barracks were ordered to march to the POW camp at North Point. About 2500 men and officers made the march. Facilities at the camp were filthy and woefully inadequate. Nearly all of the camp huts had their windows broken and the camp was a perfect breeding place for disease. There was no water in the camp and there were no cook houses yet established. Because of the water being cut off, there were no latrine facilities and the men were forced to use the sea wall.

When the POWs first came to North Point, they were allowed to go to the army food dumps and procure army rations, so for the first month or so the food was quite good since they ate these rations. Soon after the end of the first month, the Japanese took away the army rations that they had been given permission to collect. These rations would have lasted for at least three additional months with care. Almost immediately the POWs were placed on a rice diet with the rice being of very inferior quality and full of worms.

While most of the Japanese treated the prisoners with brutality or at the best with indifference, there were some noticeable exceptions where the POWs were treated with kindness and compassion by certain Japanese individuals.

In one instance there was a serious epidemic of diphtheria in the North Point Camp from October 1942 until February 1943 where three to four men died daily at the height of the epidemic. The Japanese medical officer said that no serum was available but a Japanese interpreter brought some serum into the camp later during the epidemic and thus saved the lives of many POWs. This interpreter was removed from the camp for treating the prisoners too humanely. When patients later came from Bowen Road Hospital they said the same interpreter was there and was doing what he could for extremely sick prisoners by having special food parcels sent to them. Due to his humane treatment of the prisoners this individual Japanese was sent to prison and was not released until the war was over.

Towards the end of the war, Sergeant Major Honda, the camp commandant, treated the prisoners very humanely. If it was raining, he would count the number of prisoners in the huts rather than having a muster parade or if there was a parade in the rain, he would make it as short as he could with each group being dismissed after they were counted. He also arranged for a special canteen the last Christmas that they were in the camp so that the prisoners could buy eggs, cakes, and sweets.

In his affidavit, Captain Banfill, a Canadian medical officer, stated that when the men from his First Aid Post were lined up and shot, he protested but an English speaking Japanese told him that they had been ordered to kill all captives. He also said that he had seen Japanese troops bayonet wounded officers and men, and then shoot them to make sure that they were dead.

The affidavit of one of the Volunteer Defense Corps personnel related how 25 men, after surrendering, had been ordered to leave the magazine at an anti-aircraft facility, and that when each man passed the entrance, he was bayoneted. When it came to his turn, he was bayoneted through his body, feigned death and survived.

Numerous other affidavits were introduced which told of both men and women being beaten, tortured, burned including on their private parts and executions not only for infractions of the rules but to try to get the prisoners to confess to infractions. Some told of prisoners who were removed from camps and were never seen again but it was assumed that they had been executed.

One affidavit dealt with 700 prisoners being placed aboard a boat and that they set sail in the evening. When the boat reached a point which was about 400 yards from the shore where they were to land at about 2:00 a.m. all of the people were forced into the sea by the Japanese using sticks and bayonets. About 200 men, including the witness and two or three children made it to shore. There was no food or shelter to be found and one by one the survivors died. The Japanese returned, nearly six weeks later, with the witness being the only person still alive.

One affidavit states that 120 Chinese were bayoneted to death because narcotics had been brought into a coolie camp and that these men, chosen at random, were executed as a warning for the future.

Affidavits also dealt with work at the Kankaseki Copper Mines in late 1942 on Formosa. From the camp to the minehead, the men had to descend 1,186 steps each morning and to reach the working levels of the mine was another 2,000 steps. This made for a very difficult climb after a hard days work. The prisoners were organized into working squads with civilian foremen known as 'Honchos' in charge. The Japanese guards from the camp did not enter the mine but remained in a guard room at the entrance. Due to the beatings and work conditions in the mine it had become a veritable 'hell spot' and the men dreaded each dawn when they would have to go into the mine again. It was later learned that the threat of being sent to the copper mines was used constantly in other POW camps of the island as intimidation.

Twenty or more affidavits were introduced to provide evidence of the conditions encountered on board ship by the prisoners during periods when they were being transferred from one prison camp to another. These trips ranged in length from a few days on small ships for short inter-island transfers to trips that lasted for several months on larger vessels and even extended to Japan itself.

All of these affidavits attested that sufficient space had not been allotted for prisoner transfers. In some cases as many as 50 percent of the prisoners had to stand to allow space for those persons confined to stretchers and a much smaller space which was rotated among the other POWs to allow some semblance of rest either by sitting down or lying down. Ventilation was absolutely inadequate as was the case with sanitation facilities in many instances. The lack of adequate ventilation in a tropical climate contributed much to the suffering and discomfort of the prisoners. Only a small number of latrines or in many cases buckets were allotted for the prisoners use. To further add to prisoner suffering was that many times the prisoners were not allowed on deck but were confined to remain in the holds for extended periods of time.

Food was described as being insufficient in most of the affidavits but there appeared to be little differences in the amount or the quality of the food between that provided during the ship transfers and being at a POW camp except in isolated cases or for short periods of time. The failure to provide the prisoners with adequate water was one of the worst and cruelest prisoner' deprivations. The lack of water coupled with the heat from being detained in the ship's holds in a tropical climate caused some prisoners to go out of their minds.

The lack of adequate food and water; coupled with little or no medicine, medical equipment, and care increased the spread of infectious diseases among those persons in such enforced close proximity to each other with no room for isolation of those persons suffering from such diseases and the lack of adequate medication for their treatment.

Additionally, the prisoners were still subjected to beatings, torturous treatments, and unnecessary acts of humiliation during these transfers of prisoners.

However, one of the worst violations of the Japanese was their failure to place any markings on the ships which were carrying prisoners. These ships were not only unmarked but they were intermixed with other ships carrying Japanese troops and cargo. In some cases the Japanese troops and POWs were intermixed on the same ship, and in at least one instance in the same holds, with the prisoners being on the lower levels and the Japanese troops on the upper levels of the holds. In the vernacular of today these persons would probably be called "hostages" rather than prisoners or POWs.

Some of these ships were attacked and sunk during Allied bombing raids and/or torpedo attacks by submarines. The Japanese sometimes appeared to not care if the prisoners were rescued. The prisoners were kept below decks and only so many were allowed out at a time to go to the latrines. When one ship was hit by three aerial torpedoes and machine gun fire form the attacking planes, there was complete chaos of the ship. The Japanese captain, the crew, and the guards abandoned ship by jumping overboard immediately but the prisoners were left to fend for themselves. When the ship broke in two and sank in about 5 minutes, most of the POWs had no chance as they were semi-starved, half paralyzed, were below decks and there was no way to exit the holds and escape before the ship sank. Nearly 1,000 POWs went down with the ship. The witness was one of only 217 POWs who survived.

In another incident where prisoners, being transferred by ship were killed or wounded during an air raid occurred in Formosa in January 1945. Several bombs hit the ship along the water line and three bombs exploded in the forward hold where 600 to 700 men were lined up waiting for their breakfast. Out of the 700 men were lined up waiting for their breakfast. Out of the 700 men quartered in this hold, 500 were killed and nearly 200 men were wounded in the afterhold.

A ship was hit by two torpedoes in September 1944 and was torn open. The witness who was on deck at the time the torpedoes struck, did not see the carnage that took place in the holds, but stated there must have been bast numbers of casualties in them. He also stated that he observed many POWs who had jumped overboard after the first torpedo hit, were still in the water and were killed by the second explosion. The ship sank within 20 minutes.

The witness attested that he saw the Japanese transport commander and some of the guards get into a lifeboat but they would not rescue any of the POWs many of whom had gotten hold of the lifeboat's edge. Instead of allowing these prisoners to get aboard the lifeboat, one of the Japanese used a huge ax to cut off their hands or split open their skulls.

The Japanese escort ships did not do much to rescue survivors. Depth charges were dropped as the destroyer then disappeared but returned several hours later to assist in the rescue. The corvette picked up 400 survivors and headed for shore even though there were many people still in the water. The survivors who reached shore consisted of only a small percentage of those who had embarked on the ship at the start of the trip; 276 European POWs out of 1750, 312 Ambonese POWs out of 600, and only 300 Indonesian coolies out of 5500. No mention was made as to any Japanese loss of life if there was any.

One witness stated in his affidavit that 1816 POWs were loaded aboard a ship at Hong Kong on 25 September 1942 together with 2000 Japanese troops. Conditions on this ship were basically the same as on most others with the prisoners being grossly overcrowded. The prisoners did not have adequate space to lie down in the holds.

Early in the morning of 1 October, the ship was hit by a torpedo in its coal bunkers, the ship stopped and the lights went out. After that time the prisoners were not allowed to use the latrines on deck nor were they provided with any receptacles for this purpose in the holds. Sometime after dark, when the Japanese began to batten down the hatch covers, the air in the holds became stifling as there was no air inlet, the large number of individuals present, the conditions in the holds, and the lack of latrine facilities.

The Japanese troops were disembarked from the ship sometime during the night and subsequently another vessel took the crippled ship in tow. The next day the ship stopped, gave a lurch, and it became evident that it was going to sink.

Japanese guards fired their rifles a couple of times into the hold wounding a couple of POWs slightly including the witness. The POWs cut away the hatch covers and emerged on deck form the holds as the Japanese opened fire on them from ships that were nearby and kept firing on the men after they entered the water. These ships refused to pick up anyone in the water at first but later changed this policy and rescued those POWs that they could.

In Shanghai, on 5 October, a roll call was taken and only 970 answered to their name, which meant that 846 were missing.

The witness later learned that some half dozen men had managed to escape with the help of the Chinese from some junks and sampans in the area at the time.

On 19 October 1943, a revolt broke out in Jesselton, Borneo with about 40 Japanese being killed. The Japanese retaliated by sending planes to bomb and machine gun the villages to the north of Jesselton causing much damage and loss of life and thus suppressed the revolt. A number of Kempei Tai were moved into Jesselton and a reign of terror was pursued in the following months with hundreds of men and women being arrested only on suspicion and tortured to get information on the guerrillas. Based on the information extracted from these forced confessions mass executions ensued. The Japanese admitted that on one occasion, 189 Chinese and others were executed. Several hundreds of others perished from torture, starvation, or disease while in prison.

The revolt was predominantly a Chinese affair but the Suluk people, who lived on some small islands of the West Coast of North Borneo, seem to have taken part only on the first night of the revolt. The part that they played in the revolt could not have been too conspicuous as there was no action taken against them until four months later. The Japanese appear to have selected the Suluks for extinction by executing nearly all of the adult male Suluks that they could. Very few adult male Suluks survived this reign of terror.

Dutch Borneo was occupied by the Japanese Navy in January 1942. In the area around Tarakan 32 infantry troops were captured on 11 January. When they refused to provide information on the road to Tarakan they were told they would be killed if they did not give the required data but they still would not answer. When Tarakan surrendered the following day, the POWs were tied together in groups of 10 and lead away to an area where they were blindfolded and had their hands tied behind their backs. They were then slaughtered with bayonet thrusts by Japanese soldiers, who did not stop until there were no more signs of life.

When Tarakan surrendered, the Dutch Commander of the Island sent an officer to tell one of the coastal batteries to cease fire as there was no telephone-communications to that battery. The Japanese stopped that officer and prevented his completion of his mission. As a result the gun crew was not informed of the surrender and sank two Japanese destroyers. By way of revenge, some weeks afterwards, the Japanese selected all Dutch POWs who had been members of that battery, about 215 man, and drowned them at sea.

Between October 1943 and June 1944 at Pontianak, systematic murder occurred on a huge scale. The Tokeitai, Japanese Military Police of the Navy, pretended that there was a plot, confessions were extorted after torture, and about 65 persons were tried in this fashion and executed. This pretentious legal procedure was an exception to what in fact actually took place. Altogether, 1,000 persons were executed at Mandor; 240 at Sunggei Durian; 100 at Katapang; and an unknown number at Pontianak. Several of the native rulers of West Bornea were among these victims; the first being the Sultan of Pontianak, along with two of his sons. Many well-to-do Chinese and Indonesians, and some Dutch officials were also included.

Only a very small percentage of these people who were executed had been tried by Courts Martial, 46 out of 1100 at Mandor and Katapang, and 17 out of the 100 at Sunggei Durian. The reason given was that this could not be done but that all of the suspects were dangerous to Japan and that they had to be punished.

An Australian Army Nursing sister testified that on 12 February 1942 she, 64 other nurses, 200 women and children, and a few elderly men were evacuated from Singapore on a small ship. The ship was attacked by three Japanese airplanes with bombs and machine guns which resulted with the ship beginning to sink and the order was given for the ship to be abandoned. During the air raid, the lifeboats were damaged to such an extent that when they were launched, all but two of them sunk. The witness, together with a dozen other nurses jumped into the water and swam to a life boat that was sinking where they joined three civilians and a ship's officer who were already clinging to the sides of the boat. The lifeboat still provided sufficient buoyancy to keep them afloat the nearly eight hours they drifted before landing on Banka Island and found that the two lifeboats that had not sunk were there. There were 30 to 40 women and children, 30 men from the ship's crew, and 10 nurses from these two boats. The following morning a party went to attempt to secure help for the wounded at a small native village nearby. They were refused help by the villagers who also stated that the island was already occupied by the Japanese. That night they observed a ship in the straits being shelled and two hours afterwards a lifeboat arrived with around 25 Englishmen aboard. The next morning they all decided that the only thing to do was to give themselves up and a ship's officer went to Muntok in order to bring back the Japanese to take them prisoner.

Prior to the arrival of the Japanese, the civilian women and children were sent off toward Muntok in charge of a Chinese doctor. When the ship's officer returned at mid morning with a Japanese officer in charge of a party of 15 Japanese troops, the prisoners were divided into groups with the men being in one group and the nurses and any remaining civilian women in another. The Japanese marched half of the men down to the beach and out of sight. After 10 to 15 minutes the Japanese returned and marched the remaining men to the beach. The nurses heard several shots and when the Japanese returned they were cleaning their rifles and bayonets. The nurses group was then ordered to march into the sea. The Japanese opened fire on them with machine guns when they were a few yards into the water. The witness saw some of the nurses fall one after another when she was hit in the back at waist level and the bullet passed straight through. She continued to lie at the water's edge for about 15 minutes and when she sat up and looked around the Japanese had disappeared. She dragged herself into the jungle where she became unconscious. When she regained consciousness two days later, she went to the beach to get a drink from the fresh water spring there.

On the way to the spring, a wounded Englishmen, a stretcher case, spoke to her and told her that all of the wounded had been bayoneted and left for dead. She helped him into the jungle and went to the village where the native women gave her food. When the Englishman was strong enough, after about 12 days, they decided to give themselves up and they were sent around to the coolie lines where there were other prisoners, two of them being men who had escaped the killings on the beach. On 2 March, 1942 the witness and 31 other nurses were in a group of 200 women and children who were taken across the Palembang, Sumatra.

Thus began her period of internment until they were notified that the war was over by the camp commandant on 24 August 1945. During this time frame she was held prisoner in several different camps, all of which provided inadequate space and unsatisfactory sanitary facilities, food supplied was insufficient, and they were given little or no medicine and medical equipment. During this period she was given no treatment for her wound that she had gotten on the beach but then neither did she tell the Japanese about the wound for fear that they might put her to death.

Many women were arrested and imprisoned without any suspicion. They had done nothing wrong but the fact that they had been arrested and enforced prostitution. Some married women in addition to single ones were among those taken into custody this way.

Women who refused to prostitute themselves and would not have sexual intercourse with the Japanese were subjected to various indignities including beatings, torture and the requirement for performance of manual labor.

As was specified in several affidavits and during witnesses' testimony, prisoners were often transported on board ships interspersed in convoys with cargo ships, troop carriers, oil tankers, and military warships and were not afforded the protection of displaying any indications that this was the case. This was personally confirmed by a Dutch officer who was on the submarine that torpedoed one of these ships, the Van Waerwyck, in the Malaka Straits in June 1944. Of the 700 POWs on this ship who were battened into one hatch that had only one ladder they could escape by, 250 drowned. An English witness testified that after the surrender, he had personally interrogated the Japanese troop commandant of this ship, and that the commandant admitted that there was not sufficient lifesaving equipment for POWs.

The Japanese were not always eager to rescue survivors after a ship carrying prisoners was torpedoed. In September 1944, the Junior Maru was torpedoed between Bencoolen and Padang off the west coast of Sumatra. The ship was carrying 2,300 POWs and 5,000 Javanese coolies. After the ship had been torpedoed, the Japanese machine gunned the POWs and the coolies who were in the water. Others who tried to board life rafts had their hands chopped off and/or their skulls smashed in. The loss of life in the sinking of this ship was greatly increased by these two acts of the Japanese.

From appearances it seems that the Japanese ordered their troops to kill prisoners so that they would not have to be bothered with them. On 6 March, 1942 some 80 Dutch soldiers laid down their weapons and gave up when a white flag was displayed. The Japanese troops accepted their surrender in a friendly manner, shook hands with them, and gave them chocolate and cigarettes.

A Japanese plane, which had been flying over the area at the time of the surrender, dropped a message tube, which was retrieved and given to the Japanese commander.

The Japanese commander looked through the papers contained in the tube and issued orders that caused the prisoners to have their hands bound behind their backs and to be tied together in groups of three. Another order was given and a machine gun opened fire on the fettered prisoners. When the firing stopped 25 to 30 Japanese troops with fixed bayonets went among the prisoners bayoneting anyone remaining alive. Only two of the prisoners were known to have survived this encounter, one of whom was the person who made the affidavit. He stated that some of the prisoners had their eyes put out, their heads cut off, or their abdomens ripped open.

Death rates in many of the camps throughout the areas under Japanese control reached or exceeded 50 percent. These high death rates were only possible due to the conditions that prevailed in these camps; bad food, bad medicine, massive use of beatings and torture, and the complete indifference toward the pain and suffering of the prisoners.

Based on the data contained in the affidavits presented during the trial and the sworn testimony of witnesses, it was apparent that officials at all echelons of the Japanese government were cognizant of the treatment of the POWs and internees.

Many of the defendants at the trials occupied positions at the highest level of the Japanese Imperial Government and as such must have known what the true conditions were concerning the prisoners. These defendants were not the actual perpetrators of the events described but they were lacking in the performance of their command responsibility by failing to cause any accurate investigations to be performed in response to the Allied protests received.

American witness testifies on at the War Crimes Trials in the War Ministry Building, Tokyo, on Japanese atrocities committed at Los Banos Camp, Luzon, Philippine Islands.

A former Canadian POW testifies during the War Crimes Trials at the War Ministry in Tokyo. He was captured in Hong Kong on 25 December 1941 and was liberated when Japanese Forces in Hong Kong surrendered on 15 August 1945.

The former commander of all Australian Forces in Java in 1942, Brigadier A.S. Blackburn, testifies at the War Crimes Trials in the War Ministry, Tokyo.

A former POW testifies in the War Crimes Trials, at the War Ministry Building, Tokyo. He was captured at Ambonia, Molucca Islands, 3 February 1942, while a member of the 2/21st Australian Infantry Battalion and was liberated on the same island on 10 September 1945.

A former POW who was captured at Singapore on 17 February 1942 and escaped in July 1945, testifies on the mistreatment of POWs by the Japanese at the War Crimes Trials in the War Ministry, Tokyo.

In February 1945 in Manila, a pregnant woman with an 11-month-old baby in her arms was shot and killed in her home. When the Japanese were ready to leave, they heard the baby cry, returned and killed it with two shots.

At Campos, a woman had one of her breasts hacked off.

At St. Paul's College, a baby was hurled into the air by a Japanese soldier and was impaled on another soldier's bayonet.

In Inopacaqn, Leyte, a 24-year-old girl was caught, stripped of her clothing, had her breasts slashed with a saber, and was burned on her breasts.

In Iloilo, on 18 September 1943, a man was crucified on the ground with three six-inch nails being driven through each wrist and the base of his skull.

In Tanauan, Batangas, a pregnant woman had her unborn child carved out of her stomach and beheaded.

The most shocking of atrocities against the POWs in the Philippines was the Bataan Death March. 11,000 American and 62,000 Filipino POWs, were exhausted, dispirited, and forced to march seven to eleven days without food or water, a distance of approximately 120 kilometers under a scorching tropical sun. The prisoners were so beaten, mistreated, bayoneted, or shot throughout the march, that 1,200 American and 16,000 Filipino POWs were murdered and left in the dusty, bloody road to rot.

At the march's end, the POWs were incarcerated at Camp O'Donnell, where the Japanese did not provide them with adequate food, drinking water and medical care. They were forced to labor while sick and physically unfit, subjected to punishment and torture for minor infractions, and crowded together in such a filthy, small place that was completely unfit for human habitation. Thus furthering the indirect mass annihilation of the prisoners so that 1,522 Americans and 29,000 Filipinos died there by 1 August 1942 alone. Drinking water was so scarce that it was often necessary to stand in line for six to ten hours to get a drink of water.

The prosecution submitted one document which consisting of a list of 317 separate reports containing 14,618 pages prepared by roving teams from the US Army Judge Advocate Service covering atrocities reported in the Philippines.

The Defense objected of the introduction of evidence in this manner without providing an assurance that the prosecution would provide the connection with the individual defendants against whom the evidence was intended to be directed.

The Tribunal President ruled that based on the prosecution's assurance that they would provide such a connection, the judges were satisfied in this matter even though the evidence was submitted without first hearing the connecting evidence and that the objection was overruled.

During the last dying days in Manila in February 1945, atrocities by the Japanese reached their high point. At the Bay View and three other hotels, the Japanese went on a wild orgy that culminated in the rape of many young girls who were prominent in Malate society. At the German Club, women were disrobed, raped and murdered as the rest of the crowd of 500 civilians huddled in the basement and helplessly looked on. A young girl was decapitated when she resisted advances made on her, and even then her lifeless body was violated afterward.

On 10 February 1945, Japanese marines entered the headquarters building of the Philippine Red Cross in Manila and killed or wounded many staff members, patients, and refugees by shooting or bayoneting the victims even after being told that the building belonged to the Red Cross. Appropriate markings were also displayed prominently on the building's walls, roof, and in each window. Most victims were women and children. Estimates of the number of dead ranged from a low of 20 and a high of 80 which was hard to confirm since the building was burned on 13 February.

Many documents were admitted in evidence which described the events that the witnesses had observed or which had happened to them during the rape of Manila during the early half of 1945.

One 11-year-old girl testified that both of her parents had been killed by the Japanese, and that she had been wounded by bayonet on various parts of her body 38 times. She sustained 10 wounds on her left arm, four on her right arm, one on her back, five on her legs, and wounds to her chest and abdominal area but she couldn't remember how many to each area. The same girl also gave testimony of seeing a three month old baby being thrown into the air and being caught on the Japanese soldier's bayonet when it came down, wounding but not killing the child.

Another witness provided evidence concerning the massacre of over 200 civilians at St. Paul's College. Around 250 people were placed there and the windows and doors solidly shut and barred.

Black paper was wrapped around the three hanging chandeliers and there were wires from them to the outside through the transoms.

The Japanese brought in food and liquor and told the crowd that they could partake of these items and be safe but that their houses were to be burned. Abruptly, grenade explosions proved that the chandeliers were traps and pandemonium ensued. The Japanese began firing machine guns and throwing grenades through the windows into the room. Those who were able escaped through holes in the compound wall caused by the exploding grenades. Many of those killed were sprawled across the compound wall where they were hit by the guards' bullets.

In another affidavit, the witness stated that four members from the Japanese Navy went to a house and, while two stood guard over the people there, the other two searched the house and took 5,000 pesos, jewels, watches and a revolver. When the Japanese left, they took two men and neither man was ever seen again.

Documents were submitted as evidence concerning:

- The massacre of over 2,500 civilians at Lippa, Batangas province, Luzon.
- The massacre of 194 Filipino at Santo Tomas, Batangas and the burning of the town.
- The massacre of 328 civilians at Bauan, Batangas Province.
- The massacre of 320 Filipino civilians at Taal, Batangas Province.
- The massacre of 300 civilians at Cuenca, Batangas Province.
- The massacre of at least 107 Filipino Civilians at San Jose, Batangas Province.
- The murder of 39 civilians at Lucero, Batangas Province.
- The massacre of more than 100 Filipino civilians at Tapal, Gonzaga, Cagayan.
- The murders at and the looting and burning of the town of Calauang, Laguna.
- The transcript of the testimony of Jose Havana in the trial of Yamashita regarding the massacre at Calamba, Laguna Province.
- The burning of the Barrio of Nanipil, Mountain Province, and the murder of civilians of Titig Mountain.

- The transcript of the testimony of Mariano Bayaras, Mayor of Basco, Batanes Island, in the Yamashita trial regarding atrocities in Basco, Batanes.
- The execution of Charles Putnam, Thomas Daggett, Captain Vincente Pinon, and six other unarmed Filipinos.
- The Massacre of approximately 500 Filipino civilians at Dapdap, Penson Island, Camotes Islands, Cebu Province.
- The murder of five civilians in Cervantes, Ilocos Sur, and the eating of the flesh of some of the victims by six Japanese soldiers.
- The murder, torture, and rape of civilians at Bogo, Cebu.
- The massacre of 37 civilians in Pilar, Camotes Islands, Cebu.
- The murder of 11 American Baptist teachers of the faculty of the Central Philippines College and six other Americans at Camp Hopevale, near Tapaz, Capiz.
- Summary of punitive expeditions on Panay Island by Japanese force against civilians where hundreds were massacred and buildings were burned.
- The murder of 30 or more Filipinos at San Charles
- The murder of 35 Filipinos at Malaiba, Vallehermose.
- The murder of 90 Filipino civilians on the shores of the Tagburos River, Palawan Island.

The prosecution additionally submitted nearly 60 other documents and affidavits providing evidence on the torture, rape, and/or murder of a single or couple individuals, or they might cover these type of actions against nearly 100 persons; summary of evidence of conditions which existed in certain POW camps and civilian internment camps; transcripts of testimony by witnesses at both the trials of General Yamashita and General Homma, English translations of extracts from diaries that had been kept by various Japanese individuals, English translation of captured Japanese document and statements by Japanese POWs admits to and confirms the practice of cannibalism.

Thus the Prosecution presented evidence which had been selected to provide proof that the defendants at this trial had conspired amongst themselves and with other Japanese government Officials and individuals to extend the domination of Japan over vast areas of the Pacific region.

This evidence was also presented to prove that the defendants had been instrumental in planning for and the waging of wars of aggression to further the Japanese cause without appropriate regard for compliance with the rules of international warfare particularly in matters dealing with the handling of POWs and civilian internees.

Additionally, the evidence was designed to show that once the populace indigenous to the occupied areas had been subjugated, the defendants used any and all means required to maintain Japanese control over the areas.

Defense Presentation
CHAPTER 11

General Defense

Due to the organization of the Tribunal and the method used during the court presentation, the defense phase was vastly different from that of the prosecution in that each individual accused presented evidence and testimony to refute that portion of the prosecution's presentation as it pertained to himself alone rather than as a small portion of a single conglomerate presentation. This did not mean that there was not any cooperation between the individual accused and their counsels but that it was organized in such a fashion to complete the presentation for one individual accused before proceeding to the next. A single counsel might conduct cross examination of the prosecution witnesses when appropriate during the prosecution's presentation of its case when their testimony was related and pertained to several of the accused.

The defense for each of the accused was presented in the same order as they were listed in the indictment, alphabetically by their last names.

The primary portion of each defense presentation was the individual defendant's affidavit which was prepared to provide the basis for the direct testimony during their appearance on the witness stand. These affidavits provided the background to refute those portions of the case against the defendant, was followed during direct and, if required, his redirect testimony, and was used by the prosecution to prepare any points to be used during the defendant's cross examination.

Each defendant's legal counsel also submitted statements from other witnesses and documents to attempt to disprove the Prosecution's case against their client as well as the normal direct examination of defense witnesses and the cross examination of prosecution witnesses.

Extracts from the court records of other trials of General Yamashita and General Homma were also used by the defense in some instances to assist improving specific points during some of the Defense presentations.

The defendants' affidavits varied in length with some containing only a few pages and others consisting of upwards of a couple hundred pages. To include all of these affidavits in this publication would be redundant, superfluous, and unnecessary as the case presented by the prosecution was combined. For that reason only two of these affidavits have been included as examples of the defense presentations. These affidavits are those of defendants Shimada and Tojo.

It is very appropriate that the affidavits of these two individuals be used since both were career officers in the Japanese military with Shimada being a full Admiral in the Japanese Navy and was selected to be the Navy minister in the Tojo cabinet in October 1941. Defendant Tojo advanced to the rank of full general in the Imperial Japanese Army and became a part of the political side of the Japanese government, additionally, when he accepted the Emperor's request that he head a new cabinet in October 1941. By acceding to this request so shortly before the Japanese attack on Pearl Harbor and the outbreak of hostilities in the Pacific Basin, he became one of the most hated individuals in the United States.

Tojo maintained partial, if not full control of the Japanese Army by retaining the post of war minister in addition to that of being the prime minister. During one period, in addition to these two vital posts, he was also the chief of the army general staff.

To assist in the political control, Tojo initially retained the post of home minister. From time to time he would also perform the duties for other ministerial positions temporarily. Thus an effective control was placed on the Japanese government, both politically and militarily.

The special assistant to the Secretary of State with the Consular Services testifies on the witness stand during cross examination at the War Crimes Trials in the War Ministry, Tokyo.

Former Japanese General Masao Yano displays a map describing the Manchurian border lines at the War Crimes Trials, in the War Ministry Building, Tokyo.

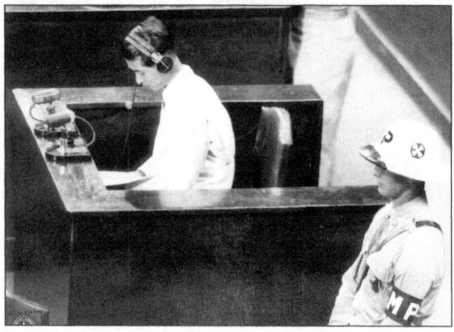

Former Japanese Imperial Headquarters staff officer testifies during Defense presentation at the War Crimes Trials in the War Ministry Building, Tokyo.

Affidavit of Shigetaro Shimada
CHAPTER 12

Shigetaro Shimada was born in Tokyo in 1883 and pursued an active career in the Japanese Navy from the time he entered the Naval Academy in 1901 and graduated as a mid shipman in 1904 until he was placed on the retired list as a full admiral on 20 January 1945.

Shimada's Career resume:

Entered the Naval Academy in 1901.

Graduated from the Naval Academy as a Mid-Shipman in 1904.

Commissioned as an Ensign in the Japanese Navy in August 1905.

Entered the Naval War College as a Lieutenant in 1913.

Graduated from Naval War College as a Lieutenant Commander in 1915.

Sent to Italy as Assistant Naval Attaché in the spring of 1916.

Appointed Naval Attaché in Italy in December 1917 and remained in that position until the end of World War I.

Designated as a staff officer of a training squadron in 1919 and toured Europe.

Returned to Japan in 1920 to become a staff officer in the Naval General Staff.

Promoted to the rank of Commander in 1920.

Assigned as second in command of the Hyuga for one year in the latter half of 1922.

Assigned duties as an instructor in the Naval War College in 1923.

Promoted to the rank of Captain in 1924.

Appointed Commander of the Seventh Submarine Unit, consisting of three submarines, in 1926.

Assigned as Captain of the cruiser Tama in August 1928.

Appointed Commander of the Battleship *Hiei* in December 1928.

Promoted to the rank of Rear Admiral and appointed Chief of Staff for the Second Fleet in November 1929.

Appointed Chief of Staff for the Combined Fleet and First Fleet in December 1930.

Designated Chief of the Submarine School at Kure in December 1931.

Appointed Chief of Staff for the Third Fleet in February 1932.

Assigned as Chief of the Naval Information Bureau of the Naval General Staff in June 1932.

Appointed Chief of the Operations Bureau of the Naval General Staff in November 1932.

Promoted to the rank of Vice Admiral in December 1934.

Appointed Vice Chief of the Naval General Staff in December 1935.

Designated Commander in Chief of the Second Fleet in December 1937.

Assigned duties as the Commander in Chief at Kure Naval Station in December 1938.

Appointed Commander in Chief of the China Fleet succeeding Admiral Oikawa in May 1940.

Promoted to the rank of Full Admiral in November 1940.

Shimada served as Commander of the China Fleet until September 1941 when he returned to Japan.

From 18-27 September 1941, Shimada toured the Naval hospitals and then assumed the post of Commander in Chief at Yokosuka Naval Station on 1 October 1941.

Appointed Navy Minister, once again succeeding Admiral Oikawa, on 18 October 1941.

Assumed the post of Chief of Naval General Staff in connection with his post as Navy Minister in February 1944.

Resigned the post of Navy Minister on 17 July 1944.

Resigned Chief of Naval General Staff post on 2 August 1944.

Appointed duties as Naval Counselor after his resignation from his Naval General Staff post.

Had his name placed on the retired list on 20 January 1945, at his own request.

At the time Shimada assumed his duties as commander in chief of Yokosuka Naval Base, he denied that he had any inkling that he was being considered as the next Navy minister, had no knowledge of any disputes within the cabinet, and that his knowledge of the political situation was dependent upon information obtained from newspapers. He stated that he was told by Admiral Oikawa on October 17th, less than three weeks after taking over duties as Yokosuka Naval Base commander, that he felt that Shimada was the best qualified of available high ranking naval officers and that he would like to submit his name in recommendation for the post of Navy minister in the new cabinet which was being formed.

Shimada refused to agree to this for the following reasons:

1. He had been away from Tokyo on routine naval assignments for a four-year continuous period and did not have ample knowledge of Japanese political situations or positions nor of their effect at that time on any international complications.

2. His past naval career had been largely on the sea or connected with the Naval General Staff and had never served any time in a Navy Ministry.

3. And lastly, that he had an emphatic distaste for politics and had no desire to become involved in that line of work.

The next day after much discussion with Admiral Oikawa, Admiral Nagano, and Fleet Admiral Prince Fushimi and receipt of several telephone calls from the Cabinet Formation Headquarters urging that the name of the Navy minister candidate be submitted as soon as possible as all of the other ministers of the new cabinet had been determined, Shimada reversed his earlier decision and agreed to accept the post.

Shimada denied the statement by the prosecution that he had joined the Tojo cabinet because he was, and was known to be, an active supporter of the Tojo policy and that his participation in the conspiracy prior to October 1941 must be inferred from his joining of the cabinet. Shimada stated that he did not know Tojo prior to accepting the position as the Navy minister, having met him only once, and then only for a few moments in Shanghai in 1940.

Shimada visited Tojo to explain a prerequisite which had to be agreed to before he would officially accept the cabinet post which was that he would insist that negotiations with the United States be pursued to the utmost with the firm determination of seeking a peaceful solution to the then existing differences between the nations involved with the United States being spoken of as the negotiating power for the others.

Emphatically agreeing that it would be the Japanese government's policy with his cabinet to start from scratch in attempting to reach a diplomatic understanding, wholeheartedly and sincerely, the aim of which, Tojo said was the prevention of war in accordance with the Emperors wish. Shimada was impressed and relieved by Tojo's attitude.

Shimada also believed that Tojo, realizing his total responsibility and full accountability as the head of the Japanese government, would do his utmost to resolve matters through diplomatic channels rather than by force of arms regardless of whatever previous stand he had taken.

In late October and early November 1941, Shimada focused his thoughts on the following two problems: how best to ease the most difficult conditions of withdrawal of troops from abroad and to reconcile this fact with the views of the Army section of the Imperial general headquarters, and what were the greatest possible concessions that Japan could afford to make in its attempt to reach an understanding with the United States.

The greatest difficulty concerned the removal of the troops from China and French Indo-China. The best solution seemed to be a compromise with each side making concessions and giving ground. An extremely strong opinion prevailed at that time, that perhaps, matters might have already progressed to far which made it a physical impossibility to withdraw all Japanese troops from China as it could be a psychological blow stunning to the Japanese people, be considered a victory over Japan by China, and relegate Japan to being in a position of dependence based on the prestige and standing of the United States and Great Britain in the Far East for their economic existence and position as a world power.

Shimada favored a compromise solution to the situation providing for an immediate withdrawal of all Japanese forces from French Indo-China but entailing a strategic withdrawal over a period of time for those forces from China proper.

Shimada went on to describe the attitude of many Japanese which led up to the decision at the Imperial Conference on November 5th to prepare for the initiation of hostilities while, continuing at the same time with all efforts toward maintaining peace through diplomacy. The reasons he gave and which he did not consider unreasonable were:

1. The Allies had effected an economic encirclement of Japan with a more telling result than what the Japanese dared to admit.

2. The increased United States armaments were viewed with alarm since they could not understand how such military steps were warranted solely on the contemplation of war with Germany alone.

3. The United States policy toward Japan had been unsympathetic and strict, revealing a determination to enforce their demands without compromise.

4. American military and economic aid which was being provided to China had caused bitter feelings among the Japanese.

5. The Allied Powers had carried on military conferences which were directly pointed against Japan.

6. The High Command advised that if diplomatic negotiations failed and they were called upon to go into action, it would have to be by early winter or not at all. Without increased oil supplies, it would render them unable to risk naval warfare at a later date.

Shimada also denied that he knew of the Pearl Harbor Attack Plan prior to his appointment as Navy minister but learned about it after he had been appointed to the post from the First Division Chief of the Naval General Staff Fukutome. He stated that he did not direct his attention to the operational procedures over which he had no jurisdiction as they were entirely within the hands of the Naval General Staff. Although it was within his power to have known when the Fleet headed for Pearl Harbor, he never knew the exact date again since it was under the operational control of the Naval General Staff and the Combined Fleet rather than the Navy Ministry.

Shimada testified that he hoped and prayed for negotiated settlement to prevent hostilities until the receipt of the note from Secretary of State Hull which was a harsh reply from the US government that was unyielding and unbending and contained no recognition of Japanese endeavors toward concessions in the negotiations. It was then that he all but lost hope for peace and felt that war was inevitable. When the final decision was made at the Imperial Conference of 1 December 1941, both Shimada and Admiral Nagano had told the Emperor the day before that the Navy had made adequate preparations.

Shimada acknowledged that part of his duties as Navy Minister entailed the issuance of regulations concerning the handling of prisoners taken by the Navy and that such regulations were issued. It became the duty of the commanders in chief of the various areas where the prisoners were located to follow and enforce these directives. These individuals could issue any orders deemed necessary for immediate circumstances as long as the orders did not violate the provisions of the Ministry's regulations.

Shimada stated that the first he had heard regarding the mistreatment of POWs was during the progression of the trial and the presentation by the Prosecution. He said that he was shocked and ashamed as he sat in the court room and heard for the first time the many accounts where Japanese Naval personnel mistreated POWs and that Japanese Naval regulations and teachings could in no way be construed to tolerate such an interpretation under any circumstance. Shimada added that although he was seated in the Navy Ministry in Tokyo, he heard nothing of these matters and lacked the command ability to control the men's conduct on the scene. Nevertheless, he felt that he had to assume moral responsibility because of his high supervisory position within the Japanese government rather than a chain of command responsibility.

Regarding the evidence presented in court which supposedly pertained to a secret order concerning submarine warfare, Shimada did not believe that such an order was issued, and if it was issued, it would not have come out of the Navy Ministry but from the Naval General Staff as this was solely within their preview of operational plans. He stated that there was very little cooperation between Germany and Japan regarding submarine warfare. The Germans may have had grounds to complain concerning the lack of naval cooperation with Germany as the Japanese Navy never viewed with favor the Japanese-German relations.

Shimada refuted the Prosecution's evidence concerning a supposed speech made by him in front of a Diet Committee in February 1942 after the start of the war on the basis that it was not a speech but rather a discussion. He contends that had the entire discussion been reported and considered rather than the few reported words, they would have provided a different light as to their context. He denied that he had ever advocated cruelty to the enemy or toward the nationals of any country. He said that he was merely explaining that the meager economy of Japan necessitated support of the war effort from the occupied countries and that he did not speak in terms of eliminating or exterminating any individuals but in the abstract sense of achieving the supply of necessary materials and the elimination of economic opposition.

On the question of whether of not the Japanese Navy favored an attack on the United States without a declaration of war or after providing such a declaration, Shimada believed that they should be able to rely upon the knowledge and skill of the foreign minister and his experts in respect to such matters. Therefore, he never had any concern on the method that was used until the question was raised after the war nor did he ever attend a conference or meeting where the Navy advocated an attack without warning.

Shimada believed the testimony of Mr. Kumaichi Yamamoto of the foreign office which indicated that the vice chief of the Naval general staff had insisted on the attack being made without warning during the liaison conference of 2 December 1941 was in error as he could not recall of any such conference on that date. He, together with Admiral Nogano not long before this date, were told of this contention and jointly they questioned each of the accused who had attended these liaison conferences, including Hoshino, Kaya, Muto Oka, Suzuki, and Tojo but none of these people could remember such an occurrence with the exception of Togo.

Shimada testified that there appeared to be some significance attached to the fact that his name appeared as a member on the Imperial general headquarters which was composed of the Army section and the Navy section controlled by their respective chief of the general staff. In as much as purely operational and strategic matters and problems were discussed there, he never attended any of these meetings as Navy minister and had no right to do so.

Shimada stated that he met his fellow accused as follows:

1. Hoshino, Kaya, Kido, Kimura, Muto, Sato, Suzuki, and Togo after he had assumed the post of Navy Minister in October 1941.

2. Tojo once, briefly around December, 1940 when he visited Shanghai during the course of a tour, prior to the time of formation of the Cabinet

3. Mr. Shigemitsu for the first time in Shanghai in 1932 and then not again until April 1943 when he assumed the office as the Foreign Minister in the Tojo Cabinet.

4. Umezu in 1932

5. Hata and Itagaki in 1940.

6. Mr. Koiso in July 1944 when he was organizing his new Cabinet.

7. His acquaintance with Admiral Oka was slight even though they had served in the Navy together and it was only after becoming Navy Minister that he talked with Admiral Oka for any great length.

8. Araki, Dohihara, Hiranuma, Matsue, Minami, Oshima, and Shiratori only after his confinement in Sugamo prison.

Hideki Tojo - Prior to Pearl Harbor
CHAPTER 13

Hideki Tojo was born in Tokyo in December 1884 into a family of seven boys and three girls. His father, Hidenori Tojo, came from rather humble feudal stock, who after the Meiji restoration of 1868, rose through the ranks of the National Army, from a non-commissioned cadet in the 1870s to the eventual honorary rank of Lieutenant General on his retirement in 1908. In some of the highlights of his father's military career included successful field duty against the Satsuma rebels in 1877, premier performance at the Army War College where he studied under the influential Prussian military during two victorious wars (the Sino-Japanese War of 1894-1895, and the Russo-Japanese War of 1904-1905, where he was a Brigade Commander).

Tojo's childhood years were affected largely by the strong maternal influence exerted by his mother, Chitose Tojo nee Tokunaga, on the large Tojo family due largely to the frequent absences of his father because of the requirements of his army service. His early life also changed when he became the oldest son after his two older brothers deaths and later after his father's early death when he had to assume full responsibility for the family.

Tojo did not consider himself to be very smart and as a 25-year-old First Lieutenant was heard to say, "I am not very intelligent, so that unless I study exceedingly hard I shall not become a great man."

Later in life when he had become a senior officer, he told a group of Japanese youths: "Endeavor and hard work have been my friends throughout life, as I am just an ordinary man possessing no brilliant talents."

Tojo rose steadily through the ranks as a career army officer after graduating from the military academy in 1905, tenth in his class out of 363. As a new 21-year-old Second Lieutenant, the Russo-Japanese War was near an end by the time he arrived in Manchuria.

Tojo was promoted to the rank of First Lieutenant in 1907. During the seven years he served in that rank, he married Katsuko Ito, and together they began to raise a family consisting of three boys and four girls born between the years 1911 and 1932.

In December 1915, Tojo, now a Captain, graduated with honors from the prestigious and difficult Army War College which was a vital requirement for an individual desirous of attaining the rank of General. Among his classmates were Hiroshi Oshima, future ambassador to Hitler's Germany and Masaharu Homma, one of the first Japanese executed after the war for his connection with the Bataan Death March in 1942.

Being an outstanding graduate conversant in German, the "elite" military language of the time, Tojo expected a leisurely trip to Berlin to study politics, economics, culture, and language the same as had been done before him by his father. However, the on-set of the First World War hostilities made Germany and Japan officially enemies, and caused a delay in his departure for Europe. While waiting for matters to clear up so that he could proceed on his assignment, he used the interim period to acquire experience and efficiency in the War Ministry's Adjutant General's Office.

He was finally ordered to Europe in August 1919 where he stayed for two years in Switzerland as Assistant Military

Attaché and then proceeded to Germany in July 1921. He was not accompanied by his family on his trip to Europe because he could not afford to take them on his existing salary even though he had been promoted to Major in 1920.

During his European assignment, Tojo expanded his circle of professional acquaintances to include Tomoyuki Yamashita, future general who later came to be known as "The Tiger of Malaya" and was one of the first Japanese executed at the end of the war; Yoshijiro Umezu, future general, Japan's last wartime army chief of staff, co-defendant at this trial; Naotake Sato, future ambassador to the Soviet Union; Shigenori Togo, future foreign minister in the Tojo cabinet, co-defendant at this trial and Tetsuzan Nagata, general staff genius who replaced Umezu as Military Attaché.

In order to observe the Washington conference proceedings which was at that time considering Far Eastern affairs in general and naval limitations in particular, Tojo traveled by way of the United States in late 1921 when he was ordered back to Japan. Being unfamiliar with the English language and anxious to return to his family and military duties in Japan, he soon left by train for San Francisco where he would board a ship to travel home to Japan. A writer felt that Tojo, based upon this single brief experience "viewed the Americans of the roaring twenties as undisciplined, unmilitary, and unconcerned with anything except the pursuit of the jazzy life."

Highlights from Tojo's military career included: a lectureship in military science at the Army War College, promotion to the rank of lieutenant colonel in 1924, assignment to the senior staff in the Military Affairs Bureau of the War Ministry in 1926, appointment as head of the Mobilization Section in 1928 and advancement to the rank of full colonel the same year.

The Marshall of the Court swears in Hideki Tojo as a witness to provide testimony in his own defense during the Tokyo War Crimes Trials at the War Ministry Building.

View of the courtroom showing Tojo providing testimony from the witness stand on his own behalf at the War Crimes Trials in the War Ministry Building, Tokyo.

The impression that Tojo conveyed to War Minister Ugaki was that he was a reliable office manager who was famous for whipping out his notebook and taking copious notes. It was about this time that the nickname of "The Razor" came to be associated with his name alluding to his rapier-like mind and mannerisms.

Tojo, at the time, was particularly disturbed, in his own outlook, by the low repute of the Army; the social and political effects of the immense catastrophic great earthquake of 1932; the subversive ideological inroads into Japan since the Bolshevik revolution; domestic economic distress; and parliament's curtailment of the 'superfluous' armed forces.

Tojo was placed in command of the First Infantry Regiment of the 1st Division in Tokyo in August 1929.

Tojo became Chief of the Organization and Mobilization Section of the Army General Staff in Tokyo in 1931.

Even though Tojo shared the hawkish aspirations of the Kwantung Army, he was not a member of any of the plotting cabals, but was involved in the high-level politicking in the search for a successor to General Minami as War Minister in September 1931. Tojo preferred garrulous, publicity-conscious General Araki who was chosen to fill the post under Premier Inukai in the Cabinet reshuffle at the end of 1931.

In March 1933, Tojo was promoted to the rank of Major General but he was not entirely satisfied with his duty assignment as the Chief of the Military Research Committee in the War Ministry. When an opportunity arose to leave this detested dull assignment, Tojo was appointed as the Deputy Commandant of the Military Academy in March 1934.

During the period of 1930 to 1936, a group called the 'Imperial Way Faction' had sprung up in the Army and sought to reform the regime and society. The resentful and insubordinate young officers in this movement did not shrink from using violence, propaganda, and terror to achieve their supposedly noble ends of elimination of party government; extermination of alleged corruption in business, high finance and politics; destruction of communism and establishment of a kind of state socialism under military auspices.

The series of crude but sensational incidents that took place at this time caused it to be called by one foreign correspondent a period of "government by assassination," while another said that Japan resembled a perpetual St. Valentines Day Massacre' in the 1930s.

Tojo thought of these young officers as "radical revolutionaries" after the war, and even though he would have been content to reform the system, he preferred that it be done from within, thereby avoiding the excesses and wild adventures that took place.

Among those assassinated during this period was Tojo's old friend and mentor General Nagata who was slain in his office by an Army malcontent in August 1935. At last the moderates became disturbed in this time of great tensions and terror. Even the Emperor was supposed to have become involved in the matter. He advised the War Minister that those young men had gone too far, and that he desired that stern measures be taken to put an end to it. When Tojo learned of Nagata's murder, he wept openly, swore to take care of Nagata's disciples, promised himself that he would do all that was within his power to "cleanup" Japanese military politics, and to avenge his old friend.

Moods and attitudes reflected by Tojo during his presentation of testimony from the witness stand in the War Crimes Trials at the Tokyo War Ministry Building.

It was at this time in 1935, that Minami, the Commanding General of the powerful Kwantung Army requested that Tojo become his Kempei Commander in Manchuria. This important post proved to be a turning point in his life for it became a stepping-stone to much bigger and better positions of authority as well as providing him close contact with General Itagaki, one of the key figures in the 1931 Manchurian Incident secret planning and the Kwantung Army Deputy Chief of Staff at the time. Tojo, was at first not enamored with the assignment but as time passed, he came to realize that it could be used as a mighty tool to crush his enemies and those individuals responsible for the killing of Nagata.

During the famous 2-26 Incident, where a large scale mutiny took place on 26 February 1936 and many important military and political figures marked for 'heavenly punishment' were systematically attacked, Tojo, on orders from General Minami, insured that all elements of the Kwantung Army remained loyal to the Government and did not side with the rebels in the homeland. In December 1936 he was promoted to the rank of Lieutenant General presumably as a reward for his accomplishments. His pleasure in this promotion was reflected in the private statement that he could now face his father without shame.

General Itagaki had been elevated from Deputy to Chief of Staff of the Kwantung Army in March 1936. When Itagaki was moved in March 1937 to become the Commander of the 5th Division, Tojo replaced him in the Chief of Staff position.

It was during Tojo's tenure in this position that he sent the telegram to the Vice Minister of War and the Vice Chief of the General Staff which he contended dealt with the subject of a point of view toward military preparations against Soviet Russia rather than operations for the war against the USSR as stated during the Prosecution's presentation.

He also said that the translation used by the Prosecution was in error when it used the phrase on delivery of a blow against China by attacking Nanking but should have been on the delivery of a blow first of all on the Nanking Regime.

At the time there was an active anti-Japanese movement sweeping over all of China, especially the menace of the Chinese Communist Party. It was determined that if conditions were not corrected, it would inevitably result in subsequent unrest and disorder in Manchuria. Since the burden of protecting Manchukuo against Soviet invasion and preserving peace in Manchuria was the responsibility of the Kwantung Army, it could not stand idly by and let such an unstable state of affairs continue at its rear.

The Japanese paramount hope in this situation was for a final, peaceful settlement with China. However, it was considered that a prerequisite for such a peaceful settlement was that the anti-Japanese policy of China had to first be abandoned.

Had the message contained information of substantial political import, it would have been communicated by the Kwantung Army commander rather than being dispatched by the chief of staff which was in accordance with the ordinary official procedure.

The actual decision as to whether the suggestion should or should not be adopted was entirely left up to the discretion of the Central Authorities, the Army general staff and the War Ministry.

Tojo testified that his appointment as the war minister in the Second Konoye cabinet in July 1940 was the first time that he held a position of political responsibility. He was notified to report to Tokyo while on tour in Manchuria in his capacity as Inspector General of the Army Air Force. He was told by the war minister in the outgoing cabinet that Prince Konoye was approaching the formation of the new cabinet with the utmost circumspection and was concerned with the basic national policy of the China Incident. During the meeting at Prince Konoye's private residence that came to be popularly called the "Ogikuro Conference," the premier-designate proposed that in view of the past course of events, the national policy to be followed by the incoming Cabinet, should emphasize the solutions of the China Incident. For this purpose, among others, it was essential that there should be better coordinated relations between the Supreme Command and the Government, and closer harmony between the Army and Navy. All present at the meeting expressed complete agreement with these proposals and even though some practical political problems were also discussed, at no time was there any discussion pertaining to the selection of Cabinet members.

The Imperial Investiture ceremony of the new cabinet took place on 22 July 1940.

During the tenure of the Second Konoye cabinet, according to Tojo, the Japanese were confronted with the following grave disturbances in foreign affairs in addition to the difficult problem in China:

- American and British aid to Chunking presented the greatest obstacle to the solution of the China Incident.
- The American and British economic strangulation of Japan increased in severity with each passing day.
- The war in Europe had brought about serious repercussions to the world in general with some European pow-

ers which had interests in East Asia, namely France and the Netherlands, having dropped out of the field of battle. With Britain in a critical position, the possibility of America entering the war became more and more likely. In that event, there was the increasingly imminent danger of the war spreading to East Asia, and it became vital, therefore, that Japan take some active measures to prepare for such a contingency.

In the area of domestic affairs, the following were applicable during this period:

- The proposal pertaining to a new political order, advocated by Prince Konoye, seemed to have been supported by the entire nation. Various political parties and factions that were in sympathy with the movement dissolved themselves of their own volition or were in the process of dissolution.

- The concept of a new order in the fields of economic and political thought were fast gathering momentum.

- Each new form of pressure brought against Japan by America, Britain, and other nations caused Japanese public opinion to gradually swing away from liberalism and towards nationalism.

The foremost aspiration of the new Cabinet, according to Tojo, was for the establishment of an enduring peace with a higher degree of prosperity for the Far East and to maintain the independence and safety of Japan with a proper and adequate national defense. These national policies did not contemplate in the slightest degree any ambitions for territorial gain or economic monopoly.

The "Outline of the Basic National Policy" was drafted by the Planning Board along ideas suggested by Prince Konoye, and was made to serve as the basis for the domestic policy of Japan with these three essential points: renovation of the domestic organization; solution of the China situation; and perfecting the national defense.

The Supreme Command prepared and presented a paper on the 'Main Points with Regard to the Handling of the Situation to Meet Changes in World Conditions' which was approved at the Liaison conference on 27 July 1940 and consisted of the following two fundamental points: ways and means for settling the China Incident; and measures for settling the problems in the southern region.

In the deliberations over these fundamental points, the following four major issues were discussed:

• Relations with Germany and Italy. In view of the resolution to find a solution of the China Incident and due to changes in the international situation, it was determined that it was urgently necessary for Japan to move from a position of world isolation to a position among the world's nations that was impregnable. It was reasoned that due to the consistent American and British attitude throughout the China Incident, Japan should make some attempt for closer political connections with Germany and Italy. At this state no thought was given to proceeding all the way toward the signing of a tripartite treaty of alliance with these two countries. There was even some argument advanced favoring the drastic improvement of relations with the Soviet Union but nothing was resolved on this item.

• Improvement of Japanese-American Relations. The effect that the negotiation of closer political ties with Germany and Italy would have on Japanese-American relations deeply concerned all members. Premier Konoye was fully aware of the Emperor's firm wishes that Japan should always be on the friendliest terms with America and Britain, was most prudent on this point, since he also believed that friendly relations with these nations was of great necessity to the ultimate solution of the China Incident. However, Foreign Minister Matsuoka insisted that due to the markedly unfriendly attitude shown toward Japan by these nations since the Washington Conference, the only policy left to follow was for Japan to take a firm attitude towards both. Mr. Matsuoka held to the view that war between Japan and America would result in world destruction, and therefore, every effort should be made to prevent such an occurrence. He reasoned that it was essential to improve the relations between the two countries and that the accomplishment of this could only be brought about by Japan taking a firm resolute position. The members decided to entrust the Foreign Minister to draw up a plan of action of this matter.

- Policy VisàVis China. With respect to China, it was decided to prevent assistance to Chiang Kai-shek and the elimination of all hostile elements. This strategy was adopted because it was felt that the reasons for delay in the solution of the China Incident were, first, the underestimation of Japan's national strength by Chunking, and, second, the active assistance to Chiang Kai-shek by third powers. It was therefore determined to be an absolute necessity that the supply route between America and Britain to Chiang's Regime be severed.

- The Problem of the Southern Region. The two absolutely essential problems facing Japan at that time were the strengthening of the national defense against the Soviet Union and the establishment of a self-sufficient nation. Obstacles blocking the accomplishment of these crucial objectives were the China Incident and the pressure from America and Britain. The controlling factor pertaining to the second obstacle was that Japan relied upon America and Britain for the major portion of her imports of essential materials and once these were cut off the very existence of the nation was endangered. Obviously, this problem was viewed with the utmost concern when it was taken in conjunction with the China Incident solution. It was believed in Japan that this critical problem could be solved only by the perfection of self-sufficiency through the importation of the essential materials from the Southern Region. However, with the China Incident still in progress, Japan desired above all else, to exclude friction with all third powers.

To summarize the feelings of the Japanese Cabinet at that time was there was no thought whatsoever of war against America or Britain, but it was feared that regardless of Japan's wishes on the matter, hostile action by force of arms from America and/or Britain was a possibility.

Tojo stressed that Foreign Minister Matsuoka was in complete charge of all negotiations leading up to the signing of the Tripartite Pact and that his participation dealt solely with matters applicable to his position as War Minister. Private discussions concerning strengthening political ties with Germany and Italy had been on going prior to the establishment of the Second Konoye Cabinet. After the formation of the Cabinet was completed, Foreign Minister Matsuoka proposed that on the subject of strengthening of the Japan-Germany-Italy axis these nations should cooperate mutually on the establishment of a new order in Europe and Asia. Matsuoka stipulated that representatives of these nations should confer to determine the best method for the accomplishment of this end and that this information then should be made known to the public at large.

This policy was confirmed at the liaison conference on 19 September and later on the same day at the Imperial Conference. Matsuoka proceeded to confer with German representative, Herr Stahmer, and together they drafted the Tripartite Pact, which in turn was submitted to the Cabinet and subsequently to the Privy Council.

The treaty was signed on the 27 September after confirmation by the Privy Council.

Tojo testified that it was his sincere belief that the purpose of the treaty was to improve the international position of Japan which would therefore become a factor in the solution of the China Incident. He believed it would assist in preventing the spread of the European War to East Asia. From the very outset of negotiations until the final stages of its ratification there was never any thought of dividing the world among the signatory powers, nor of world conquest. The "New Order in Greater East Asia" itself was based upon the basic foundations of mutual prosperity, independence, and the sovereignty of all nations concerned. Each and every treaty signed by Japan with the various states of Greater East Asia was based on the recognition of the inviolability of each other's territorial integrity and absolute sovereignty.

The above was the understanding held by Prime Minister Konoye and all members of the Cabinet.

As the War Minister, Tojo, in conjunction with the Supreme Command, participated in the stationing of troops in northern French Indo-China. The southern policy itself was one of the results of continued American and British economic strangulation of Japan. One of the aspects of this policy was to sever the coalition between America and Britain with China. Another was the establishment of economic self-sufficiency of Japan. These aspects of the southern policy were intended to be attained through peaceful means until pressure against Japan from America, Britain, and the Netherlands resulted in unforeseen developments.

During the tenure of the previous Cabinet (latter part of June 1940), the French Indo-China authorities had voluntarily agreed to prohibit the passage of supplies through their territory to the Chiang Kai-shek regime. In order to carry out this arrangement, Japan dispatched an observation force to the area and identical arrangements with Burma were made about the same time. However, after activation of the plan, it became apparent that it was impossible to insure complete stoppage of Chungking aid with such a small observation force. At the same time, Chungking announced that the route would be reopened by force and began accumulating military forces near the border regions.

The Japanese High Command felt that under the circumstances it was vital to defend North French Indo-China and since the Supreme Command desired to carry out the campaign in the interior of China as a means to speedily conclude the China Incident, they wished to have bases in northern French Indo-China for that purpose. The important items were the stationing of a specified number of troops on northern French Indo-Chinese territory and the passage of a specified number of troops through the region. Tojo did not remember the exact figures but thought they were 6,000 and 25,000, respectively. Negotiations began in August 1940 between Foreign Minister Matsuoka and the French Ambassador to Japan, M. Charles Arsene Henry.

An understanding was reached on 30 September after formal notes were exchanged. Japan recognized the sovereignty and territorial integrity of France in French Indo-China, and France, on her part, agreed to offer special facilities for the stationing of Japanese troops in the specified area. Japan further agreed that this situation would not appear to be in the nature of a military occupation.

The Matsuoka-Henry agreement set forth the basic principles and it was assumed that special instructions would be promptly issued for the local authorities to commence negotiations for the purpose of satisfying any specific requirements.

Major General Nishihara, Chief of the Japanese Observation Party, under instructions from Imperial Headquarters, began immediate discussions with local authorities and agreement on the basic items was completed by the 4 September with the detailed listing of facilities to be signed on 6 September. However, an alleged border crossing incident into China by a Japanese Battalion was cited by local French Indo-Chinese authorities as the reason for refusing to sign the detailed agreement. According to Tojo, it was determined during an investigation that the Japanese troops never actually crossed the border and that although the local authorities swore their allegiance to the Vichy Government, there was some doubt as to their true intention.

On the part of the Japanese, the policy for a peaceful settlement was maintained to the very end of the negotiations despite the fact that there was a critical urgency for the dispatch of troops to the area. Both Tojo, as the War Minister, and the Chief of the Army General Staff gave strict instructions that this must be carried out on a peaceable basis. Chief of the First Section of the Army General Staff was sent to the area to assist in the negotiations.

Despite all efforts on the part of the Japanese to reach a peacefully negotiated settlement, it became apparent that an agreement could not be accomplished due to the procrastination on the part of local authorities in spite of the agreement of the French Home Government. At that time, the Imperial Headquarters issued instructions to their negotiators to request a reply by a dead line of noon on 22 September. Both parties finally signed the detailed agreement on that date.

In summary, the dispatch of Japanese troops to North French Indo-China in September 1940 was prompted by the desire to speedily resolve the China Incident. The Japanese consistent policy was to accomplish this peacefully; the strength of the forces was held to the barest minimum with the actual number dispatched being about 4,000 troops, a figure well below the agreed total.

As evidence towards refuting the charges made by the Prosecution that these were acts of aggression against China, Tojo explained the events concerning the signing of the Sino-Japanese Basic Treaty on 30 November 1940 and the issuing of the Joint Proclamation of Japan, Manchoukuo, and China. These items were based on the 'Outline for Settlement of the China Incident' approved by the 13 November 1940 Imperial Conference. It was considered appropriate that before the signing of a basic treaty with the Nanking Government that one last effort would be made to include the Chungking regime in the overall peace. It was decided to centralize all peace negotiations with Chungking under the control of Foreign Minister Matsuoka but these negotiations ended in failure and Japan was forced to enter into the basic treaty with the Nanking Government. At the same time the Joint Proclamation of Japan, Manchoukuo, and China was issued which clarified the relations between the three countries.

Tojo, as War Minister, was concerned with three points:

1) Application of the Treaty and other instruments together with the recognition of an existing defacto state of war in China. There was no attempt by the Chungking regime to peacefully settle the issue. On the contrary, Chiang Kai-shek continued hostilities and actual warfare was in progress. In the interest of peace and order in the occupied territory, security of the Army itself, the protection of life and property of resident nationals, and the progress of the new government, it was necessary to affirm the existence of a defacto state of war and to apply the relevant rules for its conduct.

2) Withdrawal of Japanese troops. There was no objection voiced by the Supreme Command to the general principle that with the solution to the China Incident, there should be a total troop withdrawal with the exception of a small number. In order for the total withdrawal of troops there must be the termination of hostilities by means of peaceful settlement of the issues between Japan and China. If there is to be a well regulated troop withdrawal, it must first have been preceded by the establishment of peace and order in the rear. Troop withdrawal would require a period of two years to accomplish from a technical point and without peace and order in the hinterland it would be impractical to carry out any evacuation.

3) The problem of the stationing of troops. This stationing of forces was mainly a so called 'anti-communistic stationing' whereby the presence of troops in the area was to defend Japan and China from the destructive activities of the Communists. The stationing of Japanese troops was believed to be vital for the preservation of law and order in the locality in view of the intensive and violent activities of the

Chinese Communists during the Incident. The right for the stationing of troops was to be limited to the period where occupation was required, after which evacuation would take place.

This treaty did not contain normal conventional clauses found in most international treaties drawn up at the end of hostilities, such as the annexation of territory and war indemnity. The appended Protocol listed the obligations of the signatories, which bound both the Japanese and the Chinese on a reciprocal basis. The Chinese where to indemnify Japanese resident nationals for damages suffered as a result of Chinese military operations and the Japanese were to provide assistance to the Chinese refugees.

The Japanese also pledged to respect the sovereignty and the territorial integrity of China including the surrender of any territorial rights and the return of its settlements. This promise was carried out step by step by the spring of 1943. Additionally, the rights pertaining to military occupation and any others which had been reserved to Japan in the Basic Treaty were surrendered in total with the 1943 ratification of the Treaty of Alliance between Japan and China.

On 3 February 1941, an 'Outline for Negotiations with Germany, Italy, and the Soviet Union was developed at the Liaison conference just before Foreign Minister Masuoka departed for Europe. This did not constitute formal instructions but was a working plan whose central objective was the negotiations with the Soviet Union to obtain harmonious relations between that country and the Axis power so as to continue to maintain current peaceful relationship and enhance the international position of Japan. It was felt that if these two objectives could be safely completed, it would improve relations with America and that Soviet aid to Chiang Kai-shek could be curtailed. The four problems involved with these deliberations were:

- Whether the Soviet Union could be made to act in concert with the Tripartite Power. According to the working plans of the German Foreign Minister Ribbontrop, as well as in the opinion of Herr Stahmer, it would be possible to get Soviets to work harmoniously with the Tripartite Powers.

- What would be the German reaction to Japan working with the Soviet Union. It was the opinion of the cabinet that a coalition between Japan, Germany, and the Soviet Union would be welcomed by the Germans as well as any active participation by the Soviets with Germany in military operations against Britain.

- The nature and extent of compensation that could be offered by Japan to attain harmonious relations with the Soviet Union. Those that were decided upon were the restoration of fishing rights reserved to Japan in the Japan-Soviet Fishing Treaty and rights to oil fields in Northern Sakhalien. The Navy had serious concern about Northern Sakhalien oil fields but their views on this were duly considered.

- The personality and traits of the Foreign Minister himself. The Chiefs of the Army and Navy General Staffs were greatly concerned that the Foreign Minister could make commitments on questions that could involve the Supreme Command and lead to responsibilities and obligations that could cause embarrassing situations. Special precautions were placed in the outline to preclude this occurrence.

The evidence submitted by the Prosecution purporting to be extracts from German source documents were in serious conflict not only with the plan but with the Foreign Minister's oral report to the Liaison conference and the Cabinet upon his return.

When Mr. Matsuoka arrived in Europe the situation was very different from what the Japanese believed it to be at that time. Relations between Germany and the Soviets were so strained it was inconceivable that there could be any cooperation between these countries and Germany was in no position to welcome the signing of a neutrality pact between Japan and the Soviet Union. Mr. Matsuoka eventually signed a Neutrality Pact with the Soviet Union on 13 April 1941 on his way home. The trip to Europe by the foreign minister resulted in paying mere courtesy calls to Germany and Italy with Japan deriving no political benefit from the visits. The issue of "No Separate Peace" as stipulated in the plan was not even discussed. Mr. Matsuoka was restrained from even mentioning any matters that pertained to the Supreme Command from the outset. No report was ever received by Japan concerning Singapore or any other similar allegation. The prosecution's statement that Japan and Germany entered into a military agreement in the early part of February 1941 was utterly without foundation.

The Japan-Soviet Neutrality Pact concluded under these circumstances had very little effect on subsequent national policy and there was never any connection between it and the Japanese policy towards the South Seas. The defensive Japanese strength in the north against the Soviets was not reduced because of the Pact. Japan consistently lived by the terms of the Pact from beginning to end with each successive Cabinet committing itself to abide by the Pact. Japan never directed any unfriendly act against the Soviet Union despite German pressure.

In fact it was the Soviets who actually pledged themselves to enter the war against Japan on the promise of territorial gains and attacked Japan while the Neutrality Agreement was still in force.

On 18 April 1941, the Japanese government received the Proposal for Japanese-American Understanding which purported to be an unofficial and private plan. Tojo, in his capacity as War Minister, dealt with those matters concerned with military affairs, while the Prime Minister and the Foreign Minister handled all other elements involved. Prime Minister Konoye had been concerned with the effect the Tripartite Pact conclusion had on Japanese-American relations and private conversations were started as early as the end of 1940. Tojo received word from the Military Attaché to the Japanese Embassy in Washington that these preliminary negotiations were proceeding with the understanding and knowledge of Ambassador Nomura on the Japanese side, and on the American side, by the President, the Secretary of State, and the Postmaster-General. The Japanese government acknowledged this date as the start of Japanese-American negotiations on this proposal.

Upon receipt of the proposal, there was a ray of hope that a solution could be found to the very serious problems facing Japan and the Japanese government held an immediate liaison conference. Several meetings were held and finally on the 21 April a decision was reached as to what Japan's attitude should be. Japan was of the opinion that there could be harmony between the Tripartite Treaty and the Proposal through the broad interpretation of the terms of the Treaty. There was also some doubt as to whether Germany should be advised of the Japan-American negotiations but it was decided to leave this matter to the discretion of the Foreign Minster when he returned to Tokyo the following day. The Conference members decided not to notify Ambassador Nomura of this decision until then also.

Matsuoka upon his return asked to limit himself to reporting on his trip to Europe at that time and that he be allowed two weeks time to reflect on the proposal. From the time of his return until a revised proposal was submitted by Japan, Matsuoka revealed the contents of the original Proposal prematurely to the German Ambassador and insisted on issuing a statement on the European War prior to the issuance of instructions to the Japanese Ambassador. He proposed a neutrality treaty between Japan and America, believing at first that the proposal was the outcome of previous negotiations carried out by himself, but when he learned that it had developed from sources outside of the regular diplomatic channels, he adopted a cool attitude towards the proposal itself. He revealed that he was convinced after his visit to Germany and Italy and his conferences with the leaders of those countries that the Tripartite Alliance obligations should be fulfilled and that only a resolute stand by Japan would ward off the dangers of open hostilities.

All of these actions and delays by the Foreign Minister complicated the negotiations on the proposal and it was not until 12 May that a revised proposal was submitted by Japan. The main points of this revision were the problem of the application of the Tripartite Treaty of Alliance and the interpretation of the right of self-defense, as well as relations between Japan, China and American aid to the Chiang Kai-shek regime. There was no problem on troop withdrawal.

Negotiations thereafter centered around the central theme of the 12 May Japanese Proposal. Both the Government and the Supreme Command on the Japanese side exerted every effort for satisfactory progress to arrive at a successful conclusion in these negotiations. But the two countries could not reach an agreement and an American counter Proposal of 21 June 1941 resulted eventually from the negotiations.

The date of this counter proposal was one day prior to the outbreak of war between Germany and the Soviet Union. Japan naturally concluded that the sudden change in the American attitude was brought on by this event since it could be foreseen for sometime prior to the actual start of hostilities.

Attached to the proposal was a statement that there were some leaders who occupied influential official positions in Japan that definitely were supportive of Nazi Germany and its policy of conquest and indicated a lack of confidence in the Japanese foreign minister.

The second Konoye cabinet resigned en bloc because of the attitude of the foreign minister.

This resignation was designed to indicate that the Japanese desired to continue with the negotiations even if a cabinet change was necessitated since it was considered to be a matter of life or death for the Japanese nation that there be a successful conclusion to the negotiations.

Japan offered to mediate a border dispute between Thailand and French Indo-China with a satisfactory agreement being reached. A peace treaty was concluded between the two countries on 9 May 1941 and a new boundary line was determined on the spot.

Japan had to rely on these countries for obtaining supplies which were essential for existence, such as rice and rubber. Later when Japan could no longer obtain petroleum products from the United States these products had to be procured from the Netherlands East Indies.

Scrap iron was added to the list of items which were prohibited from being exported to Japan. Economic pressures were exerted by America and Britain to deny Japan open access in the procurement of these essential products not only from their countries but from areas where they could exert any influence.

Japanese troops were already in northern French Indo-China as a result of the 1940 agreement between Japan and France. Events were quiet until early 1941 when the situation in the southern portion gradually became critical.

The Japanese and French governments reached an understanding on mutual defense on 21 July 1941. Japanese troops assembled and peacefully moved to positions in Indo-China on the 29 July. The protocol on Japan-French Indo-China Mutual Defense between the Vichy Government and Japan was signed on the same day.

Japan had in actuality requested assistance from the German Government during the negotiations with the French but the German Foreign Minister refused to provide such assistance.

Also, Japan did not apply any illegal force to intimidate the Vichy Government before the start of negotiations or while they were on-going.

The Japanese advance to the South was undertaken after careful deliberation, and was not conceived or directed as a step toward an aggressive attack on America, Britain, or the Netherlands. Such a move was foreseen as an unavoidable act of Japanese self-defense.

The Japanese government and the Supreme Command did not expect this act to result in the overall rupture of economic relations but believed that Japan and America would continue to negotiate to achieve the settlement of all differences through peaceful means.

Various rumors relative to a Russo-German war had been around for some time. Even though Japan was notified by

Ambassador Oshima on 6 June that such a war was possible in reporting on an interview between Hitler and himself, it was not until an official dispatch was received in Tokyo from Ambassador Oshima on 22 June that reported the actual start of hostilities between these two countries. Prime Minister Konoye, while speaking with Tojo, stated that he was of the opinion that Germany by attacking Russia had flagrantly violated Japan's confidence and that Japan should as a result withdraw from the Tripartite Pact. Japan was totally unprepared to deal with Russo-German hostilities and it was abundantly clear that there were no prior arrangements, either politically or tactically between Japan and Germany concerning them.

Negotiations between Japan and the United States came to a standstill during the latter period of the Second Konoye Cabinet which led to its ultimate downfall. The overthrow of the Government was caused by the need to remove the Foreign Minister who had become a stumbling block towards the successful continuation of the negotiations. Rather than imply that there was political discord in the Government by demanding his resignation it was decided that the Cabinet would resign en masse on 16 July 1941.

The third Konoye cabinet was formed with the same members occupying the same positions with the exception of Admiral Toyoda replacing Matsuoka as the Foreign Minister.

When her assets in America, Great Britain, and the Netherlands were frozen on 26 July 1942, Japan faced a grave situation which involved her system of national defense and forced her to adopt immediate measures for Japan's future security and continuance as a nation. At an Imperial Conference convened on 6 September 1941 a general plan was agreed upon.

This plan consisted of proceeding along the following broad bases:

- Determined efforts be made to reach a final compromise regarding Japanese-American negotiations not later that the first of October.
- Complete preparations to ensure Japan's self-defense and continued self-preservation as a nation with such high resolve so as not to evade fighting with America and Britain no later than the end of October.
- Resolve to go to war with America, Britain, and the Netherlands if Japan's demands were not satisfied diplomatically within the time limits designated.
- Other measures should be resolved according to previous decisions.

This plan of action was decided upon based on the following existing stringent conditions and circumstances:

- Economic pressures on Japan by the American, British, and Dutch Alliance.
- Incessant intensification by these countries of an encirclement of Japan militarily and the expansion of their military preparations.
- The deadly blow to the Japanese national defense program by freezing of their assets making it extremely difficult for Japan to obtain materials for her national needs.
- The determination to break the virtual deadlock in the last stage of Japanese-American negotiations.
- The ever growing difficulties for settling of the China Incident.
- In order to satisfy the requirements of Japanese strategy on the preparations for an emergency war with America, Britain, and the Dutch East Indies.
- Relations between diplomacy and strategy.

The High Command requested at least one month's time before hostilities commenced after a national decision to engage in war was reached.

As regards to the outlook in the event of war between Japan against America and Great Britain, it was quite apparent that Japan could not be too hopeful of winning against the two greatest powers in the world. Therefore, Japan had no alternative but to advance in the Pacific and Indian Oceans, holding important strategic points, occupying regions for military resources and repulsing enemy attacks to the best of her ability.

In Japan, the Imperial High Command was independent of diplomacy as there was a complete separation and independence between the civil administration and the High Command. There was a sharp demarcation between the Army and the Navy, due to the fact that the Army and the Navy each had separate and independent objectives in point of future operations.

Tojo stated that the Army at no time undertook an armed expansion for the purpose of war in the Pacific but that he could not answer for the Navy preparations as they were beyond his scope of authority.

After the decision that was reached in the Imperial Conference of 6 September, all Japanese-American negotiations were conducted solely through Foreign Minister Toyoda but the course of the parley underwent a change and were conducted through two channels. One channel being through Ambassador Nomura and the State Department and the other being through Foreign Minister Toyoda and the American Ambassador in Tokyo.

The Third Konoye Cabinet, after vainly exhausting its efforts in the prolonged Japanese-American negotiations, collapsed in the middle of October.

The Third Konoye Cabinet had expended all of its efforts hoping to yet achieve a peaceful solution in the Japanese-American negotiations but from the Japanese military viewpoint the issues of war versus peace could no longer be delayed. Both the Government and the Imperial High Command were proceeding with their respective diplomatic negotiations and operational preparations in accordance with the 6 September Imperial Conference.

The High Command's operational preparations were advancing unevenly, but as scheduled, while the diplomatic negotiations with the United States were far from progressing smoothly.

Both the Army and Navy High Commands demanded that there be a success or failure prediction on any future negotiations at the September 25 Liaison conference. Also that a decision on the peace versus war issue not later than 15 October 1941.

The Army General Staff held views that no hope should be entertained concerning any successful progress in Japanese-American negotiations with the American Government's attitude showing no inclination to give and take, and they were not of a mind to revise any decisions reached at the 6 September Imperial Conference.

Tojo was informed by the Army General Staff that the Naval General Staff had similar concepts in this respect.

Prior to the fall of the Government, a five state ministers conference took place at Prince Konoye's villa on 12 October 1941. This meeting was attended by Prince Konoye, Navy Minister Oikawa, Foreign Minister Toyoda, President of the Planning Board Suzuki, and Minister of War Tojo, only. No other government personnel nor any responsible person from either High Command attended this meeting.

The purpose of this meeting was to provide for informal conversations among the ministers on the prospects of current Japanese-American parley as well as the decision on the peace versus war issue.

Premier Konoye and Foreign Minister Toyoda contended that if Japan held fast to the policies as before, Japan could never hope for any successful negotiation results. They also felt that on the question of evacuation of Japanese troops from China, Japan could agree to specific concessions by agreeing to wholesale troop withdrawal to conform to American requests but in future negotiations with China attempt to gain an agreement which would allow the retention of some Japanese troops in China. What neither minister mentioned was that this was tantamount to a revision of the 6 September decision.

Tojo was of the opinion that with the direction that the negotiations had so far taken no one could have the slightest hope for their being concluded successfully. By continuing to procrastinate, Japan could be placed in a precarious position if forced to wage war with the United States. He felt that the time was ripe to make the decision anticipated in the resolution of 6 September.

In reference to the withdrawal of Japanese troops from China, Japan has always been for complete evacuation from the outset and the negotiations regarding stationing of Japanese troops on Chinese territory have always been in accordance with basic treaties between the two countries. The attitude of the foreign minister is the same as stated here but the United States attitude is quite different. They intend for Japan to evacuate all troops instantaneously and entirely. Chinese contempt for Japan would ever expand if Japan retired from China unconditionally because of United States duress. Other China Incidents would certainly result, and the loss of Japanese prestige would surely be felt in Manchuria and Korea. Also, negotiations between Japan and America, should they continue, could demand more concessions on other vital matters, such as: interpretations to be placed on the Tripartite Pact; non-discrimination of international trade; etc. For these reasons, Tojo took a dim view of the possibility of there being any hope of reaching a compromise with the United States but that he was willing to reconsider if the foreign minister had any hopes.

The issue relative to peace versus war was so huge that the question should in no way be left to the discretion of the prime minister alone, which is what Navy Minister Oikawa wanted to do. With no agreement being reached, mutual consent on the following was required: No alteration was to be made about the policy concerning stationing of troops (in China) and also any other policies centered on this theme, and no impairment to the fruits reaped in the China Incident were to be permitted.

The next morning Tojo met with the chief of the general staff and told him of the results of the previous day's meeting, briefly acquainted him with the mutual consent items, and intimated for the suspension of all operational preparations while diplomatic negotiations were going on. The High Command was very much perplexed but somehow assented to it.

The 14th of October fell upon the day when a regular Cabinet Council was to be held. On that morning prior to the cabinet meeting Tojo saw the Premier at his official residence. Their conversation did not develop to anything beyond the results of the 12 October meeting. It was at this cabinet meeting that a difference of opinion between Foreign Minister Toyoda and Tojo regarding ways and means of conducting future state policy came to a head and this controversy resulted in the resignation en masse of the Konoye Ministry.

At 10 a.m. on 14 October the Cabinet Council was opened and the foreign minister expressed his opinion the same as on 12 October and Tojo stated his version. Neither the Premier nor any other minister made any remarks at all so the collision was between Tojo and the foreign minister and caused the downfall of the cabinet.

The reasons that Tojo gave for desiring the resignation of the cabinet, en bloc, were a point in Japanese-American negotiations had not yet been reached which would allow the government to determine if there was any hope of settling the matters diplomatically, and it could not yet be determined if the Navy was willing to go to war.

With these doubts it was obvious that the 6 September Imperial Conference decision was not appropriate.

On 17 October Tojo was informed by the grand chamberlain that Tojo's presence was desired at the Imperial Palace. This Imperial summons was completely unexpected and when he arrived at the palace, he was given an immediate audience with the Emperor who gave Tojo the Imperial mandate to form the Cabinet. Navy Minister Oikawa was summoned to the Palace and given an audience with the Emperor who told him to collaborate with the Army.

The Emperor desired that careful considerations be made studying the situation in broad and deep bases both at home and abroad in determining the fundamental policies of the state.

Tojo gave as his reasons for advocating a member of the Royal blood to head the new cabinet was that soon after its formation it could be placed in a position where the

6 September Imperial Conference decision might have to be revised or altered. There should be no difficulty with such a revision for a cabinet headed by a member of the Royal blood.

Tojo also foresaw a need for setting up a system of internal politics which could respond to either peace or war since no one could forecast which it was to be at that time and in that connection he concluded that he would have to assume the post of war minister as well as that of home minister. To assume the post of war minister, it was required that this person be on the active list of the Army. Tojo was again placed on the Army active list and was appointed a full general.

Once the imperial order to proceed with the cabinet formation had been received, Tojo resolved to go to the last extremity in its completion. There was to be no delay in its establishment. With the exception of the Navy minister whose selection was left to the Navy, personnel selection was to be based on each individual's merit and ability.

Tojo commenced to choose personnel to fill the posts in the cabinet on the evening of the same day that he received the imperial mandate. Tojo relied on his own choice and did not consult with anyone else in making his personnel selections. The first person chosen was Mr. Hoshino who was to act as Tojo's right hand man and was to fill the position of secretary general of the cabinet. Additionally, the following personnel gave their consent over the telephone to Tojo's request that they join the cabinet: candidate for education minister: Hashida; candidate for justice minister: Iwamura; candidate for agricultural minister: Ino; candidate for public welfare minister: Koizumi; candidate for director of the planning board: Suzuki; candidate for minister of commerce and industry: Kishi.

The following personnel consented to joining the cabinet after meeting with Tojo for consultation: candidate for finance minister Kaya; candidate for foreign minister Togo; candidate for communications and railroad minister Terajima; candidate for vice-minister for home affairs Yuzawa (although the position assigned to Yuzawa was that of vice-minister, a person of ministerial caliber was required as Tojo was going to assume the post of home minister concurrently with those of war minister and Premier).

The individual's name to fill the post as candidate for Navy minister was not received until Oikawa sent word to Tojo the next morning that Admiral Shimada was recommended for the post. Shortly thereafter Shimada gave his consent to be the candidate for Navy minister after consulting with Tojo.

At 1:00 p.m. on 18 October, Tojo tendered the proposed cabinet personnel list to the Emperor and the investiture of the new Cabinet took place before the Throne at 4:00 p.m. the same date.

From 23 October until 2 November, liaison conferences were frequently held with foreign affairs, national strength, and military matters with the exception of purely strategic problems being most conscientiously studied from all angles in view of the new light then applicable to all policies of both a domestic and foreign nature. A proposed outline on the negotiations with America was decided upon which later took the form of the decision of the 5 November imperial conference. The following three plans were derived from this decision: The first plan was to continue with Japanese-American negotiations on the basis of the newly proposed outline and even though results of these negotiations were not satisfactory, the government was to continue with its policy of patience and caution. The second plan called for the termination of negotiations at that stage and to immediately decide on war. The third plan was for continuous negotiations with America based on the outline but the war determination would be made in the event of failure of these negotiations and operational preparations were to commence accordingly.

The Japanese perceived that of all the materials vital to the existence of the nation, the one most affected as a result of the American, British, and the Netherlands embargo was that of liquid fuel. If matters were to progress at the present rate, the Japanese Navy and Air Force would come to a standstill within two years. This was a serious situation from a standpoint of national defense. Ways and means to alleviate this problem were discussed in each of these plans from the increased production of synthetic fuels to the taking of facilities through hostilities.

Tojo and both the Army and Navy chiefs of the general staff submitted this decision to the Emperor on 2 November. At that time he asked if there was any way left but to go to war if the negotiations fail to break the deadlock, but if the state of affairs is as stated, there is nothing to do but prepare for operations. He hoped that they would continue to search for a means to derive satisfactory results in the Japanese-American negotiations. The Emperor gave his approval to continue the discussions at the 5 November imperial conference.

Tojo, determined to convene a joint Army/Navy counselors' conference prior to that conference, hastened to obtain the Emperor's approval, and arranged for it to take place on 4 November. This was the first such Military Counselors' Conference since the establishment of the system in 1903.

This conference, known as the Supreme War Council, was presided over by First Marshal Prince Kanin and was held before the Emperor who submitted the question as to whether or not it was advisable for the Army and Navy High Command to draw up an operational plan to meet the eventuality where the Japanese-American negotiations failed to succeed. Tojo attended in his capacity as war minister.

Admiral Nagano, chief of the Navy general staff, explained the position concerning Naval operations as follows:

If matters continue as they currently are, the resiliency of Japan's national strength will be lost, and the country placed in the worst possible situation. The Navy agrees with the Administration that all efforts should be aimed at overcoming this crisis by means of diplomacy and felt that the Government was doing its best to attain that end. The Navy must consider, however, that Japan may be placed in such a position where there is no alternative but to decide on commencement of hostilities in case the diplomatic measures fail. The High Command desires that operational plans be prepared to meet such a contingency while in so doing, they would be contributing at the same time to expedite the diplomatic negotiations. Operational preparations and plans could be countermanded at once if the negotiations succeed. The Navy deemed that Japan had a good chance in initial operations and in the first meeting on the basis of respective actual fighting strength in the Pacific if the hostilities were to commence early in December. Where the initial operations were properly carried out, strategic points in the South-Western Pacific would be occupied by Japanese forces and be placed in a position to fight a prolonged war. Since there can be no means formulated which would induce the enemy to submit, the war with the United States and Britain is destined to become a protracted one, requiring firm resolution and thorough preparations for any eventuality. To forecast the results of a war which becomes a protracted one is difficult to predict as much depends upon incorporeal elements, the total potentials of the respective nations, and above all, how world situations will develop, which nobody knows or can currently forecast with any degree of accuracy.

Admiral Nagano made no mention of the Pearl Harbor attack at that time. Next General Sugiyama, chief of the Army general staff, expounded on matters relating to the Army command:

• Southern region armaments were steadily being strengthened day by day with total Army forces there having been increased from three to eight times over those prior to the start of the European War (more than 200,000 men and 600 planes).

• Further and more rapid increases my be added in the Southern Region area dependent on developments in the situation. In the event of war between Japan with America and Britain, reinforcements will be dispatched to the zone of battle by the Allies from Australia, New Zealand, and India, at an estimated strength of 800,000 men and 600 planes.

• The basic strength of the Japanese Army is 51 divisions. With Japan being currently engaged in China and the requirement that some divisions be held in contingency as a precaution against the Soviet Union, only a small force would be available for use during the war with

America and Britain, estimated at not more than 11 divisions. There can be no delay in the opening of hostilities considering the rapid increase in the military strength of America and Britain.

- The meteorological conditions must also be considered with early in December being the desired date.
- The essentials of Army operations consist of landing strategy, their success or failure depended much on Naval operations. The Army High Command believed in the success of its operations, regardless of how tough the task may be, if the Naval plans progress in due order.
- Japan must expect and plan for a protracted war even though every effort would be made to conclude it in the shortest possible time, utilizing every opportunity in strategy and tactics to demoralize regions. However, Japan would be able to frustrate enemy plans by assuming an invincible position and occupying and holding military and air bases to the last in conjunction with maintaining of the sea transportation route.
- Defensive measures against the USSR and China Affair strategy will remain as before, thus safeguarding the menace from the North and the continuation to attain the goal in China.
- The situation in the North arising out of operations in the South should have little effect to cause the Soviet Union to assume an offensive attitude with the exception of some diversion in the utilization of subversive or propaganda activities of the communists in Manchuria and China.
- For Japan, it is vitally important to put an end to Southern area hostilities as soon as possible and to be prepared for any even in the North.

At the end of these explanations by the chiefs of the Army and Navy general staffs, some questions were asked by the counselors pertaining to operational topics with the answers being provided by the chiefs of both staffs or by Tojo.

At the end of the conference a report unanimously adopted to the effect that the Supreme War Council deemed it proper and just that the Army and Navy High Command take appropriate measures within their respective jurisdictions to expedite operational preparations to meet the worst possible contingencies.

The Emperor seemed pleased to listen to the proceedings but he did not utter a single word from the beginning to the end of the conference.

Tojo, with the Emperor's approval, assumed the duties of presiding at the 5 November Imperial Conference and explained the measures which made the meeting necessary. The finance minister provided an account of what Japan's financial status would be attendant on the outbreak of the war; the president of the cabinet planning board spoke on the outlook of national resources following the opening of hostilities; both chiefs of the Army and Navy general staffs spoke about their respective operational plans.

These presentations were followed by questions and answers including a few questions by President Hara of the privy council with answers being provided by those members of the government or the High Command. The particulars on these questions and answers were not available since there was no record of the conference maintained and Tojo did not recall them.

Basically, the third plan formulated at the previous liaison conference with the foreign policy cited therein for use in American negotiations were adopted and approved.

Tojo then provided his views on circumstances of the times which caused Japan to reach the conclusions that they had:

1) Reports from abroad made it extremely obvious that the military and economic pressures being exerted on Japan by America, Britain, the Netherlands, and China were being intensified and that there was a growing tendency to strengthen cooperative relations among these nations. These trends were reflected by the increased travels and influential personnel not only between these nations but also to vital points within the areas concerned.

2) Greater expenditures for the enlargement of their military forces by the nations involved.

3) Offering the use of military facilities by one nation to others such as the announcement by British East Asia Fleet Commander Layton that Singapore Naval Base would be offered to the U.S. Navy for use anytime at the latter's request.

4) Speeches and statements by leading individuals directed specifically at Japan, an example of which was by the US secretary of the Navy in late October that a clash with Japan was unavoidable so long as Japan held to her present policy.

5) The Indian Government announced on 29 October 1941 the prohibition of all imports from Japan and Manchuria.

The Supreme Army Command on 6 November appointed General Terauchi to the post as Southern Army supreme commander and defined the organization of the southern area. It also issued orders on the same day to prepare for the attack on key points in the same area, and on the 15th of the month, the decision of the general strategic outline for use against the United States and Great Britain was decided on.

Tojo as the War Minister knew of this procedure and that it was only a preparatory action based on an assumption but other Cabinet members were unaware of the Supreme Army Command action.

Japan sent Ambassador Kurusu to Washington to assist Ambassador Nomura with the negotiations. He departed Tokyo on 5 November and arrived in Washington on the 15th of the month. His dispatch to America had nothing to do with a camouflage of Japan's intention to start a war but was meant to purely provide assistance to bring about a successful conclusion to the negotiations.

The Foreign Minister advised Ambassador Nomura that a rapid solution of the questions involved was required and the Japanese wish for the same effect was fully conveyed to the American Government.

Tojo, as the Premier, addressed the 77th Diet on 17 November 1941, then in session, and explained the administrative policies of the Government. These included the attitude of the Japanese government toward negotiations between Japan and America. After six months of negotiations, it should be clear to representatives of both parties that the sole remaining question is whether or not any effort should be made to keep peace in the Pacific by means of reciprocal concessions by both parties. Japan realized, that on her part for this purpose, why she must explain to the world the limits of the terms that she could bear at that time. Also, for the purpose of safeguarding her independence and sovereignty, the Japanese government expected that third powers would not disturb Japan in the disposition of the China Incident; the elimination of military and economic interference with Japan by foreign powers, and the return to customary foreign relations; the prevention of the European War spreading to East Asia.

Foreign Minister Togo then addressed the Diet while stressing these two points pertaining to the Japanese-American negotiations: There should be no necessity for prolonging the time in negotiation with the United States. That Japan, though fully desirous of concluding negotiations, would reject any matter injurious to Japanese authority as a major power.

Since both speeches were broadcast to the world on the same day they were presented, Tojo was told that the full text of the speeches had been printed in the American press; it was therefore assumed that the US Government authorities were well acquainted with them.

Tojo had much less optimism for the success of the negotiations when he was informed the United States had communicated with representatives of England, Holland, and China to establish closer contacts with these governments. Prior to this the political situation in America, England, Australia, and Holland had become very tense. Armaments had been expanded, and the leaders of these countries had been markedly provocative in their attitude towards Japan, examples of which were:

- Prime Minister Churchill of England declared on 10 November 1941 that if the United States became involved in war with Japan, the British declaration would follow within the hour.

- Two days later, King George proclaimed in His Royal message at the opening of Parliament that the British government had deep concerns about the situation in East Asia.

- President Roosevelt stated on Armistice Day, 11 November, that the United States would fight permanently for the sake of preserving liberty throughout the world.

- The President of the United States declared on 7 November that the withdrawal of the Marines stationed in China was under consideration and then announced on the 14th of the same month that the withdrawal had been decided upon.
- Iraq, then under British influence, severed all diplomatic relations with Japan on 16 November.
- It was reported around the middle of November that the Canadian Army under command of Brigadier General J. Lawson had arrived at Hong Kong for the defense of that city.
- The US government announced, on 24 November, its decision for dispatching US Army forces to Netherlands Guinea.
- Early in November, the US Navy made public the progress that had been achieved between January and October of that year in naval construction for the establishing of separate two ocean fleets.
- On 25 November, the US authorities in the Philippines announced that by the end of December mines would be laid near the fortress at the entrance to Manila Bay. At the same time, British Forces at the Straits Settlement declared that mines would be laid at the eastern entrance of Singapore Harbor.

These joint undertakings by America and Great Britain impressed Japan with what they considered to be the close imminence of war. It was under these tense circumstances that the US Government on 26 November 1941 replied to both Japanese ambassadors that they dissented from the proposal and submitted this note, which came to be known as the 'Hull Note,' as the basis for further negotiations. Included in the note were the following demands which Japan termed unreasonable and therefore unacceptable: The unconditional withdrawal of all Japanese Army and Navy forces, including police forces, from French Indo-China as well as from all parts of China including Manchuria; denial of the Manchurian Government; denial of the Nationalist Government of Nanking; making the Tripartite Alliance a dead issue.

Prior to receipt of the "Hull Note," a liaison conference was held on 22 November for discussing the negotiations, but with much less expectancy for success than before, with an exploratory study of two eventualities in view. What would Japan's attitude be if America rejected the Japanese proposals in total? In this case there could be no alternative but to act in accordance with the decision of the 5 November Imperial Conference. What would Japan's next step be in the event the United States made some concession to the Japanese request especially that which was concerned with the acquisition of oil? Japan should be prepared to propose some concrete demands to meet the current situation. It was decided to request a total of six million tons of oil from the United States and the Netherlands.

On 27 November, the government and the supreme command held a liaison conference at the Imperial Palace. The foreign minister spoke about the circumstances and difficulties associated with the negotiations. Japan had not yet received the 26 November United States proposal but had been provided with the gist of its contents by the Japanese Military and Naval attaches in Washington. The conference attendees carefully discussed the items contained in the information received and were all dumbfounded by the severity of the U. S. proposal.

The main points of the conclusions were:

1) The 26 November US memorandum amounted to an ultimatum against Japan.

2) Japan could not accept this memorandum. The United States seems to have proposed these conditions knowing full well that they would not be acceptable by Japan. Also, the memorandum was prepared with the joint understanding of the other countries concerned.

3) Due to recent events, especially those measures taken by the US, its attitude towards Japan, added to the normal Japanese conclusions from these facts, the United States appeared to have already decided on war. Japan could be attacked at any moment by the United States, and putting it bluntly, Japan should fully guard against it.

It was decided at this liaison conference that since there was not hope for any satisfactory results from future Japanese-American negotiations, it would be best to act in accordance with the 5 November Imperial Conference decisions. The final decision should not be made at a liaison conference but at the next Imperial Conference scheduled to me on 1 December to which all cabinet members would be present.

Knowing of the Emperor's deep concern over the situation and that there was probably a desire on the Emperor's part to hear the opinions of the Senior Statesmen on this matter was the reason an Imperial Conference was not convened immediately according to Tojo.

At a Cabinet meeting on 28 November, foreign minister Togo made a report in great detail concerning the negotiations. The decision of the liaison conference were under discussion and all cabinet members expressed their agreement but the cabinet did not decide on war but deferred until after the 1 December Imperial Conference.

Tojo at this point in his testimony listed facts which he did not know at that time but which came to his knowledge after the war's termination.

1) The Americans had succeeded in deciphering the Japanese secret code and knew the Japanese decision before it was presented to them.

2) That the US State Department had knowledge that Japan's proposal of 20 November 1941 would be the final one from Japan to the United States.

3) That prior to Hull's note of 26 November, the US had formulated the draft of a Modus Vivendi based on President Roosevelt's idea, which left room for negotiations, was the basis for US diplomacy to Japan, was intended to gain time for replenishment of U.S. Navy armaments, was abandoned only after opposition by Britain and China, was consequently replaced. Finally that the United States knew that this note would never be accepted by Japan.

4) The US government knew that Japan was regarding Hull's note as an ultimatum.

5) That by the end of November 1941, the United States, together with Great Britain, had decided to enter into a war with Japan, and that, moreover, the United States was intent on having Japan commit the first overt act.

The government invited the senior statesmen to convene at the Imperial Palace on 29 November 1941 where the government's intentions regarding the opening of hostilities would be explained to them and they could, at the same time, report on their opinions to the Emperor in that regard. The senior statesmen were no different from ordinary citizens except that they had all occupied the post of prime minister in the past. The gathering was designated a "senior statesmen's conference" but was actually only a meeting of these individuals since there was no president presiding at the meeting nor did those in attendance pass on any decisions. At that time included in this category were Prince

Konoye, Baron Hiranuma, General Hayashi, Mr. Hirota, General Abe, Admiral Yonai, Mr. Wakasuki, Admiral Okada, and Mr. Hara, the president of the privy council.

Representing the government at this meeting were Premier/War Minister Tojo,

Navy Minister Shimada, Foreign Minister Togo, Finance Minister Kaya, the president of the planning board, Suzuki but there was no one from the supreme command.

Tojo explained the reasons why Japan had to resort to armed conflict against the United States and Great Britain and why it was unavoidable. Some questions were asked by senior statesmen with answers being provided by government members present. Later the Emperor summoned the senior statesmen and asked for their opinions on a possible war. The lord keeper of the privy seal, Kido, also attended.

The opinions that were expressed consisted of the points: Even if the negotiations were broken off, Japan should refrain from war and make plans for the next move in the future. There was no alternative left to Japan but to rely on the government, since it has decided to finally resort to war after all of their deliberate investigations. If the war became protracted there would be much anxiety on Japan's capacity to maintain the supply of materials and the trend of public opinion as well. No person gave a definite opinion as to measures Japan should take on this point. If the war was for self-existence, Japan would be compelled to wage was even if eventual defeat was foreseen. However, if Japan went to was for a so-called East Asiatic policy, it would be extremely dangerous.

Tojo explained the government's intentions related to each point: After due consideration, the government decided that if Japan were to adopt a policy of not going to war despite the failure of the negotiations, Japan's national defense would be jeopardized and her national existence threatened. No explanation required. Japan desired that there be an early decisive battle. However, as with all warfare there would be an enemy with the same desires for their forces so that at times the war situation would not develop as was desired and the war becomes protracted. The High Command seems to be considerably confident of success at the outset of hostilities. If Japan could attain what the High Command anticipates, she should be able to mitigate her need for supplies to some extent by the securing of strategic points and the acquisition of important war materials, especially oil. Both the government and the Armed Forces planned to exert their utmost efforts towards this purpose. Japan had no recourse but to engage in a war of self-defense.

It should be noted that there was no mention of purely strategic items or matters made during the explanations, such as the projected attack on Pearl Harbor.

On 30 November, Tojo was summoned to the palace by the Emperor who told Tojo that Prince Takamatsu reported that the Navy's hands were full and they desired to avoid war. The Emperor asked for Tojo's comment on this point. Tojo answered that the Government and the High Command both desired to avoid war but that after diligent and prudent deliberations it was decided that there was no alternative. The High Command, Tojo stated, was convinced of complete victory; however, if the Emperor had any doubts on this point, then the chief of the Navy general staff and the Navy minister should be called and asked to explain.

Marquis Kido, lord keeper of the privy seal, telephoned Tojo later that evening to inform him that the Emperor would allow the Imperial Conference on 1 December to be held as scheduled.

The agenda of the conference was to determine if Japan should initiate hostilities against America, Britain, and the Netherlands based upon the failed Japanese-American negotiations. The Emperor permitted Tojo to preside over the proceedings in accordance with the usual procedure.

After Tojo opened the conference, Foreign Minister Togo reported on the results of the Japanese-American negotiations. Togo's report was followed by Admiral Nagano, chief of the Naval general staff, representing both of the Staffs at the Imperial Headquarters, who explained the situation from a military point of view with the following main points:

1) The United States, Britain, and the Netherlands were continuing to increase their armed strength while Chungking's forces had doubled their fighting power with American and British help.

2) It was obvious to Japan that the United States and Britain had already decided to fight based on the actions of these countries' leaders.

3) The Japanese Army and Navy had been preparing for war in accordance with the decision of the 5 November Imperial Conference and were ready to go into operational action as soon as the Imperial command should be issued.

4) Japanese forces are on the strictest alert to guard against Soviet Union aggression but with the aid of diplomacy, no danger from this direction was anticipated at that time.

5) The entire Army and Navy were in high spirits, burning with desire to serve their nation and the Emperor, willing to give up their lives if necessary. All armed force

members were ready to assume their duties rapidly on the issuance of the Imperial Order.

Tojo in his capacity as home minister provided an explanation about the current public sentiment, the supervision of interior affairs, the means adopted for the protection of aliens and diplomatic officials, and some other emergency precautions.

The finance minister spoke on Japanese economic and financial strength and the minister of agriculture and forestry on the question of food supplies in the case of protracted warfare.

Mr. Hara, the president of the privy council asked questions concerning the following points: The prospect of a naval victory in spite of a progressive increase and reinforcement of US armament; movement of Siam and Japan's attitude toward her; possible air attacks by the enemy on the Homeland and Japanese plans against such attacks.

The chief of the Naval general staff answered that while true that the US was pursuing a large armament plan, 40% of her Navy lay in the Atlantic and could not readily be moved to the Pacific. As for the British, they could not move a major portion of its fleet to the Far East due to the European War. Japan would be ready if they were challenged with a hopeful prospect of success. Tojo answered that Japan's Siam operations were progressing in a delicate manner both strategically as well as diplomatically, even if the British government had a latent influence upon her. In view of increased intimate relations between Siam and Japan there is every confidence that Japanese forces could pass through Siam's territory in a friendly manner in event of action against the U.S. and Britain. The chief of the Army general staff replied that the success or the failure at the start had much to do in deciding the issue not only in the beginning of the war but also in its later course. There would only be a relatively small possibility of mass raids on the homeland if Japan wins the initial battles. The US could also pressure the USSR for the use of its bases in which case infinitely better protection for the Homeland would be required. Initially, this would be difficult due to increased equipment required by the fighting front forces but this should be improved as the course of the war continues.

Mr. Hara summarized his position as follows: The US attitude was unbearably hard on Japan and it was futile to pursue further means for a peaceful settlement, consequently war was unavoidable. There can be no doubt of Japan's initial success but the country and the people must be prepared in case the war becomes prolonged. Even if it seems that a prolonged war is inevitable, it would be best if the desired assets and territory were to be conquered quickly and the war brought to an early conclusion. It is therefore requested that the government do its best to accomplish that end. If the war were to be drawn out, there could always be a danger of an inner collapse of the nation and the government needed to be very careful on this point.

Tojo replied that the government and the High Command would be very careful on the points Mr. Hara alluded to. They would do everything they could to end the war in the least possible time and even at this late date, they would still welcome the prospect of a peaceful solution to the situation. Both branches realized what a great responsibility they owed to their country and that if the Emperor decided on war, they were prepared to carry out with careful thought and foresight the plans and measure required to achieve ultimate victory. The proposal was adopted without the Emperor saying a single word.

The entire responsibility on affairs of state that were consummated by procedures such as those described rested with the appropriate members of the cabinet and the supreme command, not with the Emperor. All of the affairs of state were conducted on the advice of the cabinet and the High Command with the Emperor not taking personal action on these matters without such advice. Tojo stated that he could not recall a single time where the Emperor made an appointment in variance with the advice and the recommendation of these political counselors and military advisors nor refused to accept such advice. Also, the Emperor studiously refrained from placing a veto upon any final decision made by the cabinet and/or the supreme command.

The Imperial headquarters consisted mainly of members of the Army and Navy general staffs divided into the Army and Navy departments under the control of the respective chiefs of the general staffs. The ministers of war and Navy were not included as regular members but some members of their ministries were.

Tojo stated that during the entire period that he held the position of war minister a regular Imperial Headquarters Conference was not held. The meetings referred to by him were meetings held for the purpose of exchanging information between the Army and Navy and not true Imperial Headquarters Conferences in their proper sense.

Liaison conferences were held frequently between 1 December and the outbreak of the war where decisions were made on many issues that had important connections with the preparation for operational executions and affairs of state. As these matters lay outside the sphere of pure supreme command, some coordination was required between the High Command and military administration.

These issues included the note to be handed to the United States and the decision as to the time of its delivery. All diplomatic steps concerning the last note were to be left to the foreign minister. This was to be in the nature of a notification based upon international law, and Japan was to reserve freedom of action after the notification. The handing of the notification to the United States government had to be carried out, without fail, prior to the opening of the attack. The time of the delivery to the United States was to be decided upon after consultation between the foreign minister and the two chiefs of the general staff, since there was a distinct and precise interrelationship between diplomacy and strategy. It was a matter of great regret to the Japanese government upon learning subsequently that the actual delivery of the note was delayed.

During the liaison conference, the decision upon the matter became the guiding principle to be pursued during the conduct of the war thereafter. Agreement was reached outlining the principles which were to be followed for conducting and directing the execution of the coming war:

- Efforts were to be made through political and strategic measures to cause the fall of both Britain and the Chungking Regime immediately after the outbreak of the war.
- Key points were to be swiftly occupied according to the Supreme Command plan in the strategic districts of the Philippines, the Netherlands East Indies, British Malaya, and in Southern Burma with a foundation of selfsufficiency being established through an assured occupation of these regions as well as perfecting preparations to meet possible changes in the North. The Supreme Command estimated required time

of five months for these actions with military operations thereafter being conducted to conform with conditions obtained by that time, particularly the results of naval warfare.

- Declaration of war was to be limited at first to the United States and Britain with no declaration of war against the Netherlands for the time being. The existence of a state of war will be announced if the need arises but, regardless, simultaneous with start of the war, appropriate measures against the Netherlands will be taken and she will be treated as a quasihostile nation.

- No change was to be made with respect to the policies pursued to date on the China Incident. Simultaneously with the outbreak of the war, Hong Kong will be attacked. Other hostile nations rights and interests in China would be dealt with accordingly.

- The Japanese USSR neutrality pact was to be respected and tranquillity maintained in the North. Careful attention must be paid to SovietAmerican cooperation.

- Request for passage of Japanese troops through Thai territory was to be made prior to the advent of these troops on the Thai boarders.

- Japan would not request Manchoukuo and the Nanking Government to participate in the war but their friendly cooperation will be expected.

- A treaty of a "non-separate" peace would be concluded with Germany and Italy with an offer for such a treaty on 29 November 1941 but no date for the opening of hostilities was included. This treaty was not concluded until 11 December 1941 so according to Tojo this proved that no close cooperation existed with these nations and that Japan's decision to go to war was made purely by needs of self-defense.

- The actual time for the opening of hostilities was to be kept secret for the time being until such time as its release would be more beneficial to the Japanese cause.

- Preparations for the commencement of hostilities were to be halted in the event that Japanese-American negotiations should result in an understanding before 8 December.

In as much as the attack on Pearl Harbor at the outset of hostilities was solely the responsibility of the Navy Division of the Imperial general headquarters, Tojo had no connection with it whatsoever but that he would testify on the political phase of the matter.

The Army division of the Imperial general headquarters issued orders for commencement of preparations for opening hostilities on 1 December to the commander-in-chief of the Southern Area Army, the commander-in-chief of the Expeditionary Forces in China, and the commander of forces in the Southern Seas. It was directed at the same time that if there were to be an understanding in the Japanese-American negotiations these preparations would be terminated.

Again, Tojo announced that since all matters concerned with the Supreme Command were completely outside of his jurisdiction he could not provide factual testimony on these matters but only on how they impacted on the day-to-day operations of the Japanese government.

Listing of administrative principles concerning prospective occupied areas:

As one of the preparatory measures for military operations the conference members decided on the principles concerned with the administration of future occupied areas in the South. These principles were communicated to the respective Commanders along with the order of the Supreme Command for the commencement of preparations for the opening of hostilities.

The fundamental ideas concerned with the principles for the occupied areas administration should be in accordance with the following basic policies and in accordance with the developments of military operations: Occupied areas should be placed under military administration initially and placed under the supervision of the operational forces. Such military administrations should be abolished as soon as possible and independence or self-government should be granted as promptly as expedient in so far as local political conditions warrant with due regard to previous historical sub-division. These independent and self-ruled regions were to be required to cooperate with the establishment of the Greater Asia Co-Prosperity Sphere when directed by Japan and, depending on local conditions, asked to assist in the prosecution of the war.

Southern occupied regions outline of administration and conditions to be observed in the execution of these principles. Outline of administration highlights: The restoration of peace and order within the occupied areas, and the stabilization of life of the inhabitants; the prompt and speedy acquisition of critical natural resources needed for national defense; and the achievement of local self-sufficiency of the forces engaged in military operations.

Conditions to be observed during execution of these principles: to utilize existing governmental agencies, respect existing organizations and racial traits, customs, and habits, and recognize freedom of religion; to win over local foreigners to cooperate with the military administration; and for those who refuse to cooperate, request they withdraw; with respect to local Chinese residents, a severance of relations with Chungking was to be sought and cooperation with our policies was to be obtained; and Japanese nationals advancing to the South were to be very carefully selected.

Measures to be taken against foreign countries with respect to war: As had been previously stated, it was decided that Japan would not declare war against the Netherlands. The Netherlands declared war against Japan on 10 December 1941. On 12 January 1942, Japan proclaimed the existence of a state of war between Japan and the Netherlands.

Based on the 5 November Imperial Conference decision that in case of war with the United States, Britain, and the Netherlands, intimate military relations should be established between Japan and Thailand, it was further agreed at the 23 November liaison conference, that just prior to the advance of its forces to the Thai border, Japan should request of the Thai Government transit of its troops over Thai territory; arrange for the extending of facilities for this troop transit; and insure that suitable measures are established to avoid any unforeseen conflict between Japanese and Thai forces.

If British forces should invade Thailand prior to the arrival of its forces, Japan should immediately inform the Thai Ambassador and cross into Thai territory after an understanding was reached between both parties.

Due to delay in negotiations between Japan and Thailand because of the Thai Premier being away on a trip, and intelligence sources indicated that British forces had entered southern Thai territory. There was skirmish between Japanese and Thai forces but this was entirely concluded by the middle of the afternoon on 8 December after the Japanese-Thai agreement was signed by noon on that date.

The decision on the Imperial Rescript for the declaration of war and its promulgation.

Japan promulgated the Imperial Rescript on the declaration of war on 8 December 1941, the first day of the war.

As was clearly indicated in the first paragraph, this Rescript was solely addressed to the people of Japan.

This Rescript does not fall into the category of communication of commencement of hostilities, as contemplated by international law.

The final draft of the Imperial Rescript was decided upon at the Cabinet Council of 5 December and the 6 December Liaison conference and was submitted to the Emperor on 7 December 1941.

The transaction of the promulgation of the Imperial Rescript on the war declaration was submitted to the Privy Council for discussion. It was just past 11:00 a.m. on 8 December 1941 that the Rescript was announced by the cabinet after the privy council deliberation and the obtaining of the Imperial sanction.

General Tojo, pictured above under military guard, testifies before the International Military Tribunal.

Hideki Tojo - Subsequent to Pearl Harbor
CHAPTER 14

Japan, for the first time, made preparations for opening of hostilities on 1 December 1941. Following the strategic plans of both the Army and Navy divisions of the Imperial general headquarters, Japanese armed forces undertook the breakthrough of the enemy encirclement at four points: Hawaii, the Philippines, Hong Kong and Malaya.

The attack which began at dawn on 7 December (8 December Japanese time) with the operations being aimed at only military targets had been planned for in strictest secrecy by the supreme command. Tojo in his capacity as the war minister and Navy Minister Shimada were the only cabinet members with prior knowledge of the operation.

Tojo, based on intelligence received at the time, feared there was a high probability that the enemy might open the attack. Japan did not at that time anticipate that America was directing the war so as to force Japan to make the first overt act. Japan did not know that America had broken the Japanese secret code and therefore knew what Japan was planning prior to the occurrence.

To the best of his recollection, it was at 4:30 a.m. that Tojo received news of the successful attack on Pearl Harbor from the Navy. The Imperial general headquarters announced that Japan had entered into a state of war with America and Britain at 6 a.m. The cabinet was called into a special session at 7:30 a.m. where the complete plans of military operations were explained for the first time by the Army and

Navy ministers. Reports of the success of Japanese operations in the Malay area had been received in the meantime.

Foreign Minister Togo suddenly came to see Tojo at the Prime Minister's residence at about 1:00 a.m. on 8 December 1941 and informed him America's Ambassador Grew visited him and told him that the President of the United States had sent a personal message to the Emperor and gave Tojo a copy of the message. Togo stated that he was going to deliver the message to the Emperor.

Tojo asked if the message contained any new concessions and on being told no, he informed Togo that he had no objections to his reporting to the Emperor but that he believed the Japanese planes with the task force had already taken off from their carriers to begin the attack on Pearl Harbor. It was unthinkable that any member of the Japanese government would even consider committing such an outrageous act of lese-majeste as to willfully delay a message from the head of a nation addressed to the Emperor as the Prosecution contended.

In the Japanese military organization, the responsibility for control and direction of subordinates is divided into two categories depending on the nature of the matter involved.

The first category covers matters within the Supreme Command chain. Matters concerned with strategy, security, transport, and treatment of POWs during their transportation to the POW camps established by the supreme command and the final responsibility rests with the Chief of the general staff. Tojo cited as examples of events from this trial which would fall within this category as matters that had occurred on the Malay Peninsula, Bataan Peninsula, and on transport vessels carrying POWs prior to the transfer of their control and internment to the camps established by the minister of war. These incidents, as well as the POWs involved, fell under the jurisdiction of the individuals included within the supreme command chain of command directly involved.

The second category covers matters which occur within the jurisdictional authority of the war ministry. The treatment of POWs after their internment at detention camps under the war ministry or for civilian internees in the war zones, except for China, are of this category. An example of a matter of this classification was the POWs employed in the construction of the Burma-Siamese Railway.

Tojo assumed administrative responsibility in respect to second category matters as war minister from the beginning of the Pacific War until 22 July 1944; administrative responsibility regarding first category affairs as chief of the general staff, supreme command, from February 1944 to July 1944; administrative responsibility for any questions concerning foreign affairs such as protests from enemy countries or through the Red Cross during the period of 1 September to 17 September 1942 when he was also the minister of foreign affairs; administrative responsibility if there were any incidents concerning treatment of civilian internees within the Japan proper during the time he was also filling the position of minister of home affairs from 8 December 1941 until 17 February 1942; and political responsibility for matters relating to the promulgation of POW punishment law during his tenure as prime minister and being concurrently the war minister.

Tojo stated that any question pertaining to his legal and/or criminal liability on any of these matters rests entirely on the determination of the Tribunal and that he had nothing further to add to this point except to state frankly that at no time did he contemplate during his entire career the commission of a criminal act.

Tojo claimed to have issued orders prohibiting maltreatment of POWs, the inhabitants of occupied territories, and civilian internees. He directed that they should be treated with humanity according to the principles of international law and regulations. Also, all Army officers, soldiers, and civilian employees of the Army were given directions by war ministry. These Instructions dealt with their conduct and behavior at the front.

There were many differences in living conditions, customs, and manners between Japanese and other nationals, especially Europeans and Americans. This was part of the reason why Japan did not ratify the Geneva Protocol and why it could not be applied verbatim.

Japanese from ancient times regarded it as most degrading to be taken as a POW and all combatants were instructed to chose death rather than to be captured. The Japanese government feared that ratification of the protocol would lead the public to believe that authorities were urging combatants to be taken prisoner rather than to comply with the ancient traditions. In response to an inquiry from the foreign office, the war ministry replied that while it could not announce complete compliance with the policies specified, it could see no objection to its application with necessary reservations.

In January 1942, the foreign minister announced through the Switzerland and Argentina ministries that the protocol would be applied by Japan with modifications. These modifications pertained to changes that might be necessary to conform to domestic law and regulations as well as practical requirements of existing conditions. The Japanese government clearly stated this in its note of 22 April 1944 made to the American government in reply to a protest.

The Disciplinary Law for POWs was amended in March 1943 according to Tojo for two reasons. First, the law for POWs was enacted in 1905 and contained the classification and penalties which were in use prior to the existing penal law. The articles relating to the crimes of violence or insubordination against POW supervisors, escape in mass conspiracy, and breach of parole were adjusted in the new legislation. Secondly, new rules for penalties relating to prisoner misconduct such as mass meetings, assault, and intimidation, and the formation of bands for the purpose of insubordination against, the insulting or intimidation of, wounding, or killing of POW supervisors.

These modifications were enacted since the Japanese were convinced that their enactment did not conflict with the protocol.

For persons violating wartime laws and regulations during an air raid, penalties were specified in a vice minister communication issued in July 1942 upon orders from the war minister based on the Tokyo Air Raid by the Doolittle fliers on 18 April 1942.

Tojo stated that the atrocities, committed by these fliers against the civilian population, constituted war crimes in accordance with established international law. A huge cry arose demanding immediate harsh action, from a national defense standpoint, to prevent such future actions.

Neither did they want troops on the spot dispensing rigorous treatment of any captured fliers based on any hatred towards these individuals.

It was decided that all these cases needed to go to trial and would be disposed of only after due deliberation to decide if any particular acts constituted violations of international regulations and laws, or not.

In the name of the commander-in-chief of Japanese forces in China, based on these considerations, "Military Regulations for the Punishment of Enemy Flyers" was enacted in August 1942. This was not a new set of regulations but was a compilation of the principles then existing in international practice as contained within the rules and customs of land warfare as well as draft materials concerning aerial warfare.

For those flyers captured during the Tokyo Air Raid of 18 April 1942, a trial was held by a court established in Shanghai, and all of the eight prisoners were sentenced to death. Findings of the court were reported to the Imperial headquarters, where the chief of the Army general staff, who was in favor of carrying out the court sentences, consulted with Tojo in his capacity as the war minister. Tojo, fully aware of the Emperor's concern with such matters, commuted the sentences of five of the prisoners after making an informal report to the Emperor.

Due to relentless depredations by enemy submarines to sea borne traffic to Burma, it became imperative that a land route be established to that area and maintained to insure an adequate flow of supplies for Japanese forces there. The surveying and construction of a Thailand-Burma Railway was ordered by the Army general staff for this purpose. As war minister, Tojo was consulted and agreed to the proposal as well as the use of POWs for labor in connection with the work. In Tojo's opinion, the labor was not of a class prohibited for use of POWs by the Hague and Geneva Treaties nor was the district an uncommonly unhealthy one for that area.

The chief of the Army general staff directed the construction work on the railway but Tojo, as war minister, had administrative responsibility over the POWs as the supervising authority. When Tojo was informed in May 1943 of the deficiencies in sanitary conditions and POW treatment in the construction zone, he dispatched the chief of the POW control section, General Hamada, and a number of expert surgeons from the medical bureau to the area. One company commander who had dealt unfairly with the POWs was tried by court martial and Tojo relieved the commanding general of railway construction from duty.

A prosecution witness testified that the "Summary of the Disposal of the Prisoner of War" offered by the chief of the prisoner of war control section, Uemura and approved by the bureau directors' council, had the effect of compelling compulsory labor by the POWs. Tojo denied that the summary ordered but that it did not even suggest any compulsory labor. He did state though that the regulations on POW work left a way open for officer POWs to labor if they wanted to voluntarily. Tojo further denied that the summary was deliberated nor decided upon by the bureau director's council but that it was drafted by Uemura and adopted by Tojo. Tojo said none of the instructions, including the Summary, that he gave to the POW camp commanders ordered any compulsory or severe labor.

The Greater East Asia Policy supported by Japan came to called by different terms dependent on the period in history being referred to. Some of the terms used were: the new order in East Asia; the new order in Greater East Asia; the establishment of Great Asia; the establishment of the Co-Prosperity Sphere of Great East Asia; the Greater East Asia Co-Prosperity Sphere.

Regardless of what the policy was called, its ultimate objective was to foster an increase in the stability of the Far East. As one of the men who had actually participated in the formulation and promotion of this policy, Tojo felt he was well qualified to provide an explanation of Japan's true intentions having been concerned with this matter since the second Konoye cabinet in July 1940. Basically, the Japanese policy was an effort to establish greater economic cooperation between neighboring countries. This policy was an outgrowth of the First World War when the entire world was organized into economic zones or blocs.

The China Incident erupted as a result of the spread of Communism in Asia and China's anti-Japanese policy. Japan attempted to foster peaceful and friendly relations with China by means of anti-Communistic as well as economic cooperation. Relations between the two countries progressively deteriorated enhanced by the assistance to the Chiang regime provided by America, Britain, and the Soviets. Japan was forced to exercise her right for self preservation and resorted to use of force to break through the barrier encircling her.

Once hostilities commenced, Japan's aims included the emancipation of all Asiatic people in bondage and the establishment of a family of free and independent nations of East Asia.

Tojo cited the remarks of several delegates at the Greater East Asia Conference at Tokyo in November 1943 which denounced the colonial policies of many nations of the world and backed Japan's ideas for the formation of economic unity of Asiatic nations.

Tojo revealed the Japanese government's views on the Greater East Asia policy by quoting from a speech that he made at the opening of the Greater East Asia Conference on 5 November 1942:

- The countries comprising Greater East Asia shall through mutual cooperation secure the stability of their region, set up an order for coexistence and co-prosperity based upon justice.

- The countries of Greater East Asia shall ensure a fraternity of nations in their region by respecting one 'anthers' sovereignty and independence, and practicing mutual assistance and amity.

- The countries of Greater East Asia shall, by the respecting of one 'another' national traditions and developing the creative faculties of each race, enhance the culture and civilization of Greater East Asia.

- The nations in Greater East Asia were to endeavor to accelerate the economic development through close cooperation of reciprocity and to promote thereby the general prosperity of their own region.

- Finally, the countries of Greater East Asia should cultivate cordial and friendly relationships with the world powers to assist in the abolition of discrimination and promotion of cultural intercourse throughout the world thereby contributing towards the progress of mankind everywhere.

These were the fundamental views held by successive Japanese governments during the Greater East Asia establishment period. At no time did Japan imagine that this policy might be construed as planning for any conquest, the domination of the world or any form of aggression. Tojo maintained that after the start of the Pacific War hostilities, he made every effort for the continuance of the Greater East Asia Policy concurrently with the Japanese efforts in prosecution of the war.

Two examples of these efforts were the establishment of the Greater East Asiatic Deliberative Council in March 1942 as an advisory organ to the Prime Minister on matters pertaining to the Greater East Asia Policy, and the establishment of the Ministry of Greater East Asiatic Affairs in November 1942 to supervise business with regard to the Greater East Asia Policy.

The following measures were adopted concerning this policy in reference to external matters: The formation of a New Policy towards China by Japan. The previous unequal treaty was replaced with a new treaty which placed China and Japan on an equal footing. Giving effect to concrete measures in compliance with the Greater East Asia Policy towards the peoples and nations within Japan's occupied zone in response to their desires. The proposal for a Greater East Asiatic Conference for the purpose of promoting good understanding among the respective peoples and to provide for mutual cooperating by means of a consolidated agreement.

After the establishment of the Ministry of Greater East Asiatic Affairs on 2 November 1942, external affairs in regard to the Greater East Asia policy were exclusively placed under this Ministry's jurisdiction, while purely diplomatic affairs such as the conclusion of treaties were left, as had been heretofore, under the foreign Ministry's responsibility. This Ministry had jurisdiction mainly in the following matters: Negotiations concerning the economy, culture, and commerce between independent states within the Greater East Asiatic area; administration concerning the Kwangtung Bureau and the South Sea Bureau; business assisting military administration in occupied area.

One of the external measures of the new China Policy that was formulated on 21 December 1941, was the repeal of the unequal Japan-China treaty. The cabinet gradually developed measures outlined as follows to accomplish this purpose: The Sino-Japanese Agreement stipulating redemption of any concession in Chinese Territory and abolition of extraterritoriality, which had been held by Japan as their special interest in China was concluded and became effective on 9 January 1943. Japan transferred the right to control enemy property in China from Japan to the Nanking government on 8 February 1943. Japan and China concluded the Sino-Japanese Alliance on 30 October 1943 whereby Japan renounced all rights of occupation which had been concluded on 30 November 1940 and promised the complete evacuation of all Japanese troops after the settlement of the China Affair.

This new agreement was concluded with both nations being on equal terms and promising to respect the sovereignty and territorial integrity of the other, to affect mutual aid and an economic coalition for establishment of the Greater East Asia, and to secure an enduring peace in the Far East.

On the independence of Burma, first of all Japan recognized that Burma was an independent nation on 1 August 1943, the same day that there had been a Japan-Burma Alliance concluded with both nations on equal terms. Japan agreed to a Japanese Burma Pact on 25 September 1943 in which Japan promised to assign to Burma part of the Japanese occupied territory with which the people of Burma had a close racial association. Tojo said that the speech on administrative policy he delivered to the Diet session soon after the start of the Pacific War revealed what the Japanese government's intention was on the matter of a Burmese independent nation. From that time on, the preparations for the state were made, and the establishment, on 1 August 1943, of the independent Burmese State was accomplished.

On the subject of the independence of the Philippines, Tojo said that Japan recognized their independence on 14 October 1943 and the enactment of its constitution in accordance with the hopes and aspirations of all of its people. The two nations, on equal terms, concluded an alliance on the same day. The first article of the alliance stipulated reciprocal respect for the sovereignty and territorial integrity.

Before the start of the Pacific War, the Government of the United States had announced its intention of recognizing Philippine independence during July 1946.

Keenly aware of the desires of the Philippines according to Tojo, Japan announced its intentions of recognizing independence of the Philippines at the Diet session held on 22 January 1942 and confirmed its aims again at the 22 January 1943 Diet session. Four months later, in May 1943, Tojo went to the Philippines to assist in promoting the plan for establishing an independent nation.

In June of the same year a draft constitution was prepared and initial arrangements were progressing through the efforts of the Independence Preparation Association, an organization of Philippine people.

On 14 October 1943, The Republic of the Philippines came into being as an independent nation. A constitution based on the general consent of the people was enacted, and a president was elected in accordance with the constitutional provisions.

Japan agreed with the Philippine Republic president's proposal that they would neither participate in the war nor would they organize armed forces.

Long before the start of the Pacific War, peaceful negotiations were in progress between Japan and Thailand under the principles of the Greater East Asia Policy. Consequently on 12 June 1940 a Japan-Thailand friendship treaty was concluded, and a protocol was signed between Japan and Thailand on 9 May 1941 that assured reciprocal cooperation in friendly relations and economic matters.

After the start of the war the two nations signed a treaty of alliance on 21 December 1941 which furthered the establishment of the new order in East Asia, respecting each other's independence and sovereignty, and promised mutual political and military assistance. Enactment of the Japan-Thailand cultural agreement on 28 October 1942 that promised to strengthen the spiritual ties between the two nations. In August 1943 a treaty was concluded whereby Japan was to return to Thailand four former Malayan provinces and two Shan provinces then occupied by Japanese Troops.

Local conditions in the Netherlands Indies did not at first warrant the immediate independence for the area. Consequently, as a preliminary step based on an Imperial Conference decision, Tojo in his policy speech as Prime Minister to the Imperial Diet on 16 June 1943, made it clear that it was the Government's policy to allow political participation by the Indonesians. Based on this statement, the authorities took the necessary steps to carry out this policy on the spot and the Indonesians could then actively participate in governmental affairs.

It was after the fall of the Tojo cabinet that the Japanese government recognized the independence of the Netherlands Indies during the Koiso administration.

The Imperial Japanese government recognized the Provisional Government of Free India on 23 October 1943, two days after its establishment. This Provisional Government came into existence pursuant to the movement to secure the freedom, independence, and prosperity of India. The Japanese government gave full support to this measure in the great cause of the Great East Asiatic policy and took the opportunity at the Greater East Asia Conference to announce that Japan was ready to place the only Indian dominions under Japanese occupation at the time, the Andaman and Nicobar Islands, under their rule.

The Greater East Asia Conference was held in Tokyo on 5-6 November 1943 under the sponsorship of the Japanese government. The object of the Conference was to exchange views and to openly negotiate with each other concerning the policy of setting up a new order in Greater East Asia, and what ways and means should be used to achieve successful results in the Greater East Asia War.

The indictment charged that the internal and foreign policies of Japan were dominated and directed by a 'criminal militaristic clique.' Tojo stated that apart from the distant past there have never existed in Japan a so-called 'militaristic clique' much less any 'criminal militaristic clique' during the time of the indictment. Certain political factors occurring around this time period were the primary cause for the increase in military political involvement according to Tojo.

The military involvement in politics was basically due to the effects upon the Japanese economy of the following factors: improvement in the life of the Japanese people around the time of the Manchurian Incident, upheaval within the reformation movement against the inroads of Communism and the sympathy of the Army and the Navy with these reform movements; the voice of the military authorities was enhanced by the gradual transfer of all national activities into the general mobilization system resulting from the protraction of the China Incident and the shifting to a complete wartime posture after the start of the War; and in conjunction with these factors, the independence of the Supreme Command, an important provision of the Japanese constitution, made the military a powerful force within the political sphere.

Tojo stated that he was not in a position to influence in any way the state of affairs around the time of the Manchurian Incident but that in his opinion, the free trade system broke down after World War I caused by over production worldwide and the extremely selfish protective policy of the "Big Powers." Japan was confronted with decline of capitalism based on this collapse of free trade which could be regarded as a great turning point in her history. Japan's national economy sustained a severe blow and the lifestyle of her people was extremely impoverished. The current of worldwide unrest expanded and overflowed into Japan, thereby forcing her against her will, into an evolutionary period.

Two types of movement, generally speaking, took place in Japan during this period; one was a radical and violent revolutionary movement, and the other was a moderate movement aimed at the improvement of capitalism.

The radical group attempted to make use of Army units or soldiers and to particularly incite and involve young officers in incidents such as those of 15 May 1932 and 26 February 1936. Incidents of this type sprang from the poor miserable life of farmers, villagers, and fishermen and were then carried into the Army by soldiers drawn from this strata of society and some young officers who happened to sympathize with them. A thorough and complete military purge was performed, the offenders were punished, and individual interference in politics by military personnel was strictly forbidden. The War Minister in his capacity and upon his responsibility as a member of the cabinet, demanded that the Government formulate and implement policies to eliminate the cause for this social unrest.

One of the issues revived for this purpose was the ordinance requiring that the Army and Navy Ministers be officers on the active list. Thereby, the military authorities were provided with a voice in the political field.

The second point with regard to the natural transformation of Japan's national economy towards a general mobilization was prompted by the China Incident prolongation, and came about through the urging of the military authorities, along with the wartime organization necessitated by the start of the Pacific War.

As a natural sequence to these events and the war, the management of state affairs and administration began to move towards its final objective the successful prosecution of the war and this revolved around the Army and the Navy as its center. The Military Authorities had attained great power in politics due to these reasons, especially with the institution of the Imperial Headquarters in November 1937.

Full concentration of her national strength was logically aimed at the ultimate victory that she hoped to achieve after the start of hostilities during the Pacific War. If some individuals believed that the Military authorities were tyrannical in that situation, it could be said to be only a difference of opinion. Tojo stated that he never felt that there was a criminal element in any of this nor could he agree with the assertion that a criminal military element dominated Japanese politics.

In the matter of the independence of the supreme command, according to the old constitution, military operations and strategy (i.e., the supreme command) were not included within the meaning of state affairs and were placed independently outside the scope of it, with the exclusion of any interference from the civil administration. This was a system peculiar to Japan and, accordingly, the civil government had no authority to direct or restrict the supreme command in any way, but could merely try by means of liaison conferences, imperial conferences, or both, to coordinate their actions with them but any such coordination could not include operations and tactics. Once hostilities had commenced, all actions were carried out solely in accordance with the unilateral directives of the supreme command and the civil government served only to supply that which the High Command demanded and always had to yield to their will. In an attempt to place some controls on this matter, Tojo said he accepted the position of chief of the general staff in February 1944 in addition to the premiership but it was too late and not much was accomplished.

The deplorable incidences of 15 May 1932 and 26 February 1936 suggested a tendency of military officers to interfere in politics and to foster fractional relationships which required Army Authorities to handle these cases sternly. Upon receipt of information pertaining to the incident of 26 February 1936 from Tokyo, Tojo in his position as commander of military police for the Kwangtung Army, ordered a thorough investigation of all military as well as any civilian personnel suspected of being connected with the incident. Decisive measures were taken by War Minister Terauchi to maintain military morale, strictly prohibiting any kind of political participation by the military and preventing firmly the growth of any fractional relationships in military circles.

Tojo stated that successive war ministers, after Terauchi, including himself, supported and adhered rigidly to this policy. He further said that in order to check the growth of fictionally relationships in military circles, he made every endeavor to place the right person in the right post considering only the person's ability and experience without a regard for his individual relationships and he strictly prohibited military men from meddling in political affairs.

Above all, Tojo testified, that since he had assumed the post of prime minister, he had prevented any confusion between the war ministry and the cabinet to insure that neither would interfere with the workings of the other. While it was true, he agreed, that during his tenure of office as war minister and as prime minister, the Japanese political organization was in a state of general mobilization, there was at no time political control or domination by a military clique.

At no time did Japan even intend to invade the USSR Japans aims in East Asia were strictly of a defensive nature against Russian aggression, mainly after the establishment of Manchukuo in 1932. Additionally, Japan had never considered Siberia as part of the Great East Asia Co-Prosperity Sphere. Japan's policy towards Soviet Russia had always been based on maintaining a tranquil relationship between the nations. Especially after signing the Russo-Japanese Neutrality Treaty in April 1940, it was one of the basic fundamental principles of the Japanese peace policy towards the USSR Japan was not the one who broke the treaty and committed acts of aggression in August 1945.

Tojo recapped his affidavit by repeating the following:

- Japan realized that unless the infiltration of communistic policy into East Asia was checked, her public peace would be destroyed and the stability of East Asia upset. Japan for this reason, enacted the Public Peace Maintenance Law, under the Wakasuki cabinet, as one of her fundamental domestic policies.

- Again in the way of foreign policy, Japan realized that activities of the Chinese Communist Party were among the important causes that prevented the establishment of peace between Japan and China.

- The above points as well as making the prevention of Communism the common essential policy among the independent states in East Asia were all done with the view towards saving East Asia from the danger of World Bolshevization.

That the Pacific War was absolutely provoked by the Allied Powers to force America into the European conflict and as far as Japan was concerned it was an unavoidable war of self-defense.

That a few individuals would never be able to devise, by way of a conspiracy, plans for aggressive action to benefit Japan against her neighbors in Asia over a long period of time despite changes in the Japanese Cabinets over this period.

Tojo concluded by reiterating that the policies of Japan and her duly constituted officials involved neither aggression nor exploitation. Step by step, through numerous legally selected cabinets without a variance in the regularly constituted governmental procedures, Japan finally met face to face with stark reality. To those serving in the Government of Japan at that time, who had the duty of deciding the fate of the nation, a war of self-existence was the only alternative.

Tojo's outlook on the war could be characterized only by overconfidence. From the initiation of Pacific War hostilities Tojo exuded confidence up to the end of 1943 and early 1944. Tojo made the astonishing statement, as late as May 1944, that Saipan was now impregnable and even junior officers began to wonder if Army operations planners had misinformed Tojo, or whether he had spoken irresponsibly. When defeat followed defeat, Tojo's hitherto unchallenged star began to wane. Tojo had to back down and accept Umezu as his replacement as chief of the Army general staff instead of Ushiroku who he had proposed to fill the post.

Even though Tojo opposed any change, on 14 July 1944, his loyal ally and associate Shimada resigned as Navy minister. Regardless of how hard Tojo struggled, his cabinet, lacking the confidence of the same elders who had once installed him, finally fell.

There had already been a conspiracy against him, if he had been assassinated, his military dictatorship would have been replaced with a strong cabinet headed by a prince of the royal blood and this new Japanese government would attempt to make peace. Tojo's Government had collapsed and his cabinet had already resigned before the coup d'etate materialized.

Thus Tojo was now retired from the Army and sank into political oblivion during the remainder of the Pacific War but he was avidly interested in news of the hostilities progress. Occasionally, he would emerge from his obscurity to bolster the faltering Japanese spirits. In late February 1945, in a private audience before the Throne, during a presentation that lasted an hour, Tojo sought to point out the weaknesses in America's vast military capability. He pointed out that the closer to Japan the enemy came, the longer were their supply lines and that even though there were difficulties on the Japanese side, there was no cause for pessimism. Tojo still reflected his strong military outlook in 1945 which was the same as it was in 1941.

Tojo visited War Minister Anami in June 1945 to encourage the Army to remain strong willed in as much as Navy Minister Yonai and Tojo, once again the Foreign Minister, both gave the impression of favoring capitulation.

Tojo felt disappointment and pain as Japan was confronted by reversal after reversal following the capitulation of Germany in May 1945 until the 25th of August when the Imperial Rescript proclaimed Japan's surrender. The major reverses during this period was the destruction of the cities of Hiroshima and Nagasaki by American atomic bombs and the entry into the Pacific War by the Soviet Union.

Tojo did not follow the tradition of committing suicide that many other Japanese wartime leaders had in apology to the Throne for their failures. After General MacArthur's occupation headquarters ordered the roundup of all major Japanese war criminal suspects, Tojo shot himself below the heart with a 32 caliber colt pistol on the 11th of September. He was rushed to the American military hospital in Yokohama where his life was saved by American medical technology and the transfusion with American blood so that he could stand trial before the international tribunal.

The Prosecution began its cross examination of Tojo after he completed presenting his evidence. Normally one or two members of the Prosecution Section completed the cross examination of an accused but in the case of Tojo nearly the entire Prosecution Section was involved and a much greater period of time was required for its completion.

Court Decisions
CHAPTER 15

Court Findings

Count 1 of the indictment charged that all defendants together with other persons participated in the formulation and execution of a common plan or conspiracy. The objective of the plan was alleged that Japan was to secure military, naval, political, and economic domination of East Asia, the Pacific and Indian Oceans, and of all countries and islands there in or bordering thereon. For this purpose, Japan should, alone or in combination with other countries with similar objectives, wage an aggressive war(s) against any country(s) which might oppose that purpose.

Undoubtedly declarations were made by some of those who allegedly participated in the conspiracy which coincided with this grandiose statement, but the Tribunal was of the opinion that it had not been proved that these were more than individual declarations of their own aspirations. The Tribunal cited as an example that they did not believe the conspirators ever seriously considered an attempt to dominate North and South America. They thought that so far as the conspirator's aims being crystallized into a concrete common plan that the territory they had resolved that Japan should dominate was limited to East Asia, the Western and Southwestern Pacific Ocean, the Indian Ocean, and some of the islands in these oceans. The Tribunal treated Count 1 as if the charge had been limited to that objective.

The first consideration for the Tribunal was to determine whether a conspiracy with this objective had been proven to have existed.

Okawa, one of the original defendants, who, was discharged from trial due to his mental state, had prior to 1928 already publicly advocated that Japan should extend her Territory on the continent of Asia by the threat of or, if necessary, by the use of military force. He further advocated that Japan should seek to dominate Eastern Siberia and the South Sea Islands. He predicted that if Japan followed the course he advised it must, of necessity, result in a war between the East and the West, in which Japan would be the champion of the East. The Japanese General Staff encouraged and aided Okawa in his advocacy. This plans objective was substantially the objective of the conspiracy as defined by the Tribunal.

Subsequent conspirator declarations as to the object of the conspiracy did not vary materially from this early declaration by Okawa.

A group of military men, Okawa and civilian supporters, were advocating Okawa's policy that Japan should expand by the use of force already when Tanaka was premier from 1927 until 1929. The conspiracy had now been brought into being and it remained in being until Japan's defeat in 1945. When Tanaka was premier, the immediate question was whether Japan should attempt to expand her influence on the continent of Asia, beginning in Manchuria, by peaceful penetration, as desired by Tanaka and his cabinet, or by use of force, if necessary, as advocated by the conspirators. For the conspirators to succeed with their aims, it was essential that they have the support and control of the nation. Thus a long struggle began between the conspirators, desiring to attain their objective by force, and those politicians and bureaucrats, who wanted Japan to expand by peaceful measures or at least employ the use of force on a more discreet choice of occasions. This struggle's outcome was that the conspirators gained control of the Japanese government and began preparing and regimenting the nation's mind and material resources for aggressive wars designed to achieve the object of the conspiracy.

Propaganda and persuasion won many over to the conspirator's side but they sometimes employed methods that were totally unconstitutional and at times wholly ruthless in overcoming their opposition. These methods included military action abroad without the approval of the cabinet or in defiance of a cabinet veto, assassination of opposition leaders, plots to overthrow the government. The use of these tactics ultimately allowed the conspirators to dominate the Japanese government.

When the conspirators felt strong enough to overcome all those opposed to them, they carried out in succession the attacks necessary to allow the achievement of their ultimate objective that Japan should dominate the Far East. They launched an aggressive war against China in 1931 and captured Manchuria and Jehol. They had commenced to infiltrate into North China by garrisoning the land and establishing puppet governments designed to serve their purposes. They continued the aggressive war against China on a vast scale from 1937 onwards. Much of the country was set up, and the economy and natural resources of China were exploited to feed the Japanese military and civilian needs.

The conspirators had in the meantime been planning and preparing for a war against the USSR that they proposed to launch when a favorable opportunity occurred.

Japan's intention was the seizure of the eastern territories of that country.

The conspirators also had long realized that their exploitation of East Asia and their designs on the islands in the Southwestern and Western Pacific would bring them into conflict with the United States, Britain, France, and the Netherlands who would defend their interests and threatened territories. Plans and preparations for wars against these countries were also initiated.

Japan's alliance with Germany and Italy, who had policies that were as aggressive as their own, and whose support they desired both in the diplomatic and military fields was brought about by the conspirators. Their aggressive actions in China had brought the condemnation of the League of Nations on Japan and had left her friendless in the world councils.

Japan's proposed attack on the USSR was postponed from time to time for various reasons. Some of these reasons were Japan's preoccupation with its war in China, requiring unexpectedly large military resources, and Germany's non-aggression pact with the USSR in 1939 which for the time being freed the USSR from threat of attack on her western frontier, and might have allowed her to devote the bulk of her strength to the defense of her eastern territories if Japan had attacked her.

Then came Germany's great military successes on the European continent in the year 1940 which left Great Britain, France and the Netherlands powerless for the time being to provide adequate protection for their interests and territories in the Far East. With United States military preparations being in their initial stages the conspirators could not see a more favorable opportunity for the realization of that part of their objective which was Japan's domination of Southwest Asia and the islands in the Western and Southwestern Pacific and Indian Oceans. After extensive negotiations with the United States, in which they adamantly refused to concede any of their gains from their war against China, the conspirators launched a war of aggression against the United States and the British Commonwealth on 7 December 1941. Orders had already been issued declaring a state of war existed between Japan and the Netherlands on that date.

A jumping-off place for the attacks on the Philippines, Malaya, and the Netherlands East Indies had previously been secured in French Indo-China by threat of military force if the right to have troops in the area was refused them. The Netherlands had no recourse but to declare war against Japan in self-defense due to the imminent threat of invasion of her Far East territories.

The far reaching plans for the waging of wars of aggression and the prolonged and intricate preparation to wage these wars was not the work of one man but required the work of many leaders acting in accordance with a common plan to achieve a common objective. The common objective to secure Japan's domination by preparing and waging wars of aggression was a criminal objective. The Tribunal found that if more grave crimes could be conceived than the conspiracy to wage wars of aggression or the waging of such wars since the conspiracy threatens the security of the peoples of the world and suffering would be inflicted on countless human beings.

The Tribunal did not consider it necessary to find if the conspiracy to wage wars was in violation of treaties, agreements, and assurances since the conspiracy itself was already criminal in the highest degree.

The Tribunal found that the existence of the criminal conspiracy to wage wars of aggression as specified in Count 1 had been proved.

The conspiracy existed for and its execution occupied a period of many years. Not all of the conspirators participated in the inception of the conspiracy and some parties to the conspiracy had ceased to remain active throughout its execution to the end. All of those who were at any time a party to the criminal conspiracy or who with guilty knowledge at any time participated in its execution were guilty of charge contained in Count 1. The findings as to which defendants, if any or all, participated in the conspiracy, were dealt with by the Tribunal for each individual defendant.

The Tribunal determined that it was unnecessary to consider Counts 2 and 3, which charge the formulation and execution of conspiracies with more limited objectives that than had been found to have been proven under Count 1. The same was true regarding Count 4 which charged the same conspiracy as Count 1 but with more specifications.

Count 5 charged a conspiracy which was wider in its extent and had even more grandiose objectives than those in Count 1. The Tribunal found that although they had the opinion that some conspirators clearly desired the achievement of these grandiose objectives there was not sufficient evidence to warrant a finding that the conspiracy under this count had been proven.

The Tribunal did not consider it necessary to make a finding in 6 through 26 and 37 through 53. Therefore there remained only Counts 27 through 36 and 54 and 55 requiring findings.

Counts 27 through 36 charge the crime of waging wars of aggression in violation of international law, treaties, agreements and assurances against the countries named in the counts. The Tribunal in its statement of facts had already found that wars of aggression were waged against all those countries with the exception of Commonwealth of the Philippines (Count 30) and the Kingdom of Thailand (Count 34). The Commonwealth of the Philippines was not a completely sovereign state during the war period as it was deemed to be a part of the United States of America in as far as international relations was concerned. The Tribunal stated that beyond any doubt there had been an aggressive war in the Philippines but that they considered that as being a part of the aggressive war against the United States to be technically correct.

Count 28 charged that an aggressive war was waged against the Republic of China over a lesser period of time than that charged in Count 27. Since the Tribunal had already determined that Count 27's fuller charge had been proven there was no need for a pronouncement on Count 28.

With having determined that wars of aggression had been proven, it was not considered necessary to determine if these wars were also otherwise in violation of international law or were in violation of treaties, agreements, and assurances. The Tribunal therefore finds that wars of aggression had been waged as charged in Counts 27, 29, 31, 32, 33, 35 and 36.

Count 54 charged ordering, authorizing, or permitting the commission of conventional war crimes while Count 55 charged failure to take steps adequate to secure the observance and prevent breaches of conventions and laws of war with respect to POWs and civilian internees. Cases of crimes under both of these counts were found by the Tribunal to have been proven.

Based on these findings, the Tribunal considered charges against the individual defendants only under Counts 1, 27, 29, 31, 32, 33, 35, 36, 54 and 55.

Count 1–Conspiracy between defendants and other individuals to wage wars of aggression.

Count 27–War of aggression against the Republic of China.

Count 29–War of aggression against the United States of America and the Commonwealth of the Philippines.

Count 31–War of aggression against the British Commonwealth.

Count 32–War of aggression against the Republic of France.

Count 33–War of aggression against the Kingdom of the Netherlands.

Count 35–War of aggression against French Indo-China.

Count 36–War of aggression against the Union of Soviet Socialist Republics.

Count 54–Charged ordering, authorizing, or permitting the commission of conventional war crimes.

Count 55–Charged failure to take adequate steps to secure the observance and prevent the breaches of the conventions and laws of war pertaining to POWs and civilian internees.

Court Judgments
CHAPTER 16

The court found that excessive and unlawful punishment was imposed.

In his instructions to the chiefs of POW and civilian internee camps Tojo stated that they should tighten the control over their subordinates, supervise the prisoners rigidly, and that it was necessary to put them under strict discipline. On 30 May 1942 he repeated this charge in his instructions to the Zentsuji division commander that POWs must be placed under strict discipline in as far as it did not contravene the mistaken idea of humanitarianism. They must also take care so as not to be swayed by the long term of their imprisonment.

The Geneva Prisoner of War Convention of 1929 provided that in respect to the punishment of POWs for offenses committed while in captivity that any corporal punishment, any imprisonment in quarters without daylight, and generally any form of cruelty was forbidden and collective punishment for individual acts was also forbidden.

Other important limitations on the punishments that could be inflicted upon POWs were included. All of these were designed to insure that humane treatment was provided to the prisoners. One of these limitations dealt with escapes and attempts to escape. This provision states that escaped POWs that are retaken before they were able to rejoin their own forces or to leave the enemy occupied territory are liable only for disciplinary punishment.

The 1929 Prisoner of War Convention also provided that after there had been an attempted or accomplished escape, comrades of the escaping person who assisted in the escape would be subject to disciplinary punishment only.

Arrest was the most severe disciplinary punishment that could be imposed on a POW. A single punishment could not exceed 30 days in duration.

That the Japanese fully understood the convention is shown by their objection to its ratification in 1934. They stated that under the convention POWs could not be punished as severely as Japanese troops.

The Japanese said that to place the POWs on an equal footing with the Japanese troops would require a revision of the Japanese Military and Naval Disciplinary Codes which they felt was undesirable in the interests of discipline. The real objection to the ratification of the Convention was that the Japanese Military wanted to avoid providing any specific commitments which would hinder their policy of ill-treatment of POWs .

Early in the Pacific War, after the Japanese government had given their promise to apply the applicable provisions of the Convention to all Allied POWs and civilian internees, ordinances and regulations were enacted which were contrary to those provisions. A regulation was published in 1943 which provided that in case a POW was guilty of an act of insubordination, he would be subject to imprisonment or arrest and any other measure deemed necessary for the purpose of discipline may be added. Using this single regulation as the authority, corporal punishment as well as torture and mass punishment was administered. The infliction of corporal punishment for the least offense or for no offense was a common practice in all areas where POW and civilian internee camps were located. The mildest form of this punishment was the beating and kicking of the victim. If the victim became unconscious, he was often revived with cold water or other means, only to have the process repeated. Thousands died due to this kind of punishment.

Weakness due to starvation and disease hastened their death in many cases. Other forms of cruel punishments frequently employed were exposing the victim to the hot tropical sun without headdress or other protection; suspension of the victim by his arms in such a manner that at times would force the arms from their sockets; binding the victim where he would be attacked by insects; confining the victim in a cramped cage for days without food; confining the victim in an underground cell without food, light, or fresh air for weeks and forcing the victim to kneel on sharp objects in a cramped position for long periods of time.

Mass punishments were commonly employed in direct defiance of the rules of war as punishment for individual acts. This was especially true where the Japanese were unable to discover the offender. The usual form of mass punishment was to force all group members to assume a strained position such as sitting with the legs folded under the body or kneeling and to remain in that position during daylight hours for days at a time. Another form of mass punishment was employed at the Havelock Road Camp in Malaya where the prisoners were forced to run in a circle without shoes over broken glass while being spurred on by Japanese soldiers who beat them with rifle butts.

An ordinance was issued on 9 March 1943 which provided for the death penalty, life imprisonment or confinement for 10 years or more for a number of offenses. An important feature of this ordinance was that it provided that the death penalty or other severe form of penalty could be imposed on the so-called leader of any group's action which resulted in the commission of the offense and the same punishment or less severe penalty for all others who might be involved. Mass punishments were often inflicted upon groups of POWs or civilian internees under this ordinance for what at most amounted to no more than an individual act. The death penalty was also provided by this ordinance for POWs who defy of disobey the orders of persons supervising, guarding, or escorting them.

This ordinance is only an example, of which there were a number, where the Japanese government altered its laws concerning POWs and departed from its undertaking in respect to the Geneva Convention.

The Japanese POW regulations were amended during the Pacific War to allow an escaping prisoner to be punished in the same manner as a deserter from the Japanese Army which was in contrast to their avowed intention of abiding by the Geneva Convention.

An ordinance dated 9 March 1943 contained the provision that the leader of a group of persons acting in unison to escape would be either subject to the death penalty or imprisonment at hard labor for life or ten years minimum. Other persons that were involved in the escape would be subject to the same punishments except that the minimum could be for one year instead of ten. This provision together with the regulations covering paroles not to escape, which the POWs were forced to give, constituted the regulations governing escapes which were enforced at all prison camps.

These regulations which pertained to escapes were not only contrary to the Convention which Japan had promised to uphold but were in direct violation of international law.

The death penalty was imposed upon almost all of the prisoners without exception who attempted to escape or who had escaped and were recaptured. Under the provisions of these regulations, the comrades who assisted a prisoner to escape were also punished, many frequently by the death penalty.

The prisoners in some camps were separated into groups and the practice was to kill all members of the group if one member of the group attempted to escape or was not even provided.

The death penalty has been proven to have been imposed for escape attempts at the following camps: Mukden in Liaoning Province of China (July 1943); Hong Kong, China (July 1943); Singapore, Malaya (March 1942); Mergui, Burma (1942); Tarakan, Borneo (1942 and 1945); Pontianak, Borneo (June 1942); Banjermasin, Borneo (July 1942); Samarinda, Borneo (January 1945); Palembang, Sumatra (March 1942); Djati, Nanggor, Java (March 1942); Bandung, Java (April 1942); Batavia, Java (April 1942); Soekaboemi, Java (May 1942); Jogjakarta, Java (May 1942); Tjimahi, Java (May 1942); Makassar, Celebes (September 1942); Anboina, Moluccas Islands (November 1942 and April 1945); Oesapa Besar, Dutch Timor (February); Cabanatuan, Philippines (June 1942); Motoyama, Japan (November 1942); Fukuoka, Japan (May 1944); Wake Island (October 1943); Ranau, Borneo (August 1945).

The Japanese maintained a policy of submitting Allied POWs to violence, insults, and humiliation to impress other Asian peoples with the Japanese race's superiority. Vice-Minister of War Kimura in 4 March 1942 received a telegram from the chief-of-staff of the Korean Army requesting for the internment of 1,000 each British and American POWs in Korea, because it would be effective in stamping out the respect and admiration the Korean people had for Britain and America. This would also aid in the establishment of a strong faith in a Japanese victory by the Korean people. Minami was the governor-general of Korea at that time and Itagaki was the Commander of the Korean Army. Kimura replied on 5 March 1942 that 1000 white POWs were to be sent to Pusan, Korea. On 23 March 1942 Itagaki sent War Minister Tojo a message informing him of his plans to make use of these POWs for psychological purposes since the reason for British and American POWs to be interned in Korea prison still remained. Itagaki went on to state that the first camp would be at Seoul, Korea in the abandoned Iwamura Silk-Reeling Warehouse since Kimura objected to his former plan to confine the POWs in the theological school in Pusan by indicating that those buildings were too good for POWs. Itagaki stated that among the main points of his plan was that POWs would be used on various works in the principal cities of Korea, especially where psychological conditions were not good. Equipment for the camps would be cut to a minimum, and that the internment, supervision, and guarding of the prisoners would be carried out so as to leave nothing to be desired in the accomplishment of the purpose for which the POWs were transported to Korea.

The Chief-of-Staff of the Army in Formosa on 2 April 1942 informed the Prisoner of War Information Bureau that he planned to use POWs not only for labor to increase war production but also as material for education and guidance. Thus the plan was applied to use POWs in violation of the laws of war for pro-Japanese propaganda. The vice-minister of war on 6 May 1942 informed the chief-of-staff of the Formosa Army that white POWs would be confined in Korea, Formosa, and Manchuria and that for control purposes and security it was planned to assign special units of ethical forces, both Koreans and Formosans. The psychological effect was to be attained by providing these special units the opportunity to be a part of the plan to allow Allied POWs to be insulted and open to public curiosity.

Vice-Minister of War Kimura on 16 May 1942 notified the Southern Area Army commander-in-chief, whose headquarters were at Singapore, that the white POWs in Singapore were to be handed over to the Formosan and Korean Armies between May and August.

About 1,000 prisoners captured in the fighting in Malaya were handed over and sent to Korea. The POWs, upon their arrival in Korea, were marched through the streets of Seoul, Pusan, and Jinsen where they were paraded before 120,000 Koreans and 57,000 Japanese. The POWs had been previously subjected to malnutrition, ill treatment, and neglect in such a manner so that their physical condition would elicit contempt from any person who saw them. In reporting on what he considered a great success of this demonstration of Japanese superiority to Kimura, Itagaki's Chief-of-Staff quoted a Korean bystander as saying that 'when we look at their frail and unsteady appearance it was no wonder that they lost to the Japanese forces.'

Another Korean bystander was quoted as remarking that "when I saw young Korean soldiers, members of the Imperial Army, guarding the prisoners, I shed tears of joy."

Itagaki's Chief-of-Staff concluded his message with the observation that as a whole it seems the idea was very successful in driving all admiration for the British out of the Korean's minds and in driving into them an understanding of the situation.

This practice of parading POWs was followed as far away as in Moulmein, in Burma. Twenty-five Allied POWs were paraded through the streets of that city in February 1944. The prisoners were in an emaciated condition and were forced to carry notices in Burmese falsely stating that they had recently been captured on the Arakan front. A Japanese officer who accompanied the parade ridiculed the POWs and held then up to contempt.

Certain changes that were made by Japan regarding the enforcement of the laws of war and the Administration of POWs and civilian internees matters after the start of the Pacific War were only nominal in nature as they did nothing to insure the enforcement of the laws of war.

The Japanese government's attitude toward the enforcement of the laws of war did not substantially change after the start of the Pacific War even though there were some changes in governmental organizations and methods of procedures made. As a matter of fact, as was shown by the regulations affecting attempts to escape, changes were actually made which directed the commission of grave breaches of the laws of war.

During the China War the Japanese government did not create any special agency dealing with the administration of POWs and civilian internees nor was a Prisoner of War Information Bureau maintained as was required by The Hague and Geneva Conventions.

Muto said that the question of whether Chinese captives would be treated as POWs or not was quite a problem. In 1938 it was finally decided that because the Chinese conflict was officially known as an incident and not a war that the Chinese captives would not be regarded as POWs.

Tojo, after the start of hostilities in the Pacific War, stated that he considered that Japan was obligated to abide by The Hague and Geneva Conventions and for that reason he caused to be created a Prisoner of War Information Bureau. Tojo's statement must be interpreted based upon his comments in 18 August 1943 during an investigation committee meeting of the Privy Council at which time he said that international law should be interpreted from the viewpoint of the Japanese government's treatment of POWs and civilian internees was developed based upon this concept.

Japan agreed to apply the 1929 Geneva convention in matters pertaining to POWs and civilian internees even if Japan had never ratified the requirements contained in the convention.

The US Secretary of State on 18 December 1941 directed the American Legation in Switzerland to request that the Swiss government inform the Japanese government of the intention of the US government to abide by the Geneva POW Convention and the Geneva Red Cross Convention, both of which were signed on 27 July 1929. It further intended to extend and apply the provisions of the Geneva POW Convention to those civilian enemy aliens that it might intern, and it hoped that the Japanese government would apply the provisions of these conventions in reciprocity as indicated.

The US government further stated that it would appreciate an expression of the intention by the Japanese government in that respect with the inquiry being delivered on 27 December 1941 to Japanese Foreign Minister Togo by the Minister of Switzerland.

On 3 January 1942 the governments of Great Britain and the dominions of Canada, Australia, and New Zealand sent an inquiry through the Argentine ambassador in Tokyo in which they said that they would observe the terms of the 1929 Geneva Prisoner of War Convention toward Japan and asked if the Japanese government was prepared to make a similar declaration. The Argentine ambassador delivered another note on 5 January 1942 on behalf of Great Britain, Canada, Australia, and New Zealand which proposed that in the application of the Convention's Articles 11 and 12 relating to the provision of food and clothing for the prisoners, that both parties should take into consideration the national and racial customs of the prisoners.

Upon receiving these inquiries, Togo asked for their opinions from the War Ministry, Navy Ministry, Ministry for Home Affairs, and the Ministry of Overseas Affairs. Tojo at that time was war minister and home minister as well as being concurrently the prime minister. Muto was chief of the military affairs bureau on the war ministry. Within the bureau, Sato was Muto's assistant, Kimura was vice-minister of war, Shimada was Navy minister, Oka was chief of the Naval affairs bureau in the Naval ministry, and Hoshino was chief secretary of the cabinet.

Togo was concerned for the safety of Japanese living in Allied countries and for that reason he desired to provide a favorable reply to these inquiries and so instructed the Bureau of Treaties. He pointed out that the fate of several hundred thousands of Japanese residents in enemy countries would be affected by the Japanese treatment of the POWs and civilian internees that might be in her power.

The war ministry agreed with Togo. Kimura told Togo on 23 January 1942 that in view of the fact the Geneva Convention relating to POWs had never been ratified by His Majesty, Japan could hardly announce their observance of the same but that it would be safe to notify the world that

Japan had no objection to acting in accordance with the Convention in the treatment of POWs. He further stated that there was no objection to giving due consideration to the national or racial habits and customs of the POWs in regard to providing the prisoners with food and clothing.

Togo, on 29 January 1942, answered both the American and British inquiries. The note to the US government stated that Japan, as a signatory of the Geneva Convention of 27 July 1929 relating to the Red Cross, strictly observed that Convention. The note further indicated that since the Imperial Japanese government had not yet ratified the 27 July 1929 Convention relative to treatment of prisoners of war, Japan was not bound by that convention, but that Japan would apply *mutatis mutandis* the provisions of that Convention to American POWs in its power. Togo's note addressed to the governments of Great Britain, Canada, Australia, and New Zealand informing them that since the Imperial Japanese government had not yet ratified the agreement concerning the treatment of prisoners of war and that it was not bound to any extent by this agreement but that it would apply 'mutatis mutandis' the provisions of that agreement toward British, Canadian, Australian, and New Zealand POWs in Japanese control. It also indicated that the Imperial Japanese government would consider the national and racial manners and customs when supplying clothing and provisions to the POWs under reciprocal conditions. The same assurances were provided to the other Allied powers by Togo.

In as much as the war ministry had not agreed to extend the POW provisions to civilian internees, Togo inquired of the war ministry through his vice-minister on 27 January 1942 as to the application of the POW convention to non-combatant internees. The war ministry, after conferences, further acquiesced in Togo's plan for protection of Japanese nationals in Allied countries. Togo on 13 February 1942 informed the US government that the Imperial Japanese government would apply for the duration of the war under conditions of POWs of 27 July 1929 to enemy civilian internees, in so far as they are applicable and provided that they are not made to work without their consent.

The US government, having noted Togo's assurances to the British countries on 29 January 1942 that Japan would take into consideration the national and racial customs of POWs and supply them with clothing and provisions, addressed an inquiry pertaining to that subject on 20 February 1942.

This inquiry stated that the US government would be bound by the same provisions for POWs as for civilian internees in conformity with Articles 11 and 12 of the Geneva Convention and it expected in consequence that the Japanese government would equally conform to these provisions in the treatment of POWs and civilian internees. Togo replied to the inquiry on 2 March, 1942, by stating that the Imperial Japanese government intends to take into consideration, with regard to provisions and clothing to be distributed, the racial and national customs of the American POWs and civilian internees placed under Japanese power.

This exchange of assurances constituted a solemn agreement binding the Japanese government as well as the other combatants' governments to apply the provisions of the Geneva Prisoner of War Convention of 27 July 1929 to POWs and civilian internees when supplying them with food and clothing as required by the Convention and not to force the internees to work. The only exception to the rule established by this agreement were such which could be justified under the *mutatis mutandis* reservation. That this agreement allowed no exception to be made by reason of conflict with the municipal law of Japan was clear and was shown by Togo's testimony where he stated that the inquiries from the United States and Britain were referred in the normal course by the Foreign Ministry Treaty Bureau, which managed such matters, to the war ministry, as the ministry empowered to decide the question. The answer furnished by the war ministry was that Japan should apply the terms of the Geneva Convention "mutatis mutandis," and it was so replied to the inquiring governments. Togo further stated that although the prosecution deemed that by giving this answer Japan became bound by the convention to the same extent as if she had ratified it, but that he assumed that Japan was binding themselves only to apply the Convention so far as circumstances permitted. He said also that he assumed that where the requirements of the Convention came in conflict with the provisions of domestic law the former would prevail. The director of the Bureau of Treaties further confirmed this.

The members of the Tojo cabinet intended that the Allied powers should understand the agreement when it was made but they did not abide by the agreement and instead used it as a means to secure good treatment for the Japanese who might become POWs or be interned by the Allied powers.

In his answer to Togo's request, Vice-Minister Kimura stated that it would be safe to notify the world that Japan would observe the convention but prefaced his statement with the remark that since the Emperor had not ratified it, the Japanese government could hardly announce their intention to observe the convention.

Successive Japanese governments failed to enforce the convention even though, the ministers of state deemed the assurances to the Allies to be a promise to perform new and additional duties for the benefit of the POWs and internees, they never issued any new orders or instructions to their officers in charge of the POWs and internees to carry out the execution of this new promise nor did they set up a system which would insure the performance of the promise.

Instead of making an effort to insure compliance with all requirements of this agreement, they made efforts to conceal from the Allies their guilty non-performance by denying access to the POW and internee camps; limiting the length, content, and number of letters which a prisoner or internee might mail; suppressing all news regarding such prisoners and internees; and neglecting to answer or the making of false answers to protests and inquiries to them regarding the treatment of the POWs and internees

In an earlier part of the judgment reference was made to the effect of various conventions in relation to the treatment of POWs and civilian internees and to the obligations of belligerents in that respect. Regardless of any view that may be taken of the assurance or undertaking by the Japanese government for the compliance with the Geneva Prisoner of War Convention "mutatis mutandis," the fact remains that the customary rules of war, which are acknowledged by all civilized nations, all POWs and civilian internees must be given humane treatment. It was the grossly inhumane treatment by Japanese forces as referred to in this portion of the judgment that was particularly reprehensible and criminal. A person guilty of such inhumanities cannot escape punishment on the plea that he or his government is not bound by any convention. The general principles of the law exist independently of the conventions which merely reaffirm the pre-existing law and prescribe detailed provisions for its application.

As to the effect of the Japanese government's undertaking to observe the convention "mutatis mutandis," at no time in the defense was anything said or even suggested that these words justified the atrocities of any other grossly inhumane acts committed by the Japanese forces nor was it argued that these words could justify the looting, pillaging, and arson which was clearly established. Those accused who gave evidence on those points, for the most part, did no more than plead complete ignorance of the happenings.

Any submission which attempted to justify the atrocities would amount to nothing more than by inserting the words *mutatis mutandis* the Japanese military forces would by permitted with impunity to behave with such gross barbarity under the guise of complying with the Convention which provided for the humane treatment of POWs as its cardinal principle. Submission of such contention would never be accepted.

The ill treatment of POWs was a policy of the Japanese government. Japan signed and ratified the Fourth Hague Convention of 1907 respecting the laws and customs of war on land, which provided for humane treatment of POWs and condemned treacherous and inhumane conduct of war. The reason for the Japanese government's failure to ratify and enforce the Geneva POW Convention even though it signed this Convention at Geneva in 1929, was to be found in the fundamental training of the Japanese soldier. Long before the beginning of the period covered by the indictment, the young men of Japan had been taught that "the greatest honor is to die for the Emperor," a precept that was found to have been repeated by Araki in his speeches and propaganda motion pictures. That it was an ignominy to surrender to the enemy was another precept that was taught.

The combined effect of these precepts was to inoculate Japanese forces with a spirit of contempt for those Allied soldiers who did surrender, which, in defiance of the rules of war, was demonstrated by the treatment of the prisoners. With this attitude toward POWs the Japanese made no distinction between the soldier who fought with honor and courage up to an inevitable surrender and those who surrendered without a fight. All enemy soldiers who surrendered for any reason or under any circumstance were considered to have been disgraced and entitled to live only by the tolerance of their captors.

The Military thought that by ratification and enforcement of the Geneva Convention of 1929 it would involve abandoning this view. The Japanese Plenipotentiaries had signed the Convention at Geneva in 1929, but when the Convention came up for ratification in 1934, both military forces, the Japanese Army and Navy petitioned against its ratification. Since the military had gained sufficient political strength by then, they prevented the ratification of the convention. Some of the reasons given by the military was that the obligations imposed by the convention were unilateral, that new and additional burdens were imposed on Japan, but that Japan did not gain anything by its ratification as no Japanese soldier would ever surrender to the enemy. Tojo in giving instructions to the chiefs of the POW camps stated: "In Japan we have our own ideology concerning POWs, which should naturally make their treatment more or less different from that in Europe and America."

The Japanese purpose in all of this was the protection of Japanese nationals.

An inquiry from the International Red Cross in Geneva which was forwarded from the foreign ministry on 12 December 1941 to the war ministry prompted the creation of a Prisoner of War Information Bureau. The inquiry informed the Japanese foreign ministry that in view of the fact that the war had been extended to the Pacific the International Red Cross committee had placed the services of the Central Prisoner of War Bureau at the disposal of the belligerent states. It also inquired if the Japanese government was willing to exchange by the intermediary off the Central Bureau of Geneva lists of information on POWs and in so far as possible on civilian internees. After conferences were held by officials in the war ministry, Vice-Minister of War Kimura on 28 December 1941 informed foreign minister Togo that the war ministry was ready to exchange information. Kimura further stated that he did not declare that Japan was not prepared to apply in practice the Prisoner of War Convention of 1929 but that Japan would utilize them for convenience of transmittal of information. The International Red Cross had by 12 January 1942 received replies from Japan and the United States declaring that they were ready to proceed with the transmission of information.

The Prisoner of War Information Bureau was created on 27 December 1941 by Imperial Ordinance and was charged with making investigations on the following subjects relating to the POWs: internments, removals, releases on parole, exchanges, escapes, admissions to hospitals, and deaths.

Other duties assigned to the bureau were the maintaining of records for each POW; managing the communications and correspondence regarding POWs; and the collection of information pertaining to the POWs condition.

The bureau was established with a director and four secretaries. It was placed under the supervision and control of the war minister, and was organized as a section of the Military Affairs Bureau, where at different times it came under the control and supervision of Muto and Sato. All of the Bureau personnel were appointed on the recommendation of the war minister and Tojo appointed Lieutenant General Uemura as the bureau's first director.

On 31 March 1942 "Regulations for the Treatment of Prisoners of War" were promulgated and the Prisoner of War administration section was created in the Military Affairs Bureau of the war ministry under the supervision and control of War Minister Tojo. Tojo exercised control and supervision of the section through Muto as chief of the Military Affairs Bureau. The section was provided under the regulations to have a director and other personnel to be appointed upon the war minister's recommendation. Tojo appointed Lieutenant General Uemura as the first director of the section, thus combining in one person the administration of the Prisoner of War Information Bureau and the Prisoner of War Administration Section. As Kimura had previously stated the Prisoner of War Information Bureau was an information and records office only created to use the provisions of the Prisoner of War Convention of 1929 for the purpose of gaining information and it had no control or supervision over POWs and civilian internees. On the other hand, the Prisoner of War administration section was given authority to conduct all affairs relative to the treatment of POWs and civilian internees in the theater of war.

Control of the system set up for enforcement of the laws of war during the Pacific War was retained by the Military Affairs Bureau of the war ministry Muto and later under Sato. Although the ordinance that created the Prisoner of War Information Bureau provided that the director may demand information from any concerned military or naval unit in regard to matters falling within his jurisdiction, General Uemura and the directors following him were required to transmit all inquiries and other communications through the office of the chief of the Military Affairs Bureau.

All orders and directives relating to POWs and civilian internees were issued by the war minister according to Tojo. The Military Affairs Bureau drafted these orders and directives after the chief of that bureau had held conferences with the general staff and any other government agencies concerned. Bi-weekly conferences of all bureau chiefs in the war ministry were held and Tojo as war minister and Kimura as vice-minister of war from 10 April 1942 attended most of these conferences. Matters relating to POWs and civilian internees were discussed during these conferences with orders and regulations being formulated and then forwarded to all government agencies concerned with the treatment of POWs and civilian internees.

Imperial ordinances and regulations issued by the war ministry on 23 December 1941 which authorized detention camps provided that the camps would be administered by a commander of an Army or a commander of a garrison under the general supervision of the minister of war. However, not all of these camps were under Army commanders with some of the camps being administered by Navy officers of corresponding rank and authority in those areas under the jurisdiction of the Navy.

Civilian internees detention camps were authorized by war ministry regulations on 7 November 1943 and provided that when the commander of an Army, a term which included persons of equivalent status, had interned enemy nationals or neutrals at the front, he was to establish an army internment camp as soon as possible. The commander of an Army that establishes the internment camp was also to administer the same.

General regulations pertaining to the control and administration of camps established for civilian internees were not materially different from those applicable to the POW camps since all regulations applicable to POWs were made applicable to civilian internees. The major difference being with specific regulations that pertained to civilian internees only.

Accused who administered detention camps as military commanders during the Pacific War were Dohihara as commander of the eastern military district in Japan and as commander of the 7th Area Army at Singapore; Hata as commander of all Japanese Expeditionary Forces in China and as commander of the military districts in central and western Honshu in Japan; Itagaki as commander of the Korean Army and as commander of the 7th Area Army at Singapore; Kimura as commander of the Army in Burma; Muto as commander of the Japanese Army in Northern Sumatra; Sato as commander of the Army in French Indo-China; and Umezu as commander of the Kwangtung Army in Manchuria.

Regulations provided that an Army commander or a garrison commander may, whenever necessary, delegate authority to his subordinates for assistance in the management of a POW or civilian internment camp. Those persons so delegated under these provisions were to be under the supervision and control of the commandant. Special supervisors or chiefs to manage POW and civilian internee camps were selected and trained on Tokyo. After careful and detailed instruction, which was completed by a personal message from Prime Minister Tojo, these chiefs were sent from Japan to all places where POW civilian internees camps were located to take charge of the camps and manage them under command of the Army or Navy commander concerned. Regulations required that the camp chiefs make monthly reports to the Prisoner of War administration section in the Military Affairs Bureau of the War Ministry. These reports were discussed at the bi-weekly conferences of Bureau Chiefs in the War Ministry and were included in statistics relative to the high death rate in the camps due to malnutrition and other causes.

Tojo said this item received his particular attention. Summaries of the chiefs of camps monthly reports were filed in the office of the Prisoner of War Information Bureau.

It had been contemplated that the Navy would deliver to the Army for detention and administration all POWs and civilian internees taken by it but in many cases this was delayed for a long time or was not done.

In some occupied areas also, the Navy exercised jurisdiction for control and administration. The Navy occupied such islands as Borneo, the Celebes, the Moluccas, Timor, and other islands east of a line through Bali, as well as Wake Island. In those areas occupied by the Navy, the POWs and civilian internees were administered by the Navy minister and thus the enforcement of the laws of war became the responsibility of the Navy in those areas under the directions of Shimada and Oka.

There were some differences in control and administration of those POWs detained in Japan and those detained in other areas. POWs detained in Japan were under the war ministry in the same manner as prisoners in other areas but it was stated that the home ministry was in charge of the police in Japan and was therefore considered as the proper ministry to administer all matters that related to civilian internees in Japan proper. It should be remembered that Tojo served as home minister from 18 October 1941 until 17 February 1942 and again from 25 November 1942 until 6 January 1943. Tojo said that there was a separate body under the home ministry to deal with civilian internees but that he did not know the name of it.

Japan was divided into eight military districts for the purpose of defense and military administration with each district being occupied by an army whose commander was also the military administrator of the district and in charge of all POW camps within his district. The eastern district embraced the Tokyo-Yokohama area and was occupied by 12th Area Army. Dohihara commanded that army from 1 May 1943 until 22 March 1944 and again from 25 August 1945 until the time of the surrender on 2 September 1945. The Hiroshima area and the western tip of Honshu Island were included in the Chugoku military district which was garrisoned by the Second Army Corps. Hata commanded that Corps from 7 April 1945 until the surrender on 2 September 1945.

In the Japanese overseas possessions of Formosa, Korea, and Sakhalin which were not in a theater of operations, civilian internees were under the administration of the ministry of overseas affairs, but POWs in those possessions were under the administration of war ministry in the same manner as prisoners in other areas. The ministry of overseas affairs was established by Imperial ordinance of 10 June 1929 which provided that this ministry was to control all affairs related to the Korea governor-general's office, the Formosa governor-general's office, the Kwantung administration office, and the South Seas area administration office.

The ministry of overseas affairs was abolished in 1943 to provide for the major wartime reorganization of the Japanese government with those functions from that ministry being divided and transferred to the ministry of home affairs and the Ministry of Greater East Asia. Togo was overseas affairs minister from 18 October 1941 until 2 December 1941.

The Ministry of Greater East Asia was created on 1 November 1942 by Imperial ordinance which directed that the minister of Greater East Asiatic affairs was to administer the execution of various political affairs with the exception of purely diplomatic affairs concerning the Greater East Asia area which was defined as excluding Japan proper, Korea, Formosa and Sakhalin. The ministry was organized to govern all areas which had fallen or might fall under the military power of Japan. The minister of Greater East Asiatic Affairs was to oversee affairs concerning the Kwantung Bureau and the South Seas government and the ministry was organized with four bureaus; the General Affairs Bureau, the Manchurian Affairs Bureau, the Chinese Affairs Bureau, and the Southern Area Affairs Bureau. the Ordinance further provided that in order to extend cooperation to the Army and Navy that the Ministry of Greater East Asiatic Affairs was to conduct affairs concerning the administration of the occupied areas within the Greater East Asia Area.

Aoki was the first minister followed by Shigemitsu who took over the ministry on 20 July 1944 and remained in that position until 7 April 1945 when he was succeeded by Togo who held the office until 16 August 1945.

The following accused were among those who administered the POW/civilian internee system in the occupied territories:

- Umezu was appointed as the commander in chief of the Kwantung Army on 7 September 1939 and served in that position until 18 July 1944. During this period he was the virtual ruler in Manchukuo and the treatment of POWs and civilian internees in Manchuria were his direct responsibility.

- Hata was commander in chief if the Japanese Expeditionary Force in China from 1 March 1941 to 22 November 1944.

- Kimura resigned as Vice Minister of War on 11 March 1943. On 30 August 1944 he was appointed commander in chief of the Japanese Army in Burma where he remained until the surrender. During his time in Burma he put into practice the policies which he helped to develop during his term of office in the War Ministry. He established his headquarters first at Rangoon and at this time atrocities occurred in that area at Hsipaw, Moksokwin Reserve Forest, Henzada, Ongun Cemetery, Tharrawaddy. and at the Kempeitai Jail in Rangoon. Kimura moved his headquarters at the end of April 1945 to Moulmein and thereafter atrocities occurred at or near Moulmein. On 7 July 1945 the entire population of Kalagon, a village 10 miles from Kimura's headquarters was massacred under order of his field officers. Massacres occurred in Moulmein after Kimura's arrival, the Kempeitai became more inhumane in their treatment and internees in the camp at Tavoy were starved and beaten.

Muto made an inspection tour of the southern regions from 20 March to 12 April 1942 where he visited Formosa,

Saigon, Bangkok, Rangoon, Singapore, Palembang, Java, Manila, and other areas. Upon returning to Tokyo, he was appointed commander of the Imperial Guards Division on 20 April 1942 and was the Japanese military commander in Northern Sumatra with his headquarters at Medan until 12 October 1944 when he was transferred to the Philippine Islands. During this period while he was in command he put into practice the policies that he had been advocating as the chief of the Military Affairs Bureau in the war ministry in Tokyo. Some of the most disgraceful atrocities of the war were committed in the area occupied by his troops in Northern Sumatra. The laws of war were ignored with civilian internees and POWs being starved, neglected, tortured, murdered, and otherwise mistreated and many from the civilian populace in the area being massacred. He was transferred on 12 October 1944 to Fort McKinley and assumed the duties for that position where he remained until the Japanese surrender in September 1945. During his tenure in this position, a campaign of massacre, torture, and many other atrocities was waged by troops under Yamashita and Muto on the civilian population of the Philippines, including the massacres in Bantangas and massacres and other atrocities at Manila. These atrocities had the same features and followed the same pattern set eight years earlier at Nanking when Muto was a member of Matsui's staff where POWs and civilian internees were starved, tortured, and murdered.

Dohihara commanded the 7th Area Army at Singapore from 22 March 1944 until he was relieved by Itagaki on 7 April 1945 to become inspector general of military education. During his period of command POWs were treated as common criminals and were starved, tortured, and otherwise ill-treated.

After Itagaki assumed command of the 7th Area Army at Singapore the condition of and the treatment of POWs under the jurisdiction of that Army did not improve. During the months of June and July of 1945 not less that 17 Allied airmen were taken from their cells in the Outtam Gaul and were murdered.

Formal and informal protest and warnings against violations of the laws of war lodged by the Allied powers and the protecting power were generally ignored. When they were answered the commission of the offenses was denied or untruthful explanations were given.

Visits to the detention camps were never freely allowed throughout the war by use of one excuse of another. In the few cases where visits by protecting power's representatives to detention camps were allowed, the camps were prepared and the visits were strictly supervised. Despite the repeated objections of the protecting power, regulations were strictly enforced, including not allowing a POW to be interviewed by their delegates without a guard being present.

The fate of the POWs and civilian internees was further concealed by the refusal to provide the protecting power with a factual list of names of detained POWs and civilian internees. Failure to supply such lists of detained personnel after the capture of Wake Island is an example.

On 27 May 1942 the Swiss minister requested the names of the POWs and civilian internees that had been captured on Wake Island and their present whereabouts from the Japanese foreign ministry. When a list was finally furnished many months later, it was found that the list did not include the names of 432 American civilians who should have been on Wake Island at the time of its capture. Information on their status was requested. No information was obtained on these personnel until after the surrender of Japan when it was found that in truth 98 of these people were murdered by the Japanese Navy in October 1943.

No doubt to prevent disclosure of the ill treatment to which the POWs were being subjected news reports and mail were specially censored. POW camp officials also used the threat of not allowing the POWs to communicate by what little bit of mail that there was as another way to control them.

When Navy minister Yonai as well as Togo, now foreign minister again, had given the impression of being amenable to capitulation at any moment, Tojo in June 1945, was sufficiently agitated to visit War Minister Anami and encourage the Army to remain stouthearted.

It was obvious that some members of the conspiracy remained active and supported the aims throughout the war.

An organized effort was made to burn or otherwise destroy all documents and other evidence of ill treatment of POWs and civilian internees when it became apparent that Japan would be forced to surrender. An order was issued on 14 August 1945 by the Japanese minister of war to all Army headquarters that confidential documents should be destroyed by fire immediately. The commandant of the Kempeitai on the same day sent out instructions to all Kempeitai headquarters detailing the methods to be used for the burning efficiently of large quantities of documents. The chief of the prisoner of war camps in the Prisoner of War Administration section of the Military Affairs Bureau sent a circular telegram to the chief of staff of the Formosan Army on 20 August 1945 which said that documents which were unfavorable for us in the hands of the enemy are to be treated the same as secret documents and destroyed when finished with. This telegram was routed to the Korean Army, Kwantung Army, North China Army, Hong Kong, Mukden, Bouneo, Thailand, Malaya, and Java. It was in this telegram that the chief of the POW Camps made the statement that any camp official or guard who had ill-treated POWs and internees or who were held in extremely bad sentiment by them were to be permitted to take care of it by immediately transferring or by fleeing without a trace.

Verdicts
CHAPTER 17

Article 17 of the charter required that the judgment should give the reasons on which it was based. Those reasons were included in the facts and statements of the Tribunal's findings. The Tribunal had examined minutely the activities of each of the accused concerned in relation to these findings. Therefore, the Tribunal felt there was no need to repeat the many particular findings on which their verdicts in the case of each individual accused was based. Rather they gave their reasons in general terms for their findings in respect to each accused as these general reasons were based on the particular statements and findings.

Individual Verdict 01
Accused: Araki, Sadao

Araki, Sadao was charged with conspiracy to wage wars of aggression in violation of international law, treaties, agreements and assurances by Count 1, with waging such wars under Counts 27, 29, 31, 32, 33, 35, and 36, and with being responsible for war crimes committed in China under Counts 54, and 55. He was a military officer of high rank, became a lieutenant-general in 1927 and a general in 1933, and was prominent in the hierarchy of the Army during all material times.

Araki was an energetic proponent of the Army policy of political domination at home and military aggression abroad and, in fact was recognized as being one of the prominent leaders of that Army movement. As a member of different cabinets, he advanced the Army's policy to prepare for war by his actions, speeches, and control of the press, to incite and prepare the Japanese people for war. He was a vigorous advocate and helped to formulate the military party policy to enrich Japan at the expense of her neighbors both in and out of political office. He approved and actively supported the Japanese Army policies in Manchuria and Jehol to separate these territories politically from China, create a Japanese controlled government in the area, and place its economy under the domination of Japan. The Tribunal found him to have been one of the leaders of the conspiracy set forth in Count 1 and adjudged him guilty under that count.

Araki assumed office as the war minister in December 1931 after the aggressive war in Manchuria began and continued in that capacity until January 1934. During his tenure in office, he took a prominent part in the development and carrying out of the military and political policies pursed in Manchuria and Jehol, and gave all of his support to the steps undertaken by the military for the occupation of these territories of China. During the period he was minister of education, May 1938 until August 1939, he approved of and collaborated in military operations in other parts of China. The Tribunal ruled that the war in China from 1931 onwards to be a war of aggression and that Araki participated in the waging of that war. Accordingly, the tribunal found the defendant guilty under Count 27.

There was no evidence that Araki took an active part in any of the wars referred to in Counts 29, 31, 32, 33, 35, and 36, therefor, the defendant was found not guilty on all these counts.

The defendant was also found not guilty under Counts 54 and 55 since there was no evidence of his responsibility for any war crimes.

Individual Verdict 02
Accused: Dohihara, Kenji

Dohihara, Kenji was charged under Counts 1, 27, 29, 31, 32, 33, 35, 36, 54, and 55. At the start of the period being reviewed, Dohihara was a colonel in the Japanese Army and attained the rank of general by April 1941. Before the Manchurian affair he had been in China for 18 years and had come to be regarded as a specialist on China within the Japanese Army. He was closely involved in the start and development of the war of aggression waged against China in Manchuria and the subsequent establishment of the Japanese dominated state of Manchukuo. When the aggressive policy of the Japanese military party was pursued in other areas of China, Dohihara took a prominent part in its development by political intrigue and the threat and use of force.

Dohihara acted in close association with other military faction leaders in the development, preparation, and execution of their plans to bring East and South East Asia under influence and domination by Japan. When his special knowledge of China and the intrigue involved were no longer required, he was used as a general officer in the field in pursuit of the aims for which he conspired. He took part in the waging of aggressive war not only against China but also the USSR and those countries against whom Japan waged war from 1941 until 1945 with the exception of the Republic of France. In the war against the USSR from 1938 to 1939, Dohihara was a lieutenant general on the general staff which had overhead control of the Lake Khassan fighting. At Nomonhan elements of the army he commanded took part in the fighting. The decision to wage war against the Republic of France was made by the supreme council for the direction of war in 1945. Dohihara was not a party to that decision and there was no evidence that he took part in the waging of that war.

Dohihara commanded the 7th Area Army from April 1944 to April 1945 which included Malaya, Sumatra, Java, and for a time Borneo. The evidence concerning his responsibility for protection of POWs from murder and torture in his area of command was conflicting. However, he was at least responsible for their supplies of food and medicine. The evidence was clear that they were grossly ill-treated in respect to these supplies with the prisoners being starved and deaths from malnutrition and food deficiency diseases occurring at an alarming rate. These conditions pertained only to the prisoners and did not occur among their captors.

Evidence was presented that adequate supplies of food and medicine were available which could have been used to relieve the terrible conditions under which the prisoners were forced to exist but that these supplies were withheld under a policy for which Dohihara was responsible.

Dohihara was found guilty of conspiracy to wage wars of aggression under Count 1 and for waging aggressive wars under Counts 27, 29, 31, 32, 35, and 36. He was found not guilty under Count 33. Dohihara was also found guilty under Count 54 ordering, authorizing and permitting the commission of conventional war crimes but there was no decision made under Count 55 failure to take adequate steps in respect to prisoners of war and civilian internees.

Individual Verdict 03
Accused: Hashimoto, Kingoro

Hashimoto, was indicted under Counts 1, 27, 29, 31, 32, 54, and 55. As an Army officer he joined the conspiracy early and thereafter furthered the achievement of its objectives by all means in his power. None of the conspirators held more extreme views than he did, nor was anyone more outspoken in the statement of his views. At first he only backed the proposal for the expansion of Japan by the force of arms seizure of Manchuria. Later, as time passed, he advocated the use of force against all of Japan's neighbors for the accomplishment of the conspirators' aims.

Hashimoto was an ardent admirer of a military dictatorship form of government. He hated the political parties which, as part of the Japanese government, opposed the conspirators' schemes of conquest. He was one of the principal figures in many of the activities by which the conspirators ultimately come to suppress the opposing democratic elements in Japan and gained control of the government. Without this control of the government the conspirators aggressive schemes could not have been accomplished. He was involved in the plots of March and October 1931, the aims of which were to overthrow the existing cabinets and establish new cabinets which would support the conspirators. He was also a party to the plot of May 1932 that resulted in the assassination of Premier Inukai who had been a champion of democracy and opposed the conspirators policies. Hashimoto participated in planning of the Mukden Incident so as to give the Army a pretext for seizing Manchuria. He claimed some credit for the Manchurian seizure and for Japan leaving the League of Nations.

Subsequently, Hashimoto figured in the execution of the conspiracy mainly as a propagandist. He was a prolific publicist and contributed to the success of the conspiracy by inciting the appetite of the Japanese people for the possessions of their neighbors; inflaming Japanese opinion for war to secure these possessions; his advocacy of an alliance with Germany and Italy which were bent on similar schemes of expansion; his denunciation of treaties by which Japan had bound itself to refrain from the schemes of aggrandizement which were the aims of the conspiracy; his fervent support of the agitation for a great increase in Japanese armaments so that he might secure these aims by force or the threat of force.

Hashimoto was found guilty under Count 1 since the evidence showed that he was a principal in the formation of the conspiracy and contributed largely to its execution. He was found guilty also under Count 27 since he first plotted for the seizure of Manchuria by force of arms and later did everything in his power to secure a successful conclusion of the war with China.

The Tribunal ruled that there was no evidence which directly connected Hashimoto with any of the crimes charged in Counts 29, 31, 32, 54, or 55 and he was found not guilty under these counts.

Individual Verdict 04
Accused: Hata, Shunroko

Hata, Shunroko was charged under Counts 1, 27, 29, 31, 32, 35, 36, 54, and 55. In August 1939, Hata became the war minister with the formation of the Abe cabinet, a position which he held continuously regardless of the cabinet structure until July 1940 when the Yonai cabinet fell. He contributed substantially in the formation and execution of aggressive war plans since as war minister he exerted considerable influence on government policy. During this period the war in China was waged with renewed vigor, the Wang Ching Wei government was established at Nanking, plans for the control of French Indo-China were developed, and further negotiations with the Netherlands were conducted pertaining to matters concerning the Netherlands East Indies. Japanese domination in East Asia and the areas to the South was favored by Hata. To help achieve this objective he approved the abolition of political parties be replaced by the Imperial Rule Assistance Association and precipitated the fall of the Yonai cabinet in collaboration with other high military authorities thereby allowing the full alliance with Germany and the establishment of a virtual totalitarian state in Japan.

Hata as commander-in-chief of the expeditionary forces in China from March 1941 continued to wage war in that country until November 1944. Later as inspector general of military education, one of the highest active military posts in the Japanese Army, he continued to wage war against China and the western powers.

Hata was in central China when the Lake Khassan hostilities occurred and at the time of the Nomonhan Incident, he was the aide-de-camp to the Emperor. The Tribunal was of the opinion that he did not participate actively in either of these wars.

Hata was in command of expeditionary forces in China in 1938 and again from 1941 to 1944. During both of these periods of time, troops from units under his command were responsible for the commission of atrocities on a large scale spread over the entire time periods. Hata either knew of these atrocities and took no steps to prevent their occurrence, or he was indifferent toward their commission and made no provision to learn whether the orders for the humane treatment of POWs and civilians were being obeyed.

The Tribunal ruled that in either case he was in breach of his duty as charged under Count 55.

The Tribunal found Hata guilty under Counts 1, 27, 29, 31, 32, and 55. He was found not guilty under Counts 35, 36, and 54.

Individual Verdict 05
Accused: Hiranuma, Kiichiro

Hiranuma, Kiichiro was indicted under Counts 1, 27, 29, 31, 32, 33, 35, 36, 54, and 55. He became a member of the conspiracy if not at the beginning then shortly thereafter. He was a member of the privy council from 1936 and subsequently served as president of the council until 1939, when he became the prime minister. Later he served in succession as a minister without portfolio and the home minister in the second and third Konoye cabinets. As a member of the privy council, Hiranuma supported the various measures coming before that body which involved the carrying out of the aggressive plans of the militarists. He continued to support these plans when he was prime minister and later as a cabinet minister. From 17 October 1941, he was of the opinion that such a war was inevitable and advocated the strengthening of public opinion against the possibility of a long war. At the meeting of the senior statesmen held on 5 April 1945, he advised against and strongly opposed any overtures for peace and he advised that Japan should fight to the end.

At all times covered by the indictment Hiranuma was

not only an ardent supporter of the policy of the domination of East Asia and the South Seas by force if necessary, but was one of the leaders of the conspiracy and an active participant in the furthering of that policy. In the carrying out of that policy Hiranuma waged war against China, the United States of America, the British Commonwealth of Nations, the Netherlands, and in 1939 against the USSR. The Tribunal found Hiranuma guilty on Counts 1, 27, 29, 31, 32, and 36.

No evidence was presented during the trial which showed there to be a direct connection between Hiranuma and the crimes charged under Counts 33, 35, 54, and 55. The Tribunal therefore found Hiranuma not guilty under these counts.

Individual Verdict 06
Accused: Hirota, Koki

Hirota, Koki was indicted under Counts 1, 27, 29, 31, 32, 33, 35, 54, and 55. Hirota was foreign minister from 1933 until March 1936 when he became prime minister. After his cabinet fell in February 1937, he held no public office for four months until he again became foreign minister in the first Konoye cabinet. He held this position until May 1938, after which, his relation to public affairs was limited to attending senior statesmen meetings from time to time to advise on prime minister appointments and other important matters.

While Hirota held these high offices from 1933 to 1938, Japanese gains in Manchuria were being consolidated and turned to Japan's advantage. The political and economic life of North China was being guided in order to separate it from the rest of China in preparation for its domination by Japan.

In 1936 Hirota's cabinet formulated and adopted the national policy of expansion in East Asia and the Southern Areas. This policy had a far reaching effect and was to eventually lead to the war between Japan and the western powers in 1941. Also the aggressive policy of Japan with regard to the USSR was reiterated in 1936 and advanced so that it culminated in the Anti-Comintern Pact.

When the war in China was revived on 7 July 1937, throughout Hirota's remaining tenure in public office, the cabinet provided full support for military operations in China. Early in 1938 the real policy towards China was also clarified with every effort being made to subjugate China, abolish the Chinese national government, and replace it with a government dominated by Japan. In early 1938 the plan for mobilization of manpower, industrial potential, and natural resources was adopted. Legislation for accomplishment of this plan was also provided at that time. With little change in essentials, this plan was the basis on which the preparation for continuing the China War and waging aggressive wars were carried out during succeeding years. Hirota knew fully of all these activities and plans and supported them. Hirota, while an apparently very able man and forceful leader, was at times during his tenure of office the originator and at other times a supporter of the many aggressive plans adopted and executed by the military and various Japanese cabinets.

Defense counsel for Hirota during its final argument urged the Tribunal to consider the defendant's consistent advocacy for the resolution of all disputed questions through peaceful/diplomatic negotiation. The Tribunal agreed that Hirota, faithful to his diplomatic training, had consistently advocated attempts to first settle disputes through diplomatic channels. However, it was also abundantly clear that in so doing he was never willing to sacrifice any of the gains, real or expected, made at the expense of Japan's negotiations failed to obtain fulfillment of the Japanese demands. The Tribunal for this reason did not agree with the defense provided on this subject.

The Tribunal consequently found that Hirota, at least from 1933, participated in the common plan or conspiracy to wage aggressive wars. As foreign minister he also participated in the waging of war against China.

As pertains to Counts 29, 31, and 32, of the indictment, Hirota held no public office after 1938, his attitude and advise as a senior statesmen in 1941 was consistent with his being opposed to the start of hostilities against the Allied powers, and played no part in the direction of the wars covered by these counts, the Tribunal found him not guilty on these counts.

No proof was presented that established Hirota's participation in or support of the military operations at Lake Kassen of French Indo-China on 1945 and the Tribunal found him not guilty under Counts 33 and 35.

No evidence was presented of Hirota's having ordered, authorized or permitted the commission of any war crimes as alleged under Count 54 and the Tribunal found him not guilty under this count.

As to Count 55, the only evidence relating Hirota to such crimes deals with the atrocities at Nanking in December 1937 to February 1938. Hirota as foreign minister received reports of these atrocities immediately after Japanese forces entered Nanking. According to defense evidence credence was given to these reports. The war ministry, when questioned, assured the foreign ministry that these atrocities would cease. Reports of more atrocities came in for at least a month afterward. The Tribunal was of the opinion that Hirota was derelict in his duty in not insisting before the cabinet that immediate action be taken to put an end to the atrocities or, failing that, any other action open to him to bring about the desired result. He was content to depend on assurances he knew were unreliable while hundreds of murders, violations of women, and other atrocities were being committed daily. The Tribunal ruled that his inaction amounted to criminal negligence and found him guilty under Count 55.

Individual Verdict 07
Accused: Hoshino, Naoki

Hoshino, Naoki was charged under Counts 1, 27, 29, 31, 32, 33, 35, 54, and 55.

Hoshino was employed in the Japanese department of finance until he went to Manchuria in 1932. He was sent to Manchuria by his government to become a senior official of the Manchukuo finance ministry and of the Manchukuo General Affairs Bureau. He was able to exercise profound influence on the economy of Manchukuo in these positions and did exert that influence toward domination by the Japanese of the commercial and industrial development of that country. His duties required that he function in close cooperation with the commander of the Kwantung Army who was the virtual ruler of Manchukuo. Hosino was in effect, if not in name, a functionary of that Army whose economic policy was directed toward making the resources of Manchukuo serve the warlike purposes of Japan.

Although he had been a nominal servant of the government of Manchukuo for eight years, Hosino was recalled to

Japan in 1940 where he became a minister without portfolio and president of the planning board. In this position he became the leader of the special steps that were then being taken to equip Japan not only for the continuous progression of their aggressive war that was being waged in China but also for their aggressive wars contemplated against other countries with possessions in East Asia.

From April 1941 when Hosino left the cabinet, his official functions in connection with Japan's warlike preparations were reduced but not entirely abandoned. Upon the appointment of Tojo as prime minister in October 1941, Hosino became chief secretary of the cabinet and shortly thereafter a counselor of the planning board. From that time on he was in close association with all the preparations for the aggressive war that had already been determined upon and would shortly be waged against those countries attacked by Japan in December 1941.

Throughout the period from 1932 till 1941 Hosino was an active and energetic member of the conspiracy under Count 1 of the indictment and the Tribunal found him guilty under that count.

Not only was Hosino found guilty in the conspiracy for the waging of aggressive war but he directly participated in the waging of aggressive wars as set forth in Counts 27, 29, 31, and 32 through his actions in successive official positions and the Tribunal found him guilty under these counts.

Evidence did not prove that Hosino participated in the wars charged in Counts 33 and 35 and the Tribunal found him not guilty under these counts.

None of the evidence presented connected Hosino with any of the crimes charged in Counts 54 and 55 and the Tribunal found him not guilty on these counts.

Individual Verdict 08
Accused: Itagaki, Seishiro

Itagaki, Seishiro was charged under Counts 1, 27, 29, 31, 32, 33, 35, 36, 54, and 55.

Itagaki was a colonel on the staff of the Kwantung Army by 1931 and had already joined the conspiracy whose immediate objective was that Japan should seize Manchuria by force of arms. He promoted the agitation in support of this aim, helped in the engineering of the so-called "Mukden incident" as a pretext for military action, suppressed several attempts to prevent the military action, and authorized and directed the action.

The next principal part that Itagaki played in the intrigues was the fostering of the sham movement for the independence of Manchuria which resulted in the establishment of the puppet state of Manchukuo.

In December 1934 he became vice-chief of staff of the Kwantung Army and was active thereafter in the establishment of puppet regimes in Inner Mongolia and North China. He also wanted the extension of the Japanese military occupation into Outer Mongolia to serve as a threat to USSR territories. He was an originator of the phrase "Anti-Communism" who was eager for it to serve as a pretext for further Japanese aggression in North China.

Itagaki was sent from Japan to China when fighting commenced at the Marco Polo Bridge in July 1937 where he took part in the fighting as a division commander. During this period he again favored expansion in the area by increased aggressive military action.

In May 1938 he became minister of war in the Konoye cabinet where, under his authority and direction the attacks on China were extended and intensified. He was involved in important ministerial conferences which decided to try to destroy the National Government of China and to establish a puppet regime in its stead. He was therefore largely responsible for preliminary arrangements to establish the puppet regime headed by Wang Ching-Wei. He also took part in the arrangements for the exploitation of the occupied areas of China for the benefit of Japan.

In the Hiranuma cabinet, as the minister of war, Itagaki was again responsible for the prosecution of the war against China, the expansion of Japan's armaments, and was a strong advocate in the cabinet for an unrestricted military alliance between Japan, Germany, and Italy.

During his tenure as war minister he attempted by means of a trick to obtain the Emperor's consent for the use of force against the USSR at Lake Khassan. Subsequently he was given the authority for use of such force at a Five Ministers Conference. He was still the war minister during the fighting at Nomonhan.

Itagaki was a strong supporter for the declaration of the Japanese so-called "New Order" in East Asia and the South Seas. He realized that by the creation of this "New Order" it would inevitably lead to war with the USSR, France, and Great Britain who would defend their possessions in these areas.

He carried on the war against China as the chief of staff of the China Expeditionary Army from September 1939 to July 1941. From July 1941 to April 1945, he was commander-in-chief of the Army in Korea. From April 1945 he commanded the 7th Area Army until the date of the surrender. The 7th Area Army had its Headquarters in Singapore and its subordinate armies defended Java, Sumatra, Malaya, the Andaman and Nicobar Islands, and Borneo.

The Tribunal found Itagaki guilty in Counts 1, 27, 29, 31, 32, 35, and 36 for having conspired to wage wars of aggression against China, the United States of America, the British Commonwealth, the Netherlands, and the USSR and for having taken an active and important part in the waging of these wars which he knew were wars of aggression. He was found not guilty on Count 33.

Many thousands of prisoners of war and internees were held in camps in the area administered by the 7th Area Army which Itagaki commanded starting in April 1945. Although these camps, except for the ones in the Singapore area, were not under his direct command, he was responsible for their supply of food, medicine, and medical facilities. Conditions in these camps during this period were unspeakably bad. Deficiency diseases were rampant and many people died every day due to the grossly inadequate supplies. Those who survived until the date of the surrender were found to be in a pitiable condition. No such conditions prevailed among the guards when the camps were visited after the surrender.

Itagaki's excuse for the atrocious treatment of the POWs and internees was that Allied attacks on Japanese shipping had made the transportation of supplies to these areas very difficult and that he had done the best that he could with the supplies he had. However, after the surrender, supplies of food and medicine were made available by Itagaki's Army to the camps in Singapore, Borneo, Java, and Sumatra. The explanation tendered in evidence on behalf of Itagaki was that the Japanese were expecting a long war and were conserving supplies. This amounted to a contention that Itagaki was justified under the prevailing circumstances in treating the prisoners and internees with gross inhumanity. The Tribunal had no hesitation in rejecting this defense. If Itagaki, being responsible to insure that the supplies for the POWs and internees were provided, found himself unable to maintain them for the future, his duty under the laws of war was to distribute such supplies as he had in hand. He would also have to inform his superiors that arrangements must be made, with the Allies if necessary, for the support of the camps in the future. By adhering to the policy which he had adopted, Itagaki was responsible for the deaths and/or sufferings of thousands of people whose adequate maintenance were his duty.

The Tribunal found Itagaki guilty under Count 54 and made no finding under Count 55 the same as in the case of Dohihara.

Individual Verdict 09
Accused: Kaya, Okinari

Kaya, Okinari was charged under Counts 1, 27, 29, 31, 32, 54, and 55. Unlike most of the defendants who were military personnel, Kaya was a civilian.

During the period covered by the indictment, Kaya held the following positions in the Japanese government :

1936–counselor of the Manchurian Affairs Bureau

February to June 1937–vice minister of finance

June 1937 to May 1938–finance minister in the first Konoye cabinet

July 1938–adviser to the finance ministry

July 1939–member of the Asia development committee

August 1939 to October 1941– president of the North China Development Company

October 1941 to February 1944–finance minister in the Tojo cabinet

February 1944–adviser to the finance ministry

Evidence showed that in these positions, Kaya took part in the formulation of the aggressive policies of Japan, and the preparation of Japan, financially, economically, and industrially for the execution of these policies. Throughout this period, particularly as the finance minister in both the first Konkye and Tojo cabinets, and as president of the North China Development Company, he was actively engaged in the preparation for and carrying out the aggressive war in China and against the western powers.

The Tribunal determined that Kaya had been an active member of the conspiracy and found him guilty under Count 1 of the indictment.

The Tribunal also determined that Kaya, by virtue of his actions in the various positions held by him, was a principal in the waging of aggressive wars and found him guilty under Counts 27, 29, 31, and 32.

The Tribunal ruled that the evidence presented during the trial did not disclose any responsibility for war crimes by Kaya and he was found not guilty under Counts 54 and 55.

Individual Verdict 10
Accused: Kido, Koichi

Kido, Koichi was charged under Counts 1, 27, 29, 31, 32, 33, 35, 36, 54, and 55.

Kido was a member of the Emperor's household in the position of chief secretary to the lord keeper of the privy seal from 1930 to 1936. Being in this position, he was aware of the true actual military and political adventures into Manchuria. However, since the conspiracy was instituted by the military and their supporters, Kido was not associated with the conspiracy at that time.

Kido joined the first Konoye cabinet in 1937 as education minister and for a period he was also welfare minister. In 1939 when Hiranuma became prime minister, Kido continued as a member of the cabinet until August 1939 with the portfolio of home affairs. During the period from 1937 to 1939 Kido adopted the conspirators' views and devoted himself to this policy wholeheartedly. The war in China had entered its second phase and Kido was zealous in pursuit of that war, even resisting the efforts of the general staff to shorten the war by making terms with China. He was intent on Japan's complete military and political domination of China.

Kido not only supported the conspirators plans in China but as education minister he applied himself to the development of a strong warlike spirit in Japan.

Between the time Kido left the cabinet in August 1939 and the time he was appointed lord keeper of the privy seal in June 1940 he was active with Konoye in developing a system to replace existing political parties with a single party. Konoye was to be the president and Kido the vice president of this party. The one party system was expected to give Japan a totalitarian system and the removal of any political resistance to the plans of the conspirators.

In his position as lord keeper of the privy seal, Kido was placed in an especially advantageous position to advance the cause of the conspiracy. He could exert great influence since his principal duty was to advise the Emperor. He used the influence of his position to further the aims of the conspiracy involving the complete domination of China and the whole of East Asia as well as the areas to the south.

As time for the commencement of war against the western powers neared, Kido displayed a degree of hesitation because of doubts for complete success within the Navy. He was still determined to pursue the war in China and with some timidity and less confidence approved the projected war against Great Britain, the Netherlands and if necessary the United States of America. When the Navy's doubts were overcome Kido resumed full pursuit of the conspiracy's purposes and was largely instrumental in securing the office of prime minster for Tojo, a determined advocate of immediate war with the western powers. Kido used his position not only to provide support for such a war but he also purposely refrained from taking any action which might have prevented it by failing to advise the Emperor to take any stand against the war.

The prosecution did not provide any evidence to prove Kido's guilt for the wars under Counts 33, 35, and 36.

In the matter of war crimes Kido was a member of the Cabinet at the time the atrocities were committed in Nanking and the evidence was not sufficient to find him responsible for failure to prevent them. Kido's position during the war against the western powers from 1941 onward was such that no responsibility could be found against him for atrocities committed.

The Tribunal found Kido guilty under Counts 1, 27, 29, 31, and 32, and not guilty under Counts 33, 35, 36. 54, and 55.

Individual Verdict 11
Accused: Kimura, Heitaro

Kimura, Heitaro was indicted under Counts 1, 27, 29, 31, 32, 54, and 55.

Kimura during most of the period under consideration by the Tribunal was an army officer engaged in administrative work in the war ministry ending with his being appointed vice minister of war in April 1941. Subsequently he was appointed counselor of the planning board and counselor of the Total War Research Institute. He was relieved of his post of Vice War Minister in March 1943 and was appointed the Burma Area Army commander-in-chief in August 1944, a post which he held until the surrender of Japan in 1945.

During his tenure as vice minister where he was in almost daily contact with the war minister, other ministers and vice ministers, and bureau chiefs, he was in a position to learn about and was kept fully informed of all government decisions and actions concerning the crucial negotiations with the United States of America. He had full knowledge of the hostilities in China and the plans and preparations for the Pacific War. He collaborated and cooperated with the war minister and other ministries giving advice based on his wide experience, while he provided his wholehearted support for the aggressive plans.

Although he was not a leader, Kimura took part in the formulation and development of policies which he either initiated himself or were prepared by the general staff or other persons and that he approved or supported. He was thus a valuable collaborator or accomplice in the conspiracy to wage aggressive wars.

Kimura played a prominent part in the conduct not only of the war in China but also in the Pacific War in his positions as a division commander in 1939 and 1940, then as chief-of-staff of the Kwantung Army, and later as vice war minister as well as being one of the conspirators. He possessed full knowledge of the Pacific War when he took command of the Burma Area Army in August 1944.

Kimura was an active party to breaches of the rules of war. He approved the use of prisoners in many instances to do work that was prohibited by the rules and/or in work under conditions which resulted in the greatest hardship and the deaths of thousands of these prisoners. The Tribunal cited as an example the use of prisoners in construction of the Burma-Siam Railway, the order for which were approved and passed on by Kimura.

Prior to taking command of the Burma Area Army in 1944, Kimura had full knowledge of the extent of the atrocities that had been committed and were still being committed by Japanese troops in all theaters of the war. After his arrival at his Rangoon headquarters and later when his headquarters were moved the atrocities continued at an undiminished rate and he did not take any disciplinary measures or other steps to prevent the commission of atrocities by troops under his command.

Kimura in his own defense stated that when he arrived in Burma he issued orders to his troops that they should conduct themselves in a proper soldierly manner and to refrain from the ill treatment of the prisoners. The Tribunal found that that in view of the nature and extent of the ill treatment of prisoners, in many cases on such a large scale within a few miles of his headquarters, Kimura was negligent in his duty to enforce the rules of war. The mere issuance of routine orders, if indeed such orders were issued, does not discharge the duty of an army commander in such circumstances. His duty is to issue such orders and take such steps necessary to satisfy himself that his orders are being carried out. This Kimura did not do and he thus deliberately disregarded his legal duty to take adequate steps to prevent breaches of the laws of war.

The Tribunal found Kimura guilty on all counts under which he had been indicted; Counts 1, 27, 29, 31, 32, 54, and 55.

Individual Verdict 12
Accused: Koiso, Kuniaki

Koiso, Kuniaki was charged under Counts 1, 27, 29, 31, 32, 36, 54, and 55.

Koiso became a member of the conspiracy in 1931 by participating as one of the leaders of the "March incident" the aim of which was to oust the Hamaguchi government and install a new government that would be favorable to the occupation of Manchuria.

From August 1932 until March 1934, as chief-of-staff of the Kwantung Army, Koiso prepared or concurred in proposals and plans for the political and economic organization of Manchukuo in full accordance with the conspirator's policy to be submitted to the government through the war ministry. His defense argued that in forwarding of these plans and proposals to Tokyo he did so only because that was part of his duties as chief-of-staff and that by performing such action it did not necessarily reflect his personal approval. The Tribunal was of the opinion that in view of his knowledge of the aggressive plans of Japan he went beyond the normal duties of his position as chief-of-staff in advising on political and economic matters to further these plans.

During his tenure as chief-of-staff of the Kwantung Army there was also the military invasion of Jehol and renewed fighting in Manchuria.

Later in his position as overseas minister in the Hiranuma and Yonai cabinets, Koiso supported and took part in the direction of the war in China, the beginning of the occupation of French Indo-China, and the start of negotiations intended to obtain concessions from and eventually the economic domination of the Netherlands East Indies. During this same period he also advocated the plan for Japan to advance in all directions.

Koiso was recalled from his post as governor of Korea in July 1944 to become prime minister. In this capacity he urged and directed the waging of the war against the western powers. In April 1945 he retired as prime minister when it became clear that Japan would lose the war to make way for the Suzuki cabinet.

There was no evidence that Koiso had played any part in the hostilities at Nomonhan by either organizing or directing them.

The Tribunal was of the opinion that when Koiso became prime minister in 1944 the knowledge of the commission of atrocities and other war crimes had become so widely known that it would have been improbable that a person in his position would not have been well informed of them either by reason of their notoriety or from their being referenced in inter departmental communications. They also found that the matter was placed beyond all doubt by the presentation of the foreign minister to a meeting of the supreme council for the direction of the war, which Koiso attended, that according to recent information from enemy sources it was reported that Japanese treatment of POWs left much to be desired. The foreign minister further stated that this was a matter of importance for Japan's international reputation and future relations and he asked that directions be issued to competent authorities so that this matter could be fully discussed.

Koiso remained in office as prime minister for six months during which time the treatment of prisoners and internees by the Japanese showed no improvement whatsoever. The Tribunal felt that this amounted to a deliberate disregard of his duty.

The Tribunal found Koiso guilty under Counts 1, 27, 29, 31, 32, and 55 but not guilty under Counts 36 and 54.

Individual Verdict 13
Accused: Matsui, Iwane

Matsui, Iwane was charged under Counts 1, 27, 29, 31, 32, 35, 36, 54, and 55.

Matsui was a senior officer in the Japanese Army who attained the rank of general in 1933. His wide experience included service in the Kwantung Army and on the general staff. Although it would be presumed that due to this close association with those persons who conceived and carried out the conspiracy he must have been aware of the purposes and policies of the conspirators, evidence presented to the Tribunal did not justify a finding that he was indeed a conspirator.

Matsui's military service in China in 1937 and 1938 could not be regarded, of itself, as an indication of the waging of an aggressive war. To justify a conviction under Count 27 it was the prosecution's duty to present evidence which would provide an inference that Matsui had knowledge of the criminal character of that war. This was not accomplished by the prosecution.

Matsui was placed on the retired list in 1935 but he was recalled to active duty in 1937 to command the Shanghai Expeditionary Army. Subsequently he was appointed commander-in-chief of the Central China Army, which included both the Shanghai Expeditionary Army and the Tenth Army.

Forces under his command captured the city of Nanking on 13 December 1937. Japanese occupation of Nanking was that of a defenseless city since the Chinese forces had withdrawn before the city was captured. A long succession of horrible atrocities were committed by the Japanese Army on the helpless citizens of Nanking after the city's fall with many individual murders, wholesale massacres, rapes, looting, and arson being committed by Japanese soldiers. Denial of the extent of these atrocities was given by Japanese witnesses but contrary evidence provided by neutral witnesses of different nationalities was overwhelming. This orgy of crime started immediately after the capture of the city and did not cease until early February 1938, a period of several weeks. Thousands of women were raped, upward of 100,000 people were killed, and an untold amount of property was stolen and/or burned during this period.

Matsui made a triumphal entry into the city of Nanking on 17 December and remained there for five to seven days. He must have been aware of what was happening based upon his own observations and on the reports from his staff. He admitted to being informed by the Kempeitai and consular officials of some degree of misbehavior by members of his Army. Daily reports concerning the atrocities in Nanking were made to Japanese diplomatic personal in the city who in turn reported them to Tokyo. The Tribunal was satisfied that Matsui knew what was happening in the city and that he did nothing, or nothing that was effective to abate these horror's. He did issue orders both prior to and after the capture of the city enjoining propriety of conduct on his troops but these orders were not effective. The defense pleaded that Matsui was ill at that time but his illness did not prevent him from conducting the military operations of his command nor from his visiting the city for days while the atrocities were happening. Matsui as the commander of the Army responsible for these happenings had the power as well as the duty to control his troops and to protect the citizens of the City of Nanking. The Tribunal decided that Matsui must be held criminally responsible for his failure to discharge this duty.

The Tribunal found Matsui guilty under Count 55 and not guilty under Counts 1, 27, 29, 31, 32, 35, 36, and 54.

Individual Verdict 14
Accused: Minami, Jiro

Minami, Jiro was charged under Counts 1, 27, 29, 31, 32, 54, and 55.

In the year 1931 Minami was already a general and from April to December of that year he was the minister of war. He had aliened himself with the conspirators prior to the Mukden Incident in their advocacy of militarism, the expansion of Japan, and the concept that Manchuria was 'the lifeline of Japan.' Having been forewarned of the likelihood of the incident occurring, Minami was ordered to prevent it from happening but he did not take adequate steps to prevent it. He described the Army's action as being "righteous self-defense" when the incident must not be expanded into effect but day after day the area of operations became larger and he did not take adequate steps to restrain the Army. Minami had previously advocated Japan's withdrawal from the league of Nations if they opposed the actions of Japan in China. He knew that the Army was taking steps for the occupation of Manchuria and the establishment of a military administration in the area. Even though the Cabinet had decided this should not happen, Minami did nothing to stop it. His failure to take steps to control the Army and support the premier and foreign minister led to the cabinet's downfall. Afterward he supported the concept that the defense of Manchuria and Mongolia should be accomplished by Japan.

Minami became the commander in chief of the Kwantung Army in December 1934 and remained in this position until March 1936. It was during this period that his Army completed the conquest of Manchuria and he aided in the exploitation of that part of China for the benefit of Japan. Under threat of the use of further military action he was responsible for the establishment of puppet government in North China and Inner Mongolia.

He was partly responsible for the development of Manchuria as a base for an attack on the USSR and the plans for such an attack.

Minami was appointed governor-general of Korea in 1936. In 1938 he supported the continuing war against China which he called "the Holy War" and the destruction of the National Government of China.

The Tribunal found Minami guilty under Counts 1 and 27 but not guilty of the charges contained in Counts 29, 31, 32, 54, and 55.

Individual Verdict 15
Accused: Muto, Akira

Muto, Akira was indicted under Counts 1, 27, 29, 31, 32, 33, 36, 54, and 55.

Muto was a soldier and prior to his holding the important position of chief of Military Affairs Bureau in the ministry of war he was not in a position, alone or with other, to make high government policy. When he assumed the position of chief of the Military Affairs Bureau he joined the conspiracy. From September 1939 until April 1942 Muto held numerous other posts concurrently with his primary position. Muto was an active participant in all of the activities involved with the planning and preparation for and the waging of wars of aggression on the part of the conspirators during this period.

When he became chief of the Military Affairs Bureau the fighting at Nomonhan was finished and Muto had no part in that war.

Muto was chief-of-staff in the Philippines when Japan attacked France in French Indo-China during March 1945 and he had no part in the waging of that war.

Muto was an officer on Matsui's staff from November 1937 until July 1938 and it was during this period that the atrocities in and around Nanking were committed by Matsui's Army. The Tribunal decided that Muto knew about the atrocities but being that he was serving in a subordinate position so that he could take no steps to stop them and that he could not be held responsible for their commission.

Muto commanded the second Imperial Guards Division in Northern Sumatra from April 1942 until October 1944. Widespread atrocities were committed in the area occupied by his troops during this period. POWs and civilian internees were being starved, neglected, tortured, and murdered and many civilians were being massacred. Muto, as the commander, must share the in responsibility for the commission of these atrocities.

In October 1944 Muto became chief-of-staff to Yamashita in the Philippines and he held that post until the Surrender. This position was now different from that which he held during the so-called "Rape of Nanking" since he was now in a position where he could influence policy. During his tenure of office a campaign of massacre, torture, and other atrocities were committed by Japanese troops on the civilian population and POWs and civilian internees were starved, tortured and murdered. The Tribunal ruled that Muto must share in the responsibility for these gross breaches of the laws of war and they rejected his defense that he knew nothing of their occurrence.

The Tribunal found Muto guilty under Counts 1, 27, 29, 31, 32, 54, and 55 but not guilty under Counts 33, and 36.

Individual Verdict 16
Accused: Oka, Takasumi

Oka, Takasumi was charged under Counts 1, 27, 29, 31, 32, 54, and 55 of the indictment.

Oka was a Japanese Naval officer who was appointed chief of the Naval Affairs Bureau in the Navy ministry. During his tenure in this position until July 1944, Oka was an active member of the conspiracy. In his official capacity he was an influential member of the liaison conference where the policy of Japan was largely decided. The Tribunal ruled that he participated in the formation and execution of the Japanese policy to wage aggressive war against China and the western powers.

There was some evidence which tended to show that Oka knew or that he should have known that war crimes were being committed by naval personal against POWs with whose welfare his department was concerned. However, this evidence fell short of the standard of proof required in criminal cases to justify conviction.

The Tribunal found Oka guilty under Counts 1, 27, 29, 31, and 32 but not guilty under Counts 54 and 55.

Individual Verdict 17
Accused: Oshima, Hiroshi

Oshima, Hiroshi was charged under Counts 1, 27, 29, 31, 32, 54, and 55 of the indictment.

Oshima was an Army officer but he was engaged in the diplomatic field. First he held the post of military attaché at the Japanese Embassy in Berlin where later he was appointed to the post of ambassador. Holding no diplomatic post for about one year from 1939 he returned to Berlin as Ambassador where he remained until the Surrender of Japan.

Oshima was a believer in the success of the Hitler Regime and he exerted his full efforts toward the advancement of the plans of the Japanese Military. There were times when he went over the head of Ambassador Oshima and dealt directly with German Foreign Minister Ribbontrop in an attempt to involve Japan in a full military alliance with Germany. Upon being appointed ambassador he continued his efforts to force acceptance by Japan of a treaty which would have aligned his country with Germany and Italy against the western powers thereby opening the way to put into execution the Hirota policy. He frequently pursued a policy which was in opposition to and in direct contradiction to that of his foreign minister in the furtherance of the Army faction's aggressive plans.

Oshima's schemes were temporarily blocked by the Soviet-German Neutrality Pact. He returned to Tokyo where he supported the proponents of war by articles in newspapers and magazines and closely cooperated with the German ambassador.

Oshima was one of the principal conspirators who supported the aims of the conspiracy consistently. However, he took no part in the direction of the war in China nor the Pacific War. At no time did he hold a post whose duties involving responsibility for any prisoner of war.

In Oshima's defense it was contended that in connection with his activities in Germany he was protected by diplomatic immunity and exempt from prosecution. The Tribunal ruled that diplomatic privilege did not import immunity from legal liability but only exemption from trial by the courts of the state to which the ambassador is accredited. The Tribunal further ruled that this immunity had no relationship to crimes against international law charged before a Tribunal having jurisdiction.

The Tribunal found Oshima guilty under Count 1 and not guilty under Counts 27, 29, 31, 32, 54, and 55.

Individual Verdict 18.
Accused: Sato, Kenyro

Sato, Kenyro was charged under Counts 1, 27, 29, 31, 32, 54, and 55 of the indictment.

Sato was promoted to the rank of lieutenant colonel in 1937. At the time he was a member of the Military Affairs Bureau and in the same year he was appointed an investigator of the planning board. Thereafter he had duties, in addition to those in the Military Affairs Bureau, with other groups which were to a greater or lesser degree connected with Japan's war in China and their contemplated wars with other countries.

In February 1938 the General Mobilization Law was presented by the Konoye cabinet to the Diet and Sato was used to explain the law in addition to making a speech before the Diet in support of the measure.

Sato was appointed chief of the military affairs section in the Military Affairs Bureau in February 1941 and was promoted to the rank of major general in October of that year. He became chief of the Military Affairs Bureau in April 1942 and remained in that post until 1944. This was a position of considerable importance in the Japanese Army. Concurrently with his duties in this position he held a variety of other appointments mostly concerned with other departments of state whose activities he linked with the ministry of war.

Therefore it was not until 1941 that Sato had attained a position which by itself enabled him to influence the making of policy and no evidence was presented that indicated that prior to that date he had been involved in plotting to influence the making of such policy. The crucial question was whether Sato had by that date become aware that Japan's designs were criminal, for after that date he furthered the development and execution of these designs as much as he was able. The Tribunal ruled that this matter was put beyond a reasonable doubt by a speech which Sato delivered in August 1938 where he stated the Army's point of view on the war in China. During this speech he showed complete familiarity with the terms which had never before been revealed to China upon which Japan was prepared to settle that war.

These terms were the abolition of the legitimate government of China; recognition of the puppet state of Manchukuo whose resources had by this time been largely exploited for Japan's benefit; the regimentation of economy of China for Japan's benefit; the stationing of Japanese troops in China to ensure that these illicit gains would not be lost.

Sato also predicted that Japan would go to war with the USSR but that she would select a time when her armaments and production had been expanded.

The Tribunal ruled that by his 1938 speech Sato did not believe that Japanese actions in China had been dictated by the wish to secure protection for Japan's legitimate interests in China as the defense contended but that he knew that the motive for her attacks on China were to seize the wealth of her neighbor.

The Tribunal ruled that from 1941 onward Sato was clearly a member of the conspiracy and that thereafter in important posts in the government and as an Army commander he waged wars of aggression as charged in Counts 27, 29, 31, and 32.

There was no doubt that Sato knew of the protests against the behavior of the Japanese troops since these protests came to his bureau and they were discussed at the bi-weekly meetings of the bureau chiefs in the war ministry. Tojo presided at these meetings and he was the one who decided what action should be taken in regard to these protests. Sato could not, as Tojo's subordinate, initiate preventive action against the decision of his chief.

The Tribunal found Sato guilty under Counts 1, 27, 29, 31, and 32 but not guilty under Counts 54 and 55.

Individual Verdict 19
Accused: Shigemitsu, Mamoru

Shigemitsu, Mamoru was charged under Counts 1, 27, 29, 31, 32, 33, 35, 54, and 55 of the indictment.

In determining if he was a member of the conspiracy, the Tribunal considered Shigemitsu actions during his tenure as the Minister to China in 1931 and 1932, as a counselor of the Board of Manchurian Affairs, as the ambassador to the USSR from 1936 to 1938, as the ambassador to Great Britain from 1938 to 1941, and as the ambassador to China in 1942 and 1943. The Tribunal decided that there was no evidence that he played any part in the making of policy when he was the counselor of the Board of Manchurian Affairs. The Tribunal also ruled that during Shigemitsu's tenures of office as minister and ambassador he never exceeded the functions proper for those offices and that he was not one of the conspirators. He had repeatedly provided advice to the foreign office which was opposed to the policies of the conspirators.

By the time he became foreign minister in 1943, the policy of the conspirators to wage certain wars of aggression had been settled and in the progress of execution and that thereafter there was no further formulation nor development of that policy.

The Tribunal found Shigemitsu not guilty under Count 1 for these reasons.

When Shigemitsu became foreign minister in 1943 Japan was already engaged in the war in the Pacific. He was fully aware that so far as Japan was concerned this was a war of aggression since he had known of the policies of the conspirators which had caused the war and had often advised that they should not be put in effect. As the foreign minister he now played a principal part in the waging of that war until he resigned on April 13, 1945.

The Tribunal found Shigemitsu guilty under Counts 27, 29, 31, 32, and 33 but not guilty under Count 35.

Shigemitsu signed the surrender documents on the battleship *Missouri* as the representative of the Japanese government.

During the period Shigemitsu was foreign minister from April 1943 until April 1945, the protecting powers transmitted numerous protests which it had received from the Allies to the Japanese Foreign Office. These protests were forwarded to the protecting powers by responsible agencies of state and in many cases they were accompanied with a large amount of detail.

The matters involved in these protest were the inhumane treatment of prisoners; refusal to permit the protecting powers to inspect all save a few prisoners' camps; refusal to permit the representatives of the protecting powers to interview prisoners without the presence of a Japanese witness; failure to provide information as to names and location of prisoners.

These protests were dealt with in the foreign ministry, where, if necessary, they were passed to other ministries with requests for information that would enable the foreign minister to reply to them. The large amount of correspondence between the Japanese Foreign Office and the protecting powers would lead a reasonable person to suspect that there must have been a sinister reason for the failure of the Japanese military to supply their foreign office with satisfactory answers to these protests. At the very least, there was a case for an independent inquiry by an agency other than the military whose conduct was in question. Protest after protest went unanswered or were only answered after months of unexplained delays. Many reminders by the protecting powers went unnoticed. Those protests that were answered in all cases contained a denial that there was anything to complain about.

The Tribunal was of the opinion that Shigemitsu knew the treatment of the prisoners was not as it should have been and that he did not take adequate steps to have the matter investigated even though he, as a government member, had overhead responsibility for the welfare of the prisoners. The Tribunal felt that he should have pressed the matter, if necessary to the point of resigning, in order to quit himself of a responsibility he suspected was not being discharged.

No evidence was presented which indicated that Shigemitsu ordered, authorized, or permitted the commission of war crimes or crimes against humanity.

The Tribunal found Shigemitsu not guilty under Count 54 but guilty under Count 55.

In mitigation of the sentence the Tribunal took into account that Shigemitsu was in no way involved in the formulation of the conspiracy; waged no war of aggression until he became foreign minister in 1943, by which time his country was deeply involved in a war which would vitally affect its future; that with regard to war crimes, the military completely controlled Japan while he was foreign minister so that it would have required great resolution for any Japanese to condemn them.

Individual Verdict 20
Accused: Shimada, Shigetaro

Shimada, Shigetaro was charged under Counts 1, 27, 29, 31, 32, 54, and 55.

Prior to October 1941 Shimada had no part in the conspiracy and the only role he had was that of a Naval Officer carrying out his assigned duties. In October 1941 as a senior Naval officer he was eligible for and was appointed as Navy Minister in the Tojo cabinet a position that he held until August 1944. Shimada was also chief of the Navy general staff for a period of six months from February to August 1944.

From the formation of the Tojo cabinet until Japan attacked the western powers on 7 December 1941 Shimada took part in all of the decisions made by the conspirators in planning for and the launching of that attack. The reasons he gave for following this course of conduct were:

That the freezing orders were strangling Japan and that they would gradually have reduced her ability to fight.

That there was an economic and military 'encirclemint' of Japan.

That the United States of America were unsympathetic and unyielding in their negotiations.

That the aid provided to China by the Allies had raised bitter feelings in Japan.

What Shimada's defense failed to state according to the findings of the Tribunal was that the gains that he was determined to fight to retain were gains that Japan had acquired in years of aggressive war.

After war was declared Shimada played a principle part in the waging of that war.

The Tribunal found Shimada guilty under Counts 1, 27, 29, 31, and 32.

Some of the most disgraceful massacres and murders of prisoners were committed by members of the Japanese Navy on islands in the Pacific Ocean and on the survivors of torpedoed ships. Those persons that were immediately responsible for these acts ranged from admirals downward.

The evidence that was presented did not justify the finding that Shimada was responsible for these acts, that he ordered, authorized, or permitted the commission of war crimes of that he knew of then and failed to take action to prevent their commission in the future.

The Tribunal found Shimada not guilty under Counts 54 and 55.

Individual Verdict 21
Accused: Shiratori, Toshio

Shiratori, Toshio was charged under Counts 1, 27, 29, 31, and 32.

Shiratori entered the Japanese diplomatic service in 1914 but he first came into prominence as Chief of the Information Bureau of the Foreign Office, a post that he held from October 1930 until June 1933. It was while he held this position that he justified the seizure of Manchuria by Japan to the world press. Undoubtedly Shiratori was instructed to make that presentation, but it was characteristic of his activities then and afterwards to not be content to perform only those duties that were required of him at the moment. Shiratori had thus early expressed views on matters of policy, which had received consideration in high quarters. He had earlier advocated that Japan should withdraw from the

League of Nations and he supported the establishment of a puppet government in Manchuria. His support of the aims of the conspiracy stem from this period and he continued to support these aims for many years by all means within his power.

Shiratori was appointed minister to Sweden in June 1933 and remained in this position until April 1937. During this period certain of his letters show his views at that time. He was of the opinion that Russian influence should be expelled from the Far East by force, if necessary, and that it should take place prior to Russia becoming too strong to be attacked. He was also of the opinion that those foreign influences which might be thought to be harmful to Japanese interests should by excluded from China. He showed himself to be a wholehearted believer in aggressive war and thought that Japanese diplomats should support the policies of the militarists.

When Shiratori returned to Japan he published articles which advocated a totalitarian form of government for Japan and a policy of expansion for Japan, Germany, and Italy.

In September 1938 when negotiations for an alliance among Japan, Germany, and Italy had commenced Shiratori was appointed ambassador to Rome. During these negotiations he collaborated with Oshima then the ambassador to Berlin, in supporting the conspirators' wishes for a general military alliance between these three nations. He went so far as to refuse to comply with the instructions of the foreign minister, who wished a more limited alliance. Shiratori and Oshima threatened to resign if the wishes of the conspirators were not met.

The negotiations broke down when Japan delayed too long and Germany signed a non-aggression pact with the

USSR. Japanese opinion commonly regarded this German-USSR pact as a breach of the Anti-Comintern Pact. After these negotiations Shiratori returned to Japan where he carried on propaganda which was designed to excuse action by Germany and Italy which he still thought was required to support Japanese expansionist aims.

At one time or another during this time frame he advocated in his propaganda all of the objectives of the conspirators including. Japan should attack China; Japan should attack Russia; Japan should ally herself with Germany and Italy; Japan should take determined action against the western powers; Japan should establish the "New Order"; Japan should take the advantage offered by the European War to advance to the south; Japan should attack Singapore. Shiratori continued with this propaganda while he was an advisor to the foreign office from August 1940. He became ill in April 1941 and resigned his position in July of that year. After resigning from his position he played no important part in events.

The Tribunal found Shiratori guilty under Count 1. Since he had never occupied a position that would justify finding him guilty of waging any war of aggression the Tribunal found him not guilty under Counts 27, 29, 31, and 32.

Individual Verdict 22
Accused: Suzuki, Teiichi

Suzuki, Teiichi was charged under Counts 1, 27, 29, 31, 32, 35, 36, 54, and 55.

Suzuki as a lieutenant colonel in 1932 was a member of the Military Affairs Bureau and was already an active member of the conspiracy. When Premier Inukai was assassinated in May 1932 Suzuki stated that similar acts of violence would occur if new cabinets were organized under political leadership and that he favored the formation of a coalition government. His desire was to gain government support for the schemes of the conspirators against China.

During his service with the Military Affairs Bureau Suzuki insisted that the USSR was the absolute enemy of Japan and he assisted in the preparations then being made to wage aggressive war against that nation.

There was no evidence which indicated that Suzuki participated in the waging of the war against the USSR at Lake Kassan nor that he participated in waging war against the USSR and the Mongolian Peoples Republic at Nomonhan.

Suzuki was promoted to major general in November 1937. He was one of the organizers and the head of the political and administrative division of the Asia development board where he actively fostered the further exploitation of those parts of China occupied by Japan.

When the second Konoye cabinet was formed to complete the military domination of Japan and to further the move to the south, Suzuki became minister without portfolio and one of the counselors of the War Research Institute. Konoye replaced Hoshino with Suzuki as the president of the planning board, a position that Suzuki continued to hold until the fall of the Tojo cabinet on 19 July 1944.

In his functions as president of the planning board and minister without portfolio Suzuki regularly attended the meetings of the liaison conference, the virtual policy making body for Japan. He attended most of the important conferences which led up to the initiation and waging of aggressive wars against the Allied powers where he actively supported the conspiracy.

There was no evidence presented that indicated Suzuki was responsible for or that he allowed others to commit any atrocities.

The Tribunal found Suzuki guilty under Counts 1, 27, 29, 31, and 32, and not guilty under Counts 35, 36, 54, and 55.

Individual Verdict 23
Accused: Togo, Shigetori

Togo, Shigetori was charged under Counts 1, 27, 29, 31, 32, 36, 54, and 55 of the indictment.

Togo's principal association with the crimes he was charged with were as foreign minister in the Tojo cabinet from October 1941 until he resigned in September 1942 and later when he served also as the Foreign Minister in the Suzuki cabinet of 1945. He played no part in public life during the intervening time from his resignation until he was re-appointed.

Togo participated in the planning and preparation for war from the date of his first appointment until the outbreak of the Pacific War by attending meetings and conferences where he concurred in all decisions adopted. He played a leading role in the negotiations with the United States as the foreign minister immediately prior to the start of the war and he lent himself to the furthering of the plans of the proponents for war. After the Pacific War had begun he collaborated with other cabinet members in its conduct as well as the continued waging of the war in China.

In addition to the use of the common defense advanced by most of the accused pertaining to the encirclement and economic strangulation of Japan, Togo pleaded specifically that he joined the Tojo Cabinet only after assurances every effort would be made to bring the negotiations with the United States to a successful conclusion. He further stated that he opposed the Army from the date of his first taking office and was successful in obtaining concessions from them which allowed him to keep the negotiations alive. However, when the negotiations failed and war became inevitable, he continued in office and supported the war rather than resign in protest. He stated that to do anything else would have been cowardly. The tribunal determined that Togo's later actions completely negated this plea however.

Togo resigned in September 1942 in a dispute within the Cabinet that dealt with the treatment of the occupied countries. The Tribunal ruled that they were disposed to judge his action and sincerity in the one case by the same considerations in the other.

The Tribunal also ruled that there was no proof of any criminal act on Togo's part as alleged in Count 36. Togo's only relation to any action covered by that count was that he signed the post war agreement between the USSR and Japan which settled the boundary between Manchuria and Outer Mongolia.

The Tribunal found that Togo appeared to have endeavored to see that the rules of war were observed up to the time of his resignation in 1942. Such protests as came to him were passed on and in several instances remedial measures were taken. Atrocities committed by the Japanese troops had not become so notorious by the time of Togo's resignation as to permit knowledge of them to be imputed to him.

When Togo returned as foreign minister in the spring of 1945, there was then an accumulation of protests which he forwarded to the proper authorities. The Tribunal determined that there was insufficient proof of Togo's neglect of duty in connection with any war crimes.

The Tribunal found Togo guilty under Counts 1, 27, 29, 31, and 32 and not guilty under Counts 36, 54, and 55.

Individual Verdict 24
Accused: Tojo, Hideki

Tojo, Hideki was charged under Counts 1, 27, 29, 31, 32, 33, 36, 54, and 55.

Tojo became the chief-of-staff of the Kwantung Army in June 1937 and was associated afterwards with the conspirator's as a principal in most all of their activities.

Tojo planned and prepared for an attack on the USSR. During his planning for this attack he recommended that a further assault be made on China to relieve the Japanese Army from anxiety about its rear in the projected attack. Thereafter he never at any time abandoned the intention to launch such an attack if a favorable opportunity should occur.

In May 1938 Tojo was recalled from the field to become vice-minister of war. Since he held numerous other posts in addition to that office of the Japanese people and economy for war. He opposed all suggestions at this time for a compromise peace with China. Tojo became the minister of war in July 1940 and thereafter his history was largely that of the successive steps taken by which the conspirators planned for and waged wars of aggression against Japan's neighbors for he was a principal in making the plans for and the waging of the wars. The conspiracy's aims were advocated by him and he furthered their accomplishment by means of his ability, resolution, and persistency.

In October 1941 Tojo became prime minister and held that office until July 1944.

During the periods that Tojo held both positions of war minister and premier he consistently supported the policy of conquering the National Government of China, the development of the resources of China on behalf of Japan, and the retaining of Japanese troops in China to safeguard the results won by Japan in the war against China.

During the negotiations which preceded the 7 December 1941 Japanese attacks Tojo's position was that Japan must secure terms which would preserve for her the benefits gained during her war with China and which would be conducive to the establishment of Japan's domination in East Asia and the southern areas. He threw all of his great influence in support of that policy. The Tribunal was of the opinion that the importance of the leading part that Tojo had in securing the decision to go to war in support of that policy could not be overestimated and that he bore the major responsibility for the criminal attacks by Japan on her neighbors.

On his behalf Tojo defended these attacks by alleging that they were legitimate measures of self-defense. The Tribunal determined that this was totally unfounded.

There was no evidence that Tojo held any official position which would render him responsible for the war in 1939 as charged in Count 36.

The Tribunal found Tojo guilty under Counts 1, 27, 29, 31, 32, and 33 but not guilty under Count 36.

The war ministry of which Tojo was the head was charged with the care of POWs and civilian internees in the theater of war and was responsible for the supply of billets, food, medicine, and hospital facilities for them. He was also the head of the home ministry which had similar duties toward civilian internees within Japan. Above all else he was the head of the government which had overall continuing responsibility for the care of POWs and civilian internees.

The Tribunal ruled that Tojo knew of the barbarous treatment of the POWs and inductees and that no adequate steps were taken by him to punish the offenders nor to prevent the commission of similar offenses in the future. They cited his actions with regard to the Bataan Death March as an example of his attitude toward the captives. He knew of some of the conditions of that March in 1942 and that many prisoners died as a result of these conditions but that he did not call for a report of the incident. He explained that a Japanese Army commander in the field was given a mission in the performance of which he was not subject to specific orders from Tokyo.

The head of the government of Japan thus knowingly and willfully refused to perform the duty which was required of that government in enforcing performance of the laws of war.

The Tribunal also cited as another outstanding example reflecting his culpability in was crimes was when Tojo advised that prisoners of war should be used in the construction of the Burma-Siam Railway which had been designed for strategic purposes. No proper arrangements for the billeting and feeding of the prisoners was made nor for caring for those who became ill in that trying climate. Tojo upon learning of the poor conditions of the prisoners employed on this project sent an officer to investigate. As a result of that investigation the only step taken was the trial of one company commander for the ill treatment of prisoners. Nothing was done to improve these conditions and prisoners continued to be killed off by starvation and deficiency diseases until the end of the project.

Tojo presided over conferences at which statistics relative to the high death rate from malnutrition and other causes in POW camps were discussed. The shocking condition of the prisoners as well as the enormous number of prisoners who died from lack of food and medicine provided conclusive proof that Tojo took no proper steps to care for them.

The Tribunal further referred to the Japanese Army's attitude toward the Chinese POWs. The Japanese government did not recognize the "incident" in China as a war and argued that the rules of war did not apply to that fighting and Chinese captives were not entitled to the status and rights of POWs. Tojo knew of that shocking attitude and did not disapprove of it.

The Tribunal ruled that Tojo was responsible for the instruction that prisoners who did not work should not eat. They had no doubt that his repeated insistence on this policy led in large measure to the sick and wounded being driven to work and to the resultant suffering and death.

It was further ruled that Tojo bore the full responsibility for the measures taken to prevent knowledge of the ill treatment of prisoners from reaching the outside world.

The Tribunal found Tojo guilty under Count 54 but made no ruling under Count 55.

Individual Verdict 25
Accused: Umezu, Yoshijiro

Unezu, Yoshijiro was charged under Counts 1, 27, 29, 31, 32, 36, 54, and 55.

Umezu was an Army officer who while in command of Japanese troops in North China from 1934 to 1936 continued the Japanese aggression in that country against the northern provinces, set up a pro-Japanese local government, and compelled the Chinese in June 1935 to enter into the Ho-Umezu agreement which for a time limited the power of the legitimate government of China.

Umezu was appointed vice-minister of war in March 1936 and remained in that office until May 1938. During this period the National Policy Plans of 1936 and the Plan for Important Industries of 1937 were decided upon. These two plans were Army plans and were one of the prime causes of the Pacific War.

When the Imperial mandate to form a new cabinet was given to General Ugaki in January 1937, Umezu had an important part in the Army's refusal to support Ugaki as Hirota's successor. Ugaki was unable to form his cabinet because of this opposition.

In July 1937 when fighting in China started again at Marco Polo Bridge, Umezu knew of and approved the plans of the conspirators to carry on that war. Umezu as a member of the cabinet planning board as well as many other boards and commissions contributed immeasurably to the formulation of these aggressive plans and to the preparations that were required for the execution of these plans.

In December 1939, Tojo as chief-of-staff of the Kwantung Army, sent to Umezu plans for the preparation for an attack on the USSR. Afterwards Tojo also forwarded plans for the strengthening of the Kwantung Army and installations in Inner Mongolia which he stated were of vital importance both in the preparation for war with the USSR and in connection with the war in China.

From 1939 to 1944 Umezu was commander of the Kwantung Army. During his tenure in this position he continued with steering the economy of Manchukuo to serve the purposes of Japan and plans were made for the occupation of Soviet territories including the military administration of these territories. Officers were sent to occupied areas in the south to study the military administration there with the intention of using this information in the Soviet territories.

Umezu served as chief of the Army general staff from July 1944 until the surrender of Japan. He thereby played a principal part in waging of the wars against China and the Western Powers.

Umezu signed the surrender documents aboard the battleship *Missouri* as the representative of the Japanese military forces.

The Tribunal ruled that the evidence was overwhelming that Umezu was a member of the conspiracy.

With reference to the charges under Count 36 the Tribunal took note of the fact that the fighting at Nomonhan had begun before Umezu took command of the Kwantung Army and that he had been in command for only a few days when the fighting ceased.

Military Tribunal in session.

The Tribunal also ruled that there was not sufficient evidence to indicate that Umezu was responsible for any atrocities.

The Tribunal found Umezu guilty under Counts 1, 27, 29, 31, and 32 and not guilty under Counts 36, 54, and 55.

Charges vs. Verdicts RECAP

Charges and verdicts against the accused were limited to ten counts.

Indictment counts:

Accused	01	27	29	31	32	33	35	36	54	55
Araki, S.	X	X	X	X	X	X	X	X	X	X
	G	G	NG	NG	NG	NG	NG	NG	NG	NG
Dohihara, K.	X	X	X	X	X	X	X	X	X	X
	G	G	G	G	G	NG	G	G	G	G
Hashimoto, K.	X	X	X	X	X	-	-	-	X	X
	G	G	NG	NG	NG	-	-	-	NG	NG
Hata, S.	X	X	X	X	X	-	X	X	X	X
	G	G	G	G	G	-	NG	NG	NG	G
Hiranuma, K.	X	X	X	X	X	X	X	X	X	X
	G	G	G	G	G	NG	NG	G	NG	NG
Hirota, K.	X	X	X	X	X	X	X	-	X	X
	G	G	NG	NG	NG	NG	NG	-	NG	G
Hoshino, N.	X	X	X	X	X	X	X	-	X	X
	G	G	G	G	NG	NG	NG	-	NG	NG

Accused	01	27	29	31	32	33	35	36	54	55
Itagaki, S.	X	X	X	X	X	X	X	X	X	X
	G	G	G	G	G	NG	G	G	G	NF
Kaya, O.	X	X	X	X	X	-	-	-	X	X
	G	G	G	G	G	-	-	-	NG	NG
Kido, K.	X	X	X	X	X	X	X	X	X	X
	G	G	G	G	G	NG	NG	NG	NG	NG
Kimura, H.	X	X	X	X	X	-	-	-	X	X
	G	G	G	G	G	-	-	-	G	G
Koiso, K.	X	X	X	X	X	-	-	X	X	X
	G	G	G	G	G	-	-	NG	NG	G
Matsui, I.	X	X	X	X	X	-	X	X	X	X
	NG	NG	NG	NG	NG	-	NG	NG	NG	G
Minami, J.	X	X	X	X	X	-	-	-	X	X
	G	G	NG	NG	NG	-	-	-	NG	NG
Muto, A.	X	X	X	X	X	X	-	X	X	X
	G	G	G	G	G	-	-	-	NG	NG
Oshima, H.	X	X	X	X	X	-	-	-	X	X
	G	NG	NG	NG	NG	-	-	-	NG	NG
Sato, K.	X	X	X	X	X	-	-	-	X	X
	G	G	G	G	G	-	-	-	NG	NG

Accused	01	27	29	31	32	33	35	36	54	55
Shigemitsu, M.	X	X	X	X	X	X	X	-	X	X
	NG	G	G	G	G	G	NG	-	NG	G
Shimada, S.	X	X	X	X	X	-	-	-	X	X
	G	G	G	G	G	-	-	-	NG	NG
Shiratori, T.	X	X	X	X	X	-	-	-	-	-
	G	NG	NG	NG	NG	-	-	-	-	-
Suzuki, T.	X	X	X	X	X	-	X	X	X	X
	G	G	G	G	G	-	NG	NG	NG	NG
Togo, S.	X	X	X	X	X	-	-	X	X	X
	G	G	G	G	G	-	-	NG	NG	NG
Tojo, H.	X	X	X	X	X	X	-	X	X	X
	G	G	G	G	G	G	-	NG	G	NR
Umezu, Y.	X	X	X	X	X	-	-	X	X	X
	G	G	G	G	G	-	-	NG	NG	NG

Ind:										
Charged	25	25	25	25	25	10	11	13	24	24
Not Charged	0	0	0	0	0	15	14	12	1	1

Ver:										
Guilty	23	22	18	18	17	2	2	3	5	8
Not Guilty	2	3	7	7	8	8	9	10	19	14
No Ruling	0	0	0	0	0	0	0	0	0	1
No Finding	0	0	0	0	0	0	0	0	0	1

Sentences
CHAPTER 18

After the verdicts for each accused had been read in open court, the accused were removed from the courtroom. Each of the accused was then returned to the courtroom individually for sentencing in the order in which their names appeared in the title of the indictment. The three accused who were too ill to be present in the court at the time of the sentencing had their sentences read in court in their absence after all of the accused who were present in the court had been sentenced.

The President of the Tribunal made the announcement that in accordance with Article 15-h of the Charter, the International Military Tribunal for the Far East would then pronounce the sentences on the accused that had been convicted on any of the counts of the indictment. Since all of the accused were found guilty of at least one or more of the counts of the indictment, there were only three sentences that were adjudged: imprisonment for a specific term; imprisonment for life; death.

The president of the Tribunal announced the sentences in the following manner.

1) "Accused (Name), on the counts of the indictment on which you have been convicted, the International Military Tribunal for the Far East sentences you to imprisonment for (number) years from the date of the arraignment."

2) "Accused (Name), on the counts of the indictment on which you have been convicted, the International Military tary Tribunal for the Far East sentences you to imprisonment for life."

3) "Accused (Name), on the counts of the indictment on which you have been convicted, the International Military Tribunal for the Far East sentences you to death by hanging."

The accused sentences fell within these categories as follows: two of the accused were sentenced to imprisonment for a specific term; 16 of the accused were sentenced to imprisonment for life; seven of the accused were sentenced to death.

The individual accused sentences were: Araki, Sadao–imprisonment for life; Dohihara, Kemji–death; Hashimoto, Kingoro–imprisonment for life; Hata, Shunroku–imprisonment for life; Hiranuma, Kiichiro–imprisonment for life; Hrota, Koki–death; Hoshino, Naoki–imprisonment for life; Itagaki, Seichiro–death; Kaya, Okinori–imprisonment for life; Kido, Koichi–imprisonment for life; Kimura, Heitaro–death; Koiso, Kuniaki–imprisonment for life; Matsui, Iwane–death; Minami, Jiro–imprisonment for life; Muto, Akira–death; Oka, Takazumi–imprisonment for life; Oshima, Hiroshi–imprisonment for life; Sato, Kenryo–imprisonment for life; Shigemitsu, Mamoru–imprisonment seven years; Shimada, Shigetaro–imprisonment for life; Shiratori, Toshio–imprisonment for life; Suzuki, Teiichi–imprisonment for life; Togo, Shigenori–imprisonment 20 years; Tojo, Hideki–death; and Umezu, Yoshijiro–imprisonment for life.

After the sentencing had been completed, the prisoners made a last trip from the war ministry to Sugamo Prison where those sentenced to specific terms or life imprisonment would begin serving their sentences and those sentenced to death would await their appointment with the hangman.

Executions
CHAPTER 19

As the trial dragged on, Tojo seemed to be increasingly turning toward religion. On the date that Tojo and six other prisoner were sentenced to death Tojo wrote this verse: "Looking up, I hear reverently the voice of Buddha calling me from the limitless clear sky."

The sentences were appealed by defense counsel, over Tojo's objection to the whole "monkey show," to General MacArthur and the US Supreme Court.

Tojo admitted to Hanayama, the Buddhist chaplain at Sugamo Prison, that he was glad he had not succeeded in killing himself. "First because I have been able to bring religion into my life; second because I have learned to understand the beauty of human life as never before; and third because I was able to clear up certain points during the trial."

He also admitted to the chaplain that he was glad to be killed in Japan rather than to be taken abroad to be humiliated.

The appeal to Washington was rejected on 20 December 1948 because of jurisdictional reasons and General Mac-Arthur thereupon ordered that the condemned Class A prisoners were to be executed promptly on 23 December.

When Tojo was told on 21 December, a week before his 64th birthday, that he would be executed at one minute past midnight on the 23rd, he replied "Okay...Okay," in English several times and bowed low. He thanked the prison colonel for honoring most of his personal requests but he complained that the precautionary measures were "too strict." He said that they would never try to kill themselves and that they would show that they could die noble deaths. He also said that the prisoners were guarded at all times, even when they used the latrine and that this to a Japanese was an unbearable thing. He requested at least one Japanese meal, however simple, and at least one drink of sake.

Tojo was also greatly troubled by the pitiful condition of the condemned men's families.

The day before his death, Tojo told the chaplain that only his faith in Buddha had probably saved him from a nervous breakdown induced by the 100-watt light bulb that burned in his cell day and night.

He also observed to the chaplain, "I am dying at a very opportune time. For one thing, I can tender my apologies to the people. Next, I am able to offer myself as a sacrifice to peace and can become one stone in the foundation for the rebuilding of Japan. Thirdly, I can die in peace of mind because no trouble was brought upon the Emperor. Fourthly, is the fact that I can die on the gallows as my death would have had no meaning if it had come through suicide. Fifth, I was physically weak as a child, and have lived too long as it is. I have only one or two teeth left, I cannot see well, and my brain doesn't function well any more. I couldn't go on living like this and it's just about time that I should die. Sixth, the accusation that I helped myself from the public funds has been disproved and I can die in peace. Seventh, it is more fortunate to die in one instant than to suffer a lingering illness. If I had been given a life-sentence, I would have been tormented with worldly passions and it would have been intolerable. The most important thing is that through faith I can die and go to the Paradise of Buddha. Last night, when the execution date was announced, I felt very cheery at heart."

Tojo's only specific questions concerned the method of hanging and the chaplain explained that he would die instantaneously as the spinal cord would be severed.

Tojo commented that he was grateful that he would be reabsorbed into the soil of Japan.

Tojo had been working for weeks on a long political testament for the world at large that he read aloud to the Chaplain on 22 December. His comments included: A plea for Far Eastern unity; a prediction of the Third World War involving America versus the USSR on the battlefields of China, Japan, and Korea; and a poem:

> And now, as in the fullness of my heart
> I hurry west
> Not a cloud besmirches
> Or shadows my soul

Shortly before midnight on the 22 December the condemned prisoners were brought to the hallway of the tiny Buddhist chapel at Sugamo Prison, enroute to the gallows. There were two guards for each man. Both hands were handcuffed, and the cuffs were thrust through a band, fastened in loincloth style which made it terribly uncomfortable and inconvenient. Their clothes were the usual American Army fatigue uniforms and they wore Japanese laced shoes on their feet. The condemned men painfully lit incense sticks and then inked their names on heavy Japanese paper. They sipped their last wine but could not eat the cookies offered by the chaplain as their dentures had been removed. After a brief reading from the Buddhist sutra, they shouted "Banzai for the Emperor!" and "Long live the Japanese Empire!" three times. Not a sign of grief or agitation was visible as they were led to the gallows. Tojo went to the gallows smiling with the chant of supplication to the Buddha of Unlimited Light on his lips.

Japan's General Hideki Tojo listens to preceedings during War Crimes Trial.

Annex A:

Names Changes and Abbreviations

Name Changes: The names of some countries, territories, provinces, and cities were changed during the period covered by the trial or since then due to the structure of the countries, etc., or the predominant religion of the area. Another reason depended on which nation's name for the area was to be used; i.e., Japanese versus Chinese. Some of these changes were:

Manchuria (Chinese) vs Manchukuo (Japanese) (1931-1945).

Formosa (Japanese) (1895-1945) vs. Taiwan (Chinese) (Seat of the Nationalist Republic of China since 1949, Capital Taipei).

French Indo-China. Two states of the French Union were Laos and Vietnam. Kingdom of Laos, Administrative Capital: Vientianne. Royal Capital: Luang Prabang. After a civil war in 1954, Vietnam was divided at the 17th parallel with the Capital of North Vietnam being in Hanoi and for South Vietnam being in Saigon. South Vietnamese rebel forces, the Viet Cong, assisted by the North Vietnamese Army fought a civil war for over 20 years against the South Vietnamese Army who were aided by the United States until the US Forces withdrew from the country and the South Vietnamese surrendered. Vietnam combined as one country with its Capital at Hanoi. Saigon was renamed Ho Chi Minh City.

When Burma gained her independence, the country was renamed Miramar.

Singapore city and Port Singapore, formerly a British Crown Colony, became an independent republic in 1965.

Netherlands East Indies consisted of most of the islands of the Malay archipelago (Sumatra, Java, South and East Borneo, Celebes, West Timor, West New Guinea, the Moluccas, and many adjacent smaller islands. It became the Republic of Indonesia in 1949, with it's capital at Djakarta, formerly Batavia).

During the 1970s-1990s the Chinese changed the spelling of most of their cities and towns to those using the Chinese spelling; example: Peking became Beijing.

South Korea followed the Chinese example in changes of the spelling of certain names; Example: Pusan and Taegu became Busan and Daegu, respectively.

The predominant religious affiliation of the area's populace could designate the name of the country; i.e., when India gained her independence from Great Britain, she retained the name India as most of her people were of Hindu religion whereas the majority of the people of the Muslim religion resided in those areas which were to become part of Pakistan therefore the Muslim name for the area.

Abbreviations

NEI	Netherlands East Indies
POW(s)	Prisoner(s) of War
SSR	Soviet Socialist Republic
US	United States
USA	United States of America
USSR	Union of Soviet Socialist Republics

Tribunal members from eleven nations preside over the War Crimes Trials.

INDEX

Printed in the USA
CPSIA information can be obtained
at www.ICGtesting.com
JSHW022208140824
68134JS00018B/923